Blender 2.6 Cycles: Materials and Textures Cookbook

Over 40 recipes to help you create stunning materials and textures using the Cycles rendering engine with Blender

Enrico Valenza

[PACKT] open source ✺
PUBLISHING   community experience distilled

BIRMINGHAM - MUMBAI

Blender 2.6 Cycles: Materials and Textures Cookbook

First published: June 2013

Production Reference: 1180613

Published by Packt Publishing Ltd.
Livery Place
35 Livery Street
Birmingham B3 2PB, UK.

ISBN 978-1-78216-130-1

www.packtpub.com

Cover Image by Enrico Valenza (envval@gmail.com)

Credits

Author

Enrico Valenza

Reviewers

Ken Beyer

Darrin Lile

Acquisition Editors

Sam Birch

Sarah Cullington

Andrew Duckworth

Lead Technical Editor

Arun Nadar

Technical Editors

Sumedh Patil

Dominic Pereira

Pragati Singh

Project Coordinator

Arshad Sopariwala

Proofreaders

Claire Cresswell-Lane

Mario Cecere

Indexer

Tejal R. Soni

Production Coordinator

Nilesh R. Mohite

Cover Work

Nilesh R. Mohite

About the Author

Enrico Valenza, also known on the Web as "EnV", is an Italian freelance illustrator, mainly collaborating with publishers, such as Mondadori Ragazzi and Giunti, as a cover artist for sci-fi and fantasy books.

He graduated at Liceo Artistico Statale in Verona (Italy) and later was a student of illustrator and painter Giorgio Scarato.

When he started to work, computers weren't that popular among the masses, and he spent the first 15 years of his career doing illustrations with traditional media, usually on cardboards. Particularly, he specialized in the use of the air-graph, a technique particularly esteemed for advertising work.

But this was only until the moment *Jurassic Park* came to the theaters: he then decided to buy a computer and try his hand at this "computer graphic" thing everyone was talking about. Totally self-taught in the many aspects of CG, it was his encounter with the open source philosophy that actually opened a brand new world of possibilities—in particular, Blender.

In 2005, he won the Suzanne Awards for "Best animation, original idea, and story" with the animation *New Penguoen 2.38*.

In 2006, he joined the Orange Team for the last two weeks of production in Amsterdam, to help in finalizing the shots of the first open source CG-animated short movie produced by the Blender Foundation, named *Elephants Dream*.

From 2007 to 2008, he was a Lead Artist in the Peach Project Team for the production of *Big Buck Bunny*, the Blender Foundation's second open movie.

From 2010 to 2011, he was an Art Director at CINECA (Bologna, Italy) for the *Museo della Città di Bologna* project, that is, the production of a stereoscopic CG-animated documentary made in Blender and explaining Bologna's history.

Being also a Blender Certified Trainer, he collaborates as a CG artist with Italian production studios that have decided to switch their pipeline to the open source.

He uses Blender almost on a daily basis for his illustration jobs, rarely to have the illustration rendered straight by the 3D package, more often as a starting point for painting over with other open source applications such as The Gimp or, more recently, MyPaint.

He has presented several presentations and workshops about Blender and its use in productions.

I would like to say thanks to my family: my father Giuseppe and my mother Licia, for giving me the possibility to follow what I always thought was my path in life, my wonderful wife Micaela and my beautiful daughter Sara, just for being there and encouraging me while writing this book.

Then, I would like to thank, obviously, Ton Roosendaal for creating Blender and Brecht Van Lommel for Cycles. I would also like to thank all the blender-heads at the BlenderArtist and at the Kino3d forums for all the testing, experimentations, explanations, and examples about the Cycles features and materials creation that were (and still are) often posted almost at the same time they are implemented in the software. Especially on BlenderArtist.org, there is a very long and informative thread at this address, which, at this moment, has already reached 540 pages:

http://blenderartists.org/forum/showthread.php?216113-Brecht-s-easter-egg-surprise-Modernizing-shading-and-rendering

And another one at this address, which is already more than 200 pages long:

http://blenderartists.org/forum/showthread.php?216866-Cycles-tests-the-new-blender-CPU-GPU-renderer-of-awesomeness

About the Reviewers

Ken Beyer is a Blender Foundation Certified Trainer, and at `KatsBits.com` has been providing tutorials, training, downloads, and other information and resources on using Blender for content creation and production relative to games and other real-time interactive products to hobbyists, amateur artists, Indie developers, and small studios for nearly 15 years.

`KatsBits.com` itself is a site and community dedicated to making game content and general game development using Blender 3D, where members can post questions, comments, and read information important for taking that next step from "gamer" to "creator".

He has served as a Technical Reviewer on (both full and partial reviews) the following books:

- *Blender 2.5 Hotshot (Packt Publishing, 2011)*
- *Blender 2.5 Materials and Textures Cookbook (Packt Publishing, 2011)*
- *Blender 3D 2.49 Architecture, Buildings and Scenery (Packt Publishing, 2010)*
- *Blender 2.5 Lighting and Rendering (Packt Publishing, 2010)*

Darrin Lile is an animator, writer, and full-time faculty member in the Media Arts and Animation Program at The Art Institute of Wisconsin. He teaches courses in computer animation, including Principles of 3D Modeling, Materials and Lighting, Advanced Lighting and Texturing, and Advanced Modeling and Animation. He received Bachelor's and Master's degrees in Film and Media Studies from the University of Kansas and has worked as a producer of educational films, as a sound editor for film and television, and as a computer security analyst. He currently lives in Wisconsin with his wife and children near the shores of Lake Michigan. Check out his latest work at `www.darrinlile.com`.

www.PacktPub.com

Support files, eBooks, discount offers and more

You might want to visit www.PacktPub.com for support files and downloads related to your book.

Did you know that Packt offers eBook versions of every book published, with PDF and ePub files available? You can upgrade to the eBook version at www.PacktPub.com and as a print book customer, you are entitled to a discount on the eBook copy. Get in touch with us at service@packtpub.com for more details.

At www.PacktPub.com, you can also read a collection of free technical articles, sign up for a range of free newsletters and receive exclusive discounts and offers on Packt books and eBooks.

http://PacktLib.PacktPub.com

Do you need instant solutions to your IT questions? PacktLib is Packt's online digital book library. Here, you can access, read and search across Packt's entire library of books.

Why Subscribe?

- ▸ Fully searchable across every book published by Packt
- ▸ Copy and paste, print and bookmark content
- ▸ On demand and accessible via web browser

Free Access for Packt account holders

If you have an account with Packt at www.PacktPub.com, you can use this to access PacktLib today and view nine entirely free books. Simply use your login credentials for immediate access.

Table of Contents

Preface

Since the Blender interface and code was totally rewritten from scratch, starting with the 2.5 series and throughout the production of the "Durian" open movie "Sintel", a lot of good things happened to this famous open source 3D modeling and animation suite.

One of them has been the announcement, in April 2011, of Cycles, a new rendering engine developed by Brecht Van Lommel with the goal of modernizing Blender's shading and rendering systems and to be used as alternative to the Blender Internal rendering engine.

Cycles has finally been fully integrated in Blender with the 2.61 release as an add-on, which is a Python script, enabled in the Preferences panel by default: it's enough to set it as the active render engine in the UI's top header.

Just as Blender Internal is a scan-line rendering engine, Cycles is instead a physically based path tracer; this approach permits the simplification of materials' creation, the support for Global Illumination, and in the end much more realism in the results.

But the best Cycles feature is probably the rendering interactivity you have in the 3D viewport. By setting the draw mode of any 3D viewport to Rendered, an interactive rendering starts in the viewport itself and since then the pre-visualization rendering of the scene is continuously updated almost in real time (depending on the power of your graphic card) as a material, a light, an object, or the whole scene gets modified.

Currently, BI is still maintained (even though, no more developed) and there are no real plans to drop it, at least for the moment. It's not clear if in the future Cycles will totally replace BI or if both will be (hopefully) kept as possible choices. What is clear is that presently Cycles is still missing several of the features possible with BI, such as smoke simulations, stress mapping, and others.

This doesn't mean that Cycles is not production-ready; a lot of astonishing images have already been produced, both for testing purposes and for real productions as well. You can find most of them on the BlenderArtist forum (`http://blenderartists.org/forum/`), but it's enough to mention "Tears of Steel", the fifth open movie produced by the Blender Foundation with the codename "Mango": a science fiction short movie entirely rendered in Cycles to accomplish the visual special effects. Well, maybe not entirely but actually at 95 percent: the team still used BI for the unsupported features. In fact, being included in the same software also provided with an integrated compositor, both the Blender Internal and the Cycles render engines can actually be used in tandem to get full use of all the needed features from both of them.

The best of two different worlds.

What this book covers

Chapter 1, Overview of Materials in Cycles, explains the way Cycles materials work, their main characteristics, and how to build a basic Cycles material, add textures, how to use lamps, or light-emitting objects and set the World.

Chapter 2, Managing Cycles Materials, explains how to better manage and organize the Cycles materials to build libraries to link or append the materials from.

Chapter 3, Creating Natural Materials in Cycles, explains the creation process of several types of basic natural materials by using both image textures and procedurals, but mainly dwells on procedurals.

Chapter 4, Creating Man-made Materials in Cycles, explains the creation process of several types of man-made materials by using procedurals textures.

Chapter 5, Creating Complex Natural Materials in Cycles, explains the creation process of more complex natural materials by using both image textures and procedurals, but mainly dwells on procedurals.

Chapter 6, Creating More Complex Man-made Materials, explains the creation process of some more elaborate man-made material by mainly using procedurals textures.

Chapter 7, Creating Organic Materials, explains the creation process of several types of organic shaders, trying to use only procedural textures wherever possible.

Chapter 8, Human Skin Materials and Faking Sub Surface Scattering in Cycles, explains some ways to simulate the Sub Surface Scattering effect in Cycles and teaches how to build simple and layered human skin shaders. This chapter is available as a free download and can be downloaded from `http://www.packtpub.com/sites/default/files/downloads/Chapter_8.pdf`.

Chapter 9, Special Materials, explains the usage of the Cycles "hair" experimental feature and the creation process of some special effects material. This chapter is available as a free download and can be downloaded from `http://www.packtpub.com/sites/default/files/downloads/Chapter_9.pdf`.

What you need for this book

The only software strictly needed for following along the recipes of this book is the official 2.66a Blender release, although the just released 2.67 and 2.67a Versions work perfectly fine (but if you use the latter ones, be aware that something in the graphic look of the nodes has changed, especially for node groups. In any case, the working principles are the same). You only need to download it from `www.blender.org/download/get-blender`. Any particular texture needed for the exercises in the book is provided as a free download on the Packt Publishing website itself.

Not essential but also handy can be an image editor, in case you want to adapt your own textures to replace the provided ones. I suggest trying The Gimp, an open source image editor that you can download from `www.gimp.org`. Any other software you prefer is perfect anyway.

Who this book is for

This book is aimed mainly at the average – intermediate Blender user who already knows Blender but still hasn't dealt with the new Cycles rendering engine. It's taken for granted that you already know how to move inside the Blender interface and that you already have at least some basic knowledge of the standard Blender material creation interface, although this is actually not strictly necessary.

Conventions

In this book, you will find a number of styles of text that distinguish between different kinds of information. Here are some examples of these styles, and an explanation of their meaning.

Code words in text, database table names, folder names, filenames, file extensions, pathnames, dummy URLs, user input, and Twitter handles are shown as follows: "Start Blender and open the `1301OS_08_start.blend` file, where there is a Suzanne mesh leaning on a plane and two mesh-light planes."

New terms and **important words** are shown in bold. Words that you see on the screen, in menus or dialog boxes for example, appear in the text like this: "In the **Material** window switch the **Diffuse BSDF** shader with a **Mix Shader** node. In the first **Shader** slot, select a **Diffuse BSDF** shader and in the second one a **Glossy BSDF** shader node."

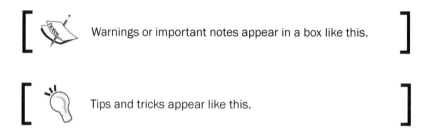

Warnings or important notes appear in a box like this.

Tips and tricks appear like this.

Reader feedback

Feedback from our readers is always welcome. Let us know what you think about this book—what you liked or may have disliked. Reader feedback is important for us to develop titles that you really get the most out of.

To send us general feedback, simply send an e-mail to feedback@packtpub.com, and mention the book title via the subject of your message.

If there is a topic that you have expertise in and you are interested in either writing or contributing to a book, see our author guide on www.packtpub.com/authors.

Customer support

Now that you are the proud owner of a Packt book, we have a number of things to help you to get the most from your purchase.

Downloading the example code

You can download the example code files for all Packt books you have purchased from your account at http://www.packtpub.com. If you purchased this book elsewhere, you can visit http://www.packtpub.com/support and register to have the files e-mailed directly to you.

Errata

Although we have taken every care to ensure the accuracy of our content, mistakes do happen. If you find a mistake in one of our books—maybe a mistake in the text or the code—we would be grateful if you would report this to us. By doing so, you can save other readers from frustration and help us improve subsequent versions of this book. If you find any errata, please report them by visiting http://www.packtpub.com/submit-errata, selecting your book, clicking on the **errata submission form** link, and entering the details of your errata. Once your errata are verified, your submission will be accepted and the errata will be uploaded on our website, or added to any list of existing errata, under the Errata section of that title. Any existing errata can be viewed by selecting your title from http://www.packtpub.com/support.

Piracy

Piracy of copyright material on the Internet is an ongoing problem across all media. At Packt, we take the protection of our copyright and licenses very seriously. If you come across any illegal copies of our works, in any form, on the Internet, please provide us with the location address or website name immediately so that we can pursue a remedy.

Please contact us at copyright@packtpub.com with a link to the suspected pirated material.

We appreciate your help in protecting our authors, and our ability to bring you valuable content.

Questions

You can contact us at questions@packtpub.com if you are having a problem with any aspect of the book, and we will do our best to address it.

1

Overview of Materials in Cycles

In this chapter, we will cover:

- ▶ Material nodes in Cycles
- ▶ Procedural textures in Cycles
- ▶ How to set the World material
- ▶ Creating a mesh-light material
- ▶ Using displacement (aka bump)

Introduction

Cycles materials work in a totally different way than in Blender Internal.

In Blender Internal, you can build a material by choosing a diffuse and a specular shader from the **Material** window, by setting several surface options, and then by assigning textures (both procedurals or image maps as well) in the provided slots—all these steps make one complete material. After this, it's possible to combine two or more of these materials by a network of nodes, thereby obtaining a lot more flexibility in a shader's creation. But, the materials themselves are just the same you used to set through the **Material** window, that is, shaders made for a scan-line rendering engine as Blender Internal is, and their result is actually just an approximation of a simulated light absorption-reflection surface behavior.

In Cycles the approach is quite different: all the names of the closures describing surface properties have a **Bidirectional Scattering Distribution Function** (**BSDF**), which is a general mathematical function that describes the way in which the light is scattered by a surface in the real world. It's also the formula that a path tracer such as Cycles uses to calculate the rendering of an object in a virtual environment. Basically, light rays are shot from the camera, they bounce on the objects in the scene and keep on bouncing until they reach a light source or an "empty" background. For this reason, a pure path tracer such as Cycles can render in reasonable times an object set in an open environment, while instead the rendering times increase a lot for closed spaces. For example, furniture set inside a room, and this is just because the light rays can bounce on the floor, the ceiling, and the walls a good many times before reaching one or more light sources.

In short, the main difference between the two rendering engines is due to the fact that, while in Blender Internal the materials use all the traditional shader tricks of a scan-line rendering engine such as, for example, the simulated specular component, the Cycles rendering engine is a path tracer trying to mimic the real behavior of a surface as closely as possible as in real life. This is the reason why in Cycles we don't have, for example, the arbitrary Spec factor simulating the reflection point of the light on the surface, but a glossy shader actually mirroring the light source and the surrounding, to be mixed to the other components in different ratios and so behaving, in this respect, in a more correct way.

In any case, just for explanatory purposes, in this book I will still refer to the more or less blurred point of light created by the reflection of the light source on a mirroring glossy surface as **Specularity**.

Be aware that the rendering speed in Cycles depends on the device—CPU or GPU—you use to render your scenes. That is, basically you can decide to use the power of the CPU (default option) or the power of the graphic card processor, the GPU.

To set this:

1. Call the **User Preferences** panel (*Crtl + Alt +U*) and go to the **System** tab, the last one to the right of the panel.

2. Under the **Compute Device** tab to the bottom-left of the panel, select the one to be used for the computation; to make this permanent, click on the **Save User Settings** button or press *Crtl + U*. Now close the **User Preferences** panel.

3. In the **Properties** panel to the right of the interface, go to the **Render** window and, under the **Render** tab, it's now possible to configure the GPU of the graphic card instead of the default CPU (the option is present only if your graphic card supports CUDA, that is, for NVIDIA graphic cards; OpenCL, which is intended to support rendering on AMD/ATI graphics cards, is still in a very incomplete and experimental stage and therefore not of much use yet).

A GPU-based rendering has the advantage of literally increasing the Cycles' rendering speed several times, albeit with the disadvantage of a small memory limit, so that it's not always possible to render big complex scenes made by a lot of geometry; in such cases, it's better to use the CPU instead.

There are other ways to reduce the rendering times and also to reduce or avoid the noise and the fireflies (white dots) produced in several cases by the glossy, transparent, and light-emitting materials. All of this doesn't strictly belong to shaders or materials, by the way, you can find more information related to these topics at the following addresses:

 ▸ Cycles Render Engine: `http://wiki.blender.org/index.php/Doc:2.6/Manual/Render/Cycles`

 ▸ Reducing Noise – Cycles Wiki page: `http://wiki.blender.org/index.php/Doc:2.6/Manual/Render/Cycles/Reducing_Noise`.

 ▸ A list of supported graphic cards for Cycles can be found at: `https://developer.nvidia.com/cuda-gpus`.

Material nodes in Cycles

A Cycles material is basically made up of distinct components, initially named **closures** and later more traditionally renamed **shaders** (by Brecht Van Lommel himself), which can be combined together to build even more complex surface shaders.

In this recipe, we'll have a look at the basic necessary steps required to build a basic Cycles material, to activate the rendered preview in the 3D window, and to finally render a simple scene.

Getting ready

In the description of the following steps, I'll assume that you are starting with a brand new Blender with the default factory settings; if not, start Blender and just click on the **File** menu item to the top main header bar to select **Load Factory Settings** from the pop-up menu.

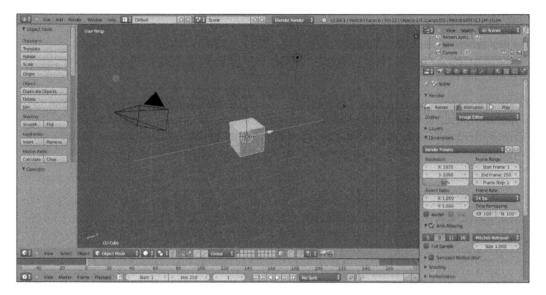

1. In the upper menu bar, switch from **Blender Render** to **Cycles Render** (hovering with the mouse on this button shows the **Engine to use for rendering** label).

2. Now split the 3D view into two horizontal rows and change the upper one in to the **Node Editor** window by selecting the menu item from the **Editor type** button at the left-hand corner of the bottom bar of the window itself. The **Node Editor** window is, in fact, the window we will use to build our shader by mixing the nodes (it's not the only way, actually, but we'll see this later).

3. Put the mouse cursor in the 3D view and add a plane under the cube (press *Shift + A* and navigate to **Mesh | Plane**). Enter edit mode (press *Tab*), scale it 3.5 times bigger (press S, digit *3.5*, and hit *Enter*) and go out of edit mode (press *Tab*). Now, move the plane one Blender unit down (press G, then Z, digit *-1*, and then hit *Enter*).

4. Go to the little icon (**Viewport Shading**) showing a sphere in the bottom bar of the 3D view and click on it. A menu showing different options appears (**Bounding Box**, **Wireframe**, **Solid**, **Texture**, **Material**, and **Rendered**). Select **Rendered** from the top of the list and watch your cube being rendered in real time in the 3D viewport.

5. Now, you can rotate or/and translate the view or the cube itself and the view gets updated in real time (the speed of the update is only restricted by the complexity of the scene and by the computing power of your CPU or of your graphic card).

6. Let's learn more about this:

7. Select **Lamp** in the **Outliner** (by default, a **Point** lamp).

8. Go to the **Object Data** window under the **Properties** panel on the right-hand side of the interface.

9. Under the **Nodes** tab, click on **Use Nodes** to activate a node system for the selected light in the scene; this node system is made by an **Emission** closure connected to a **Lamp Output** node.

10. Go to the **Strength** item, which is set to **100.000** by default, and start to increase the value—as the intensity of the Lamp increases, you can see the cube and the plane rendered in the viewport getting more and more bright, as shown in the following screenshot:

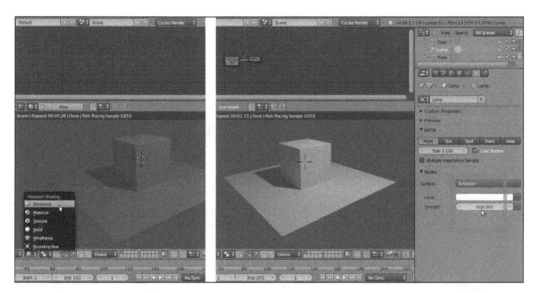

How to do it...

We just prepared the scene and had a first look at one of the more appreciated features of Cycles: the real-time rendered preview. Now let's start with the object's materials:

1. Select the cube to assign the shader to, by left-clicking on the item in the **Outliner**, or also by right-clicking directly on the object in the **Rendered** viewport (but be aware that in **Rendered** mode, the object selection outline usually around the mesh is not visible because, obviously, it's not renderable).

2. Go to the **Material** window under the **Properties** panel: even if with the default **Factory Settings** selected, the cube has already a default material assigned (as you can precisely see by navigating to **Properties | Material | Surface**). In any case, you need to click on the **Use Nodes** button under the **Surface** tab to activate the node system; or else, by checking the **Use Nodes** box in the header of the **Node Editor** window.

3. As you check the **Use Nodes** box, the content of the **Surface** tab changes showing that a **Diffuse BSDF** shader has been assigned to the cube and that, accordingly, two linked nodes have appeared inside the **Node Editor** window: the **Diffuse BSDF** shader itself is already connected to the **Surface** input socket of a **Material Output** node (the **Volume** input socket does nothing at the moment, it's there in anticipation of a volumetric feature on the to-do list, and we'll see the **Displacement** socket later).

4. Put the mouse cursor in the **Node Editor** window and by scrolling the mouse wheel, zoom in to the **Diffuse BSDF** node. Left-click on the **Color** rectangle: a color wheel appears, where you can select a new color to change the shader color by clicking on the wheel or by inserting the RGB values (and take note that there are also a color sampler and the Alpha channel value, although the latter, in this case, doesn't have any visible effect on the object material's color):

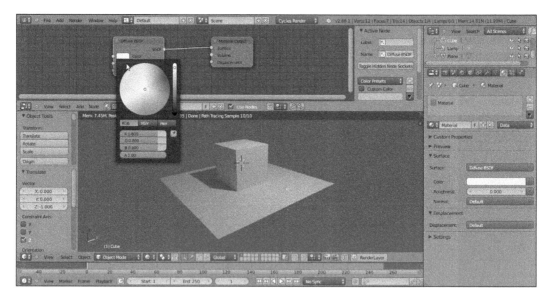

5. The cube rendered in the 3D preview changes its material's color in real time. You can even move the cursor in the color wheel and watch the rendered object switching the colors accordingly. Set the object's color to a greenish color by setting its RGB values to 0.430, 0.800, and 0.499 respectively.

6. Go to the **Material** window and, under the **Surface** tab, click on the **Surface** button, which at the moment is showing the **Diffuse BSDF** item. From the pop-up menu, select the **Glossy BSDF** shader item. The node now also changes in the **Node Editor** window and so does accordingly the cube's material in the **Rendered** preview, as shown here:

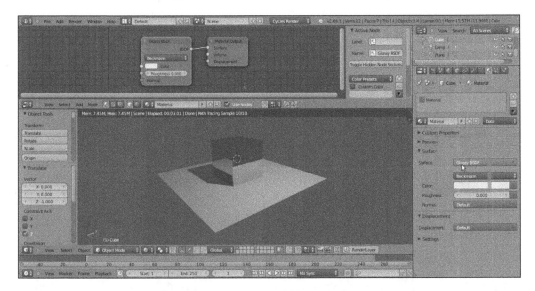

Note that although we just switched a shader node with a different one, the color we set in the former one has been kept also in the new one; actually, this happens for all the values that can be kept from one node to a different one.

Now, because in the real world a material having a 100 percent matte or reflective surface could hardly exist, a more correct basic Cycles material should be made by mixing the **Diffuse BSDF** and the **Glossy BSDF** shaders blended together by a **Mix Shader** node, in turn connected to the **Material Output** node.

1. In the **Material** window, under the **Surface** tab, click again on the **Surface** button that is now showing the **Glossy BSDF** item and replace it back with a **Diffuse BSDF** shader.

2. Put the mouse pointer in the **Node Editor** window and, by pressing *Shift + A* on the keyboard, make a pop-up menu appear with several items. Move the mouse pointer on the **Shader** item, it shows one more pop-up where all the shader options are collected.

3. Select one of these shader menu items, for example, the **Glossy BSDF** item. The shader node is now added to the **Node Editor** window, although not connected to anything yet (in fact, it's not visible in the **Material** window but is visible only in the **Node Editor** window); the new nodes appear already selected.

4. Again press *Shift + A* in the **Node Editor** window and this time add a **Mix Shader** node.

5. Press *G* to move it on the link connecting the **Diffuse BSDF** node to the **Material Output** node (you'll probably need to first adjust the position of the two nodes to make room between them). The **Mix Shader** node gets automatically pasted in between, the **Diffuse** node output connected to the first **Shader** input socket, as shown in the following screenshot:

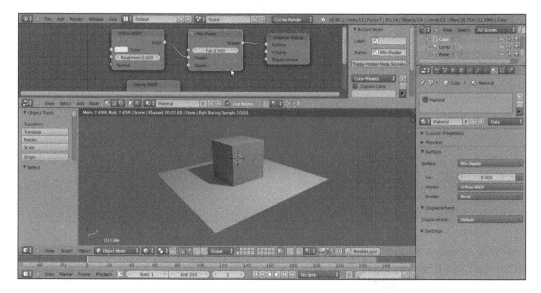

6. Left-click with the mouse on the green dot output of the **Glossy BSDF** shader node and grab the link to the second input socket of the **Mix Shader** node. Release the mouse button now and see the nodes being connected.

7. Because the blending **Fac** (*factor*) value of the **Mix Shader** node is set by default to 0.500, the two shader components, **Diffuse** and **Glossy**, are now showing on the cube's surface in equal parts, that is, each one at 50 percent. Left-click on the **Fac** slider with the mouse and slide it to 0.000. The cube's surface is now showing only the **Diffuse** component, because the **Diffuse BSDF** shader is connected to the first **Shader** input socket that is corresponding to a value set to 0.000.

Downloading the example code

You can download the example code files for all Packt books you have purchased from your account at http://www.packtpub. com. If you purchased this book elsewhere, you can visit http://www.packtpub.com/support and register to have the files e-mailed directly to you. The high resolution colored images of the book can also be found in the code bundle.

8. Slide the **Fac** slider value to `1.000` and the surface is now showing only the **Glossy BSDF** shader component, which is, in fact, connected to the second **Shader** input socket corresponding to a value set to `1.000`.

9. Set the **Fac** value to `0.800`. The cube is now reflecting on its sides, even if blurred, the white plane, because we have a material that is reflective at 80 percent, matte at 20 percent, and so on:

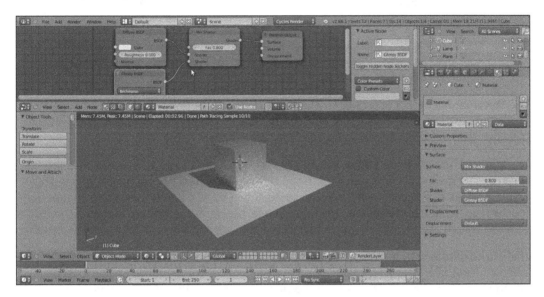

10. Lastly, select the plane, go to the **Material** window and click on the **New** button to assign a default whitish material.

How it works...

So, in its minimal form, a Cycles material is made by a closure (a node shader) connected to the **Material Output** node; by default, for a new material, the node shader is the **Diffuse BSDF** with RGB color set to 0.800, and the result is a matte whitish material (with the **Roughness** value at `0.000` actually corresponding to a **Lambert** shader). The **Diffuse BSDF** node can be replaced by any other one of the available shader list. For example, by a **Glossy BSDF** shader as in the former cube scene, which produces a totally mirrored surface material.

As we have seen, the **Node Editor** window is not the only way to build the materials; in the **Properties** panel on the right-hand side of the UI, we have access to the **Material** window, which is usually divided as follows:

- ▶ The material name, user, and the datablock tab
- ▶ The **Surface** tab, including in a vertical ordered column only the shader nodes added in the **Node Editor** window and already connected to each other
- ▶ The **Displacement** tab, which we'll see later
- ▶ The **Settings** tab, where we can set the object color as seen in the viewport in not-rendered mode (**Viewport Color**), the material **Pass Index**, and a **Multiple Importance Sample** option

The **Material** window not only reflects what we do in the **Node Editor** window and changes accordingly to it (and vice versa), but also can be used to change the values, to easily switch the closures themselves and to some extent to connect them to the other nodes.

The **Material** and the **Node Editor** windows are so mutual that there is no prevalence in which one to use to build a material; both can be used individually or combined, depending on preferences or practical utility. In some cases, it can be very handy to switch a shader from the **Surface** tab under **Material** on the right (or a texture from the **Texture** window as well, but we'll see textures later), leaving untouched all the settings and the links in the node's network.

There is no question, by the way, that the **Material** window can become pretty complex and confusing as a material network grows more and more in complexity, while the graphic appearance of the **Node Editor** window shows the same network in a much more clear and comprehensible way.

There's more...

Looking at the **Rendered** viewport, you'll notice that the image is now quite noisy and that there are white dots in certain areas of the image; these are the infamous fireflies, caused mainly by transparent, luminescent, or glossy surfaces. Actually, they have been introduced in our render by the glossy component.

Follow these steps to avoid them:

1. Go to the **Render** window under the **Properties** panel. In the **Sampling** tab, set **Samples** to **100** both for **Preview** and **Render** (they are set to **10** by default).

2. Set the **Clamp** value to **1.00** (it's set to **0.00** by default). Go to the **Light Paths** tab and set the **Filter Glossy** value to **1.00** as well. The resulting rendered image, as shown here, is now a lot more smooth and noise free:

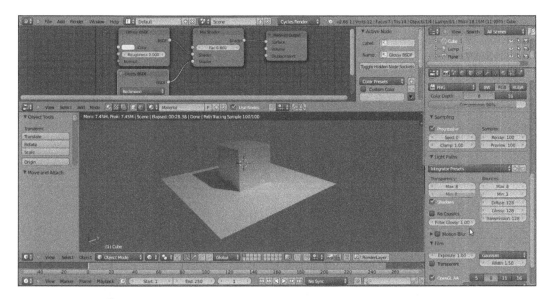

3. Save the blend file in an appropriate location on your hard drive with a name such as `start_01.blend`.

Samples set to **10** by default are obviously not enough to give a noiseless image, but are good for a fast preview. We could also let the **Preview** samples as default and increase only the **Render** value, to have longer rendering times but a clean image only for the final render (that can be started, as in BI, by pressing the *F12* key).

By using the **Clamp** value, we can cut the energy of the light. Internally, Blender converts the image color space to linear. It then re-converts it to RGB, that is, from 0 to 255 for the output. A value of 1.00 in linear space means that all the image values are now included inside a range starting from 0 and arriving to a maximum of 1, and that values bigger than 1 are not possible, so usually avoiding the fireflies problem. **Clamp** values higher than 1.00 can start to lower the general lighting intensity of the scene.

The **Filter Glossy** value is exactly what the name says, a filter that blurs the glossy reflections on the surface to reduce noise.

Be aware that even with the same samples, the **Rendered** preview not always has a total correspondence to the final render, both with regards to the noise as well as to the fireflies. This is mainly due to the fact that the preview-rendered 3D window and the final rendered image usually have very different sizes, and artifacts visible in the final rendered image may not show in a smaller preview-rendered window.

Procedural textures in Cycles

In this recipe, we'll see the several kinds of textures available in Cycles and learn how to use them with the shaders.

Similar to Blender Internal, we can use both procedural textures and image textures in Cycles. However, the Cycles procedural textures are not exactly the same as in Blender Internal; some are missing because of being replaced by an improved version (for example, Clouds has been replaced by particular settings of the Noise Texture) and a few are new and exclusive to Cycles.

Getting ready

We have already seen a simple construction of a basic Cycles material by mixing the diffuse and the glossy ("specular") components of a surface. Now let's have a look at the textures we can use in Cycles to further refine a material.

Because Cycles has a node-based system for the materials, the textures are not added in their slot under a tab as it is in Blender Internal, but they just get added in the **Node Editor** window and directly connected to the input socket of the shaders or other kind of nodes. This gives a lot more flexibility to the material creation process, because this way a texture can be used to drive several options inside the material network.

1. Starting from the previously saved `start_01.blend` blend file, where we already had set a simple scene with a cube on a plane and a basic material, select the cube and go to the **Object Modifiers** window under the **Properties** panel to the right of the UI.

2. Assign to the cube a **Subdivision Surface** modifier, set the **Subdivisions** level to **4**, both for **View** as for **Render**.

3. In the **Object Tools** panel to the left of the 3D window, under **Shading**, set the subdivided cube (let's call it **spheroid** from now on) to **Smooth**.

4. Just to make things clearer, click on the color box of the **Glossy BSDF** shader to change it to a purple color (**RGB** set to **0.800**, **0.233**, and **0.388** respectively). Note, only the glossy reflection part on the spheroid is now purple, whereas the rest of the surface, the diffuse component, is still greenish.

5. Save the blend file and name it `start_02.blend`.

How to do it...

1. Put the mouse pointer in the **Node Editor** window and press *Shift + A*.

2. In the contextual menu pop-up, go to the **Texture** item, just under **Shader**, and left-click on **Wave Texture** to add the texture node to the **Node Editor** window.

3. Grab and connect the **Color** yellow output socket of the texture to the yellow input socket of the **Diffuse** shader, the one close to the **Color** rectangle that we had formerly set as a greenish color:

4. In the **Wave Texture** node, change the **Scale** value to 8.500, **Distortion** to 12.000, **Detail** to a maximum value of 16.000, and the **Detail Scale** value to 6.000.

5. Now disconnect the texture color output from the **Diffuse** node and connect it to the color input socket of the **Glossy** shader:

6. Now disconnect the texture color output from the **Glossy** shader. Grab and connect the texture node's **Fac** output to the **Roughness** input socket of the **Glossy BSDF** shader, as shown in the following screenshot:

7. Save the file.

8. Delete the **Wave Texture** node (*X* key), press *Shift + A* with the mouse pointer in the **Node Editor** window and add a **Checker Texture** node.

9. Connect the **Fac** output of the **Checker Texture** node to the **Fac** input socket of the **Mix Shader** node, as shown here:

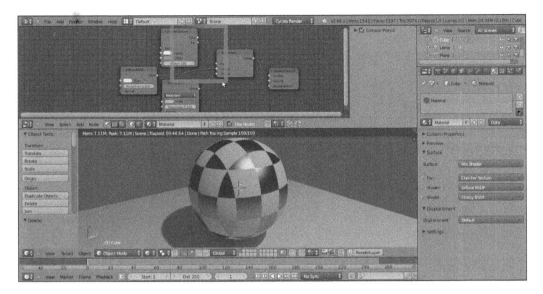

10. Save the file as `start_03.blend`.

How it works...

As is immediately visible in the **Rendered** viewport, at the moment the **Wave Texture** node color output is connected to color input of the **Diffuse BSDF** shader node, the spheroid looks as if it's painted in a black and white series of bands; actually, the black and white bands output of the texture node override the green color of the diffuse component of the shader, while keeping the material's pink glossy component unaltered (steps 1 to 3).

Exactly the opposite as you disconnect the texture output from the diffuse to connect it to the **Glossy** shader color input. Now we have the diffuse greenish color back and the pink has been overridden, while the reflection component is visible only inside the white bands of the wave texture (step 4 and 5).

In addition to the color output, every texture node has also a **Fac** output socket, outputting gray-scale linear values: connected to the **Roughness** input socket of the **Glossy** shader, the texture is working has a factor for its reflectivity. The working texture has a factor for its reflectivity; the spheroid keeps its colors and gets the specular-mirrored component only in the white-colored areas on the surface (that is, white bands equal to total reflecting and black bands equal to no reflection; step 6).

The **Checker Texture** fac (*factor*) output connected to the **Fac** input socket of the **Mix Shader** node works in a similar way: the numeric slider for the mixing factor on the **Mix Shader** node has disappeared, because now we are using the black and white linear values of the **Checker Texture** fac output as a factor for the mixing of the two components—the **Diffuse** and the **Glossy**—which, therefore, appear on the spheroid surface accordingly to the black and white quads (steps 8 and 9).

Every texture node has several setting options; all of them have the **Scale** value to set the size, the others change accordingly to the type of texture.

There's more...

At this point you could wonder: "ok, we just mapped a texture on the spheroid, but what's the projection mode of this mapping?"

Good question. By default, if not specified and if the object doesn't have any UV coordinates yet, the mapping is **Generated**, which is the equivalent of the **Original Coordinates** mode (now renamed **Generated** as well) in Blender Internal.

But what if I want to specify a mapping method? Then, just follow these steps:

1. Press *Shift + A* on the keyboard with the mouse pointing in the **Node Editor** window again, go to the **Input** item and select the **Texture Coordinate** item, which is a node with several mapping modes and their respective output sockets.

2. Try to connect the several outputs to the **Checker Texture | Vector** input (the blue socket on the left-hand side of the node) to see the texture mapping on the spheroid change in real time, as shown in the following screenshot:

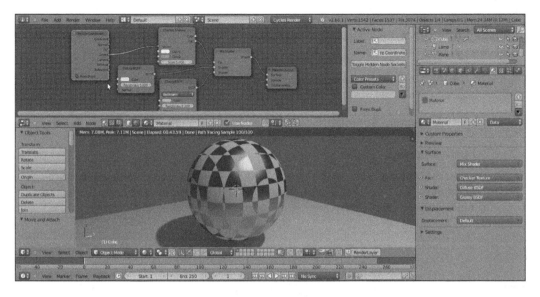

By the way, I'd like to point your attention to the UV coordinates output. Connect the link to the texture's vector socket and see the mapping on the spheroid disappear. Why is this? Put simply, because we haven't assigned any UV coordinates to our spheroid yet. Follow these steps to do so:

1. Go in the **UV Maps** tab in the **Object Data** window under the **Properties** panel on the right and click on the **+** sign. This just adds a one-to-one **Reset UV projection UV** layer to the object, that is, every face of the mesh is covering the whole area of the UV window (remember that although the cube looks like a spheroid now, this is only due to the effect of the assigned **Subdivision Surface** modifier; the UV coordinates work at the lowest level of subdivision, which is still a six-face cube).

2. A second option is to just place the proper seams on the cube's edges and directly unwrap the object in an **UV/Image Editor** window. Press *Tab* to go to edit mode, press *A* to select all the vertexes (if the vertexes are deselected). Now, press *U* and chose an unwrapping method from the pop-up menu (**Smart UV Project** and **Cube Projection** don't even need the seams), then go out of edit mode to update the Rendered preview.

The **Texture Coordinate** node is not needed in the case you unwrap an object and then use an **Image Texture** node, because in that case Cycles will automatically use the available UV coordinates to map the image map.

Obviously, the **Texture Coordinate** node alone is not enough. What we need now is a way to offset, rotate, and scale this texture on the surface:

1. Select the **Texture Coordinate** node and grab it to the left of the window, as far as suffices to make room for a new node. In the **Add** menu, go to **Vector** and choose **Mapping**.

2. Grab the **Mapping** node on the middle of the link that is connecting the **Texture Coordinate** node to the **Checker Texture** node; it will be automatically pasted in-between them, as shown in the following screenshot:

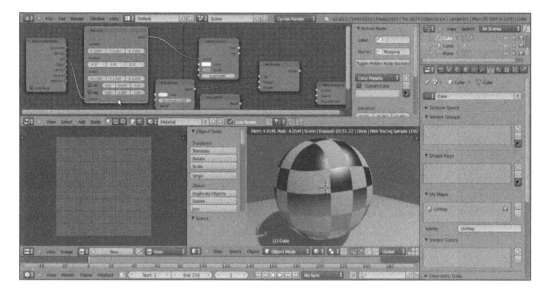

3. Now, start playing with the values inside the **Mapping** node. For example, set the **Z Rotation** value to 45°, the **X Scale** value to 2.000 and then slide the **X Location** value, while looking at the texture changing orientation, dimension and actually sliding on the x axis in the **Rendered** viewport.

4. Save the blend file as start_04.blend.

The **Min** and **Max** button on the bottom of the **Mapping** node are used to clip the extension of the texture mapping. That is, check both **Min** and **Max** to avoid the texture to be repeated n times on the surface and shown only once. A minimum value of 0.000 and a maximum value of 1.000 give a correspondence of one to one with the mapped image. You can tweak these values to even limit or extend the clipping. This is useful to map, for example, logos or labels on an object and avoiding repeating.

Setting the World material

In this recipe, we'll see the properties and the settings of the **World** window in Cycles.

The main characteristic of the Cycles **World** is that it can emit light, so it practically behaves as a light source. Actually, its effect is the famous "Global Illumination" effect.

As in Blender Internal, it is considered as a virtual dome at a large distance from the camera and never touching the scene's objects. Nothing in the 3D scene can affect the **World**. Actually, only the **World** can emit light on the scene and on the objects.

Getting ready

1. Open the start_04.blend file and go to the **World** window under the **Properties** panel to the right of the interface. This is where we see the usual **Use Nodes** button under the **Surface** tab.

2. Although no node system for the **World** window is set by default, the **World** window has a dark medium gray color already slightly lighting the scene. Delete the default lamp or put it on a different and disabled layer to see that the spheroid in the scene is dark but still visible in the rendered 3D viewport.

3. It's already possible to change this gray color to some other color by clicking on the **Color** button right under **Use Nodes** (color at the horizon). This brings up the same color wheel we have seen for the shader colors. Set the color to R 0.179, G 0.152, and B 0.047 and save the file as start_05.blend.

Note that both the intensity as well as the general color graduation of the World are driven by this color. To have more light, just move the **Value** slider (the vertical one) towards a whiter hue. To give a general color mood to the scene, pick a color inside the wheel. This will affect all of the scene's illumination but will show mainly in the shadows, as shown in the following screenshot:

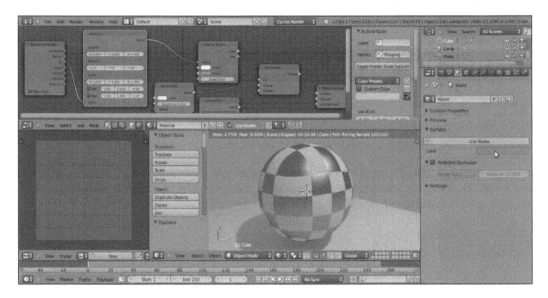

How to do it...

However, to have access to all the options for the **World**, we have to initialize it as a node system:

1. Look in the bottom header of the **Node Editor** window, on the left-hand side of the material datablock, there are two little icons: a little cube and a little world and, yes, the cube icon is used for creating materials, while the world icon is for the **World** window. At the moment, because we were working on the spheroid material, the cube icon is the one selected.

2. Click on the little world icon. The material's node disappears and the **Node Editor** window is empty now, because we entered the **World** mode. Check the little **Use Nodes** box on the right of the datablock to make a default world material appear. Or else, go to the **World** window under the **Properties** panel and click on the **Use Nodes** button under the **Surface** tab, as shown here:

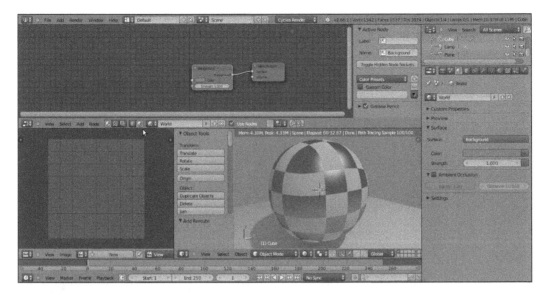

Also, for the **World**, the default material is simply made up of two nodes: a **Background** node connected to a **World Output** node. In the **Background** node, there are two setting options: the **Color** box and the **Strength** slider, both of which are quite self-explanatory.

3. Go to the **World** window under the **Properties** panel and click on the little square with a dot to the right side of the **Color** slot. From the resulting menu, select the **Sky Texture** node item. This replicates a physical sky model, with an atmospheric **Turbidity** value slider and the **Strength** slider, as shown here:

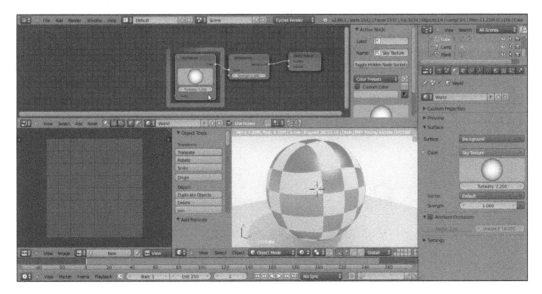

Note that you can also modify the incoming direction of the light, that is, the location of the sun, by rotating the sphere icon inside the node interface.

4. Save the file as `start_06.blend`.

5. Click on the **Color** button, which is now labeled as **Sky Texture** under the **Surface** tab in the **Properties** panel and select the **Environment Texture** node to replace it:

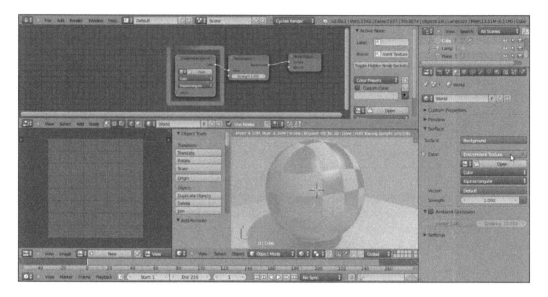

6. Looking in the **Rendered** view, you'll see that the general lighting has turned to a pink color. This is to show that the **World** material is now using a texture to light the scene, but that at the moment there is no texture yet.

7. Click on the **Open** button both in the **World** window under the **Properties** panel or in the just added node inside the **Node Editor** window. Browse to the `texture` folder and load the `Barce_Rooftop_C_3k.hdr` image (a free high dynamic range image licensed under the Creative Commons Attribution-Noncommercial-Share Alike 3.0 License from the **sIBL Archive** `http://www.hdrlabs.com/sibl/archive.html`).

8. To better appreciate the effect, click on the little eye icon on the side of the **Lamp** item in the **Outliner** to disable its lighting. The spheroid is now exclusively lit by the .hdr image assigned to the **World** material. Actually, you can also see the image as a background in the **Rendered** preview. You can also rotate the viewport and watch the background texture, "pinned" to the **World** coordinates, rotate accordingly in real time.

9. As for object's materials, the mapping of any texture you are going to use for the **World** can be driven by the usual **Mapping** and **Texture Coordinates** nodes we have already seen. Generally, for the **World** materials, only the **Generated** coordinates output should be used, and actually it's the one used by default if no mapping method is specified. Add the **Mapping** and **Texture Coordinates** nodes and connect them to the **Vector** input socket of the **Environment Texture** node, as shown in the following screenshot:

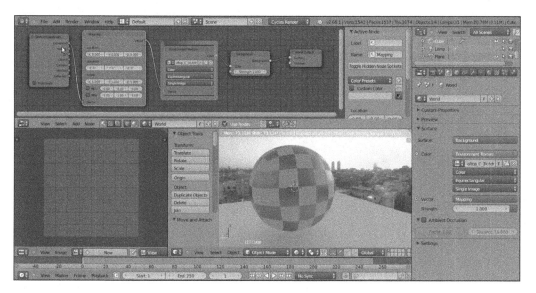

10. Save the file as start_07.blend.

But now, let's imagine a case in which we want to assign a texture to the **World** material and use it for the general lighting of the scene, but we don't want it to show in the background of the render. That is, for example, we are using the hdr image to light the spheroid and the plane, but we want the two objects rendered on a uniform blue background, then how to do it? This is how we do it:

1. One way is to go in the **Render** window and, under the **Film** tab, check the **Transparent** option. This will show our spheroid and plane rendered both in the 3D viewport as well as in the effective final rendered image on a transparent background, that is, with a pre-multiplied alpha channel:

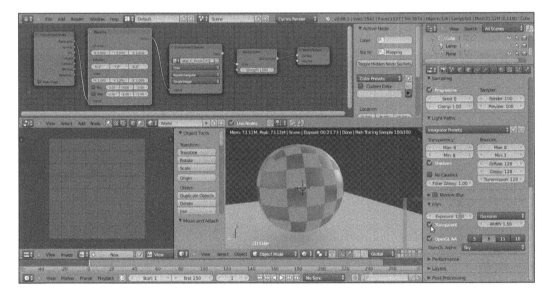

2. It's enough, then, to compose the rendered objects with a blue background image, both in an external image editing software (such as The Gimp, to stay inside F/OSS) or directly in the Blender compositor.

But the simplest way to render the two objects on a uniform blue background is to use a **Light Path** node:

1. If it's the case, uncheck the **Transparent** box in the **Render** window to restore the sky in the preview and in the render.

2. Left-click the **World Output** node in the **Node Editor** window, and press G and move it to the right.

3. Add a **Mix Shader** node (press *Shift + A* and select **Shader** | **Mix Shader**) and move it to the link connecting the **Background** node to the **World Output** node, to paste it automatically between the two nodes. Connect it to the **Surface** input socket of the **World Output** node.

4. Select the **Background** node in the **Node Editor** window. Press *Shift + D* to duplicate and move it down.

5. Connect its output to the second input socket of the **Mix Shader** node. Click on its **Color** box to change the color to R 0.023, G 0.083, and B 0.179.

6. Now, add a **Light Path** node (press *Shift + A* and go to **Input | Light Path**).

7. Connect the **Is Camera Ray** output of the **Light Path** node to the **Fac** input socket of the **Mix Shader** node, and voilà—the objects in the scene are lit by the hdr image connected to the first **Background** node, but they appear on a "sky" that is colored as set in the **Color** box of the second **Background** node:

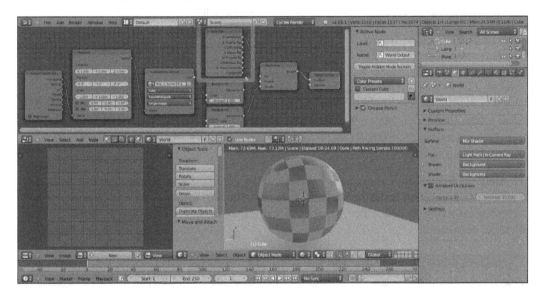

8. Save the file as start_08.blend.

How it works...

To better explain this "trick", let's say we just created two different **World** materials: the first one with the texture and the second one with a plain light blue color (this is not literally true, actually the material is just one containing the nodes of both the "ideally" different worlds).

We mixed these two materials by using the **Mix Shader** node. The upper green socket is considered equal to a value of 0.000, while the bottom green socket is considered as a value of 1.000. As the name itself suggests, the **Light Path** node can set the path for the rays of light that, if you remember, are shot from the camera. **Is Camera Ray** means that only the rays directly shot from the camera have a value of 1.000, that is, not the reflected ones, or the transmitted ones, or whatever, which instead have a value of 0.000.

So, because the textured world is connected to a socket equal to the value 0.000, we don't see it directly as a background but only see its effect on the objects lit from the reflected light or from the hdr image. The blue sky world that is connected to the value 1.000 input socket instead shows as a background because the light rays shot from the camera directly hit the sky.

There is more...

Just after the **Surface** tab, in the **World** window, there is the **Ambient Occlusion** (AO) tab. **AO** is a lighting method used to emphasize the shapes or the details of a surface, based on how much a point on that surface is occluded by the nearby surfaces. Although not exactly the same thing, **AO** can replace, in some cases, the Global Illumination effect. For example, to render interiors having fast and noise-free results, **AO** is a cheap way to get an effect that looks a bit like indirect lighting.

There is a checkbox to enable AO along with the following two sliders:

> ▸ **Factor**: Used for the strength of the AO. A value of 1.00 is equivalent to a white World.

> ▸ **Distance**: Is the distance from a shading point to the trace rays. Shorter distance emphasizes nearby features, a longer distance makes it take objects further away into account.

The **Ambient Occlusion** feature is only applied to the **Diffuse BSDF** component of a material. **Glossy** or **Transmission BSDF** components are not affected. Instead, the transparency of a surface is taken into account. For example, a half transparent surface will only half occlude the other surfaces.

Creating a mesh-light material

In this recipe, we will see how to create a mesh-light material to be assigned to any mesh object and used as source light to light the scene.

Getting ready

Until now we have used the default lamp (a **Point** light) already present in the scene for lighting the scene. By enabling the node system for the lamp, we have seen that the lamp uses a material created by connecting an **Emission** node to the **Lamp Output** node.

The good news is that, exactly because it's a node material, we can assign an **Emission** shader also to a mesh. For example, to a plane conveniently located, scaled, and rotated to point to the scene. Such a light emitting mesh is called a **Mesh-light**. Being a mesh, the **Emission** shader node output must be connected to the **Surface** input socket of a **Material Output** node instead of the **Lamp Output** node.

The light emission, coming from a surface and not from a point, is a lot more diffuse and softer than a lamp. A mesh-light can be any mesh of any shape and, therefore, can be easily used as an object taking part in the scene and being, at the same time, the real light source of the rendering—for example, a table lamp, or a neon sign, or a television screen. As a pure light-emitting plane, it's usually used as a sort of photographic diffuser. Two or three mesh-lights strategically placed can realistically simulate a photo studio situation.

1. Starting from the `start_07.blend` file, click on the eye lamp icon in the **Outliner** to enable it again.

2. Right-click the lamp in the 3D view and press *Shift + S* to bring up the **Snap** menu. Left-click on the **Cursor to Selected** item.

3. Press *Shift + A* with the mouse pointer in the 3D view and add a plane to the scene at the cursor's location.

4. Come out of edit mode (press *Tab*). *Shift* select the lamp; now you have both the just added plane and the lamp selected, and the latter is the active one.

5. Press *Crtl + C* to bring up the **Copy Attributes** menu and select the **Copy Rotation** item.

6. Rename this plane to **Emitter**.

7. Right-click the lamp in the 3D view and press *X* to delete it.

8. Put the mouse pointer in the 3D view and press *0* from the numpad to go to **Camera** view.

9. From the **Viewport Shading** menu in the window header, select the **Rendered** mode:

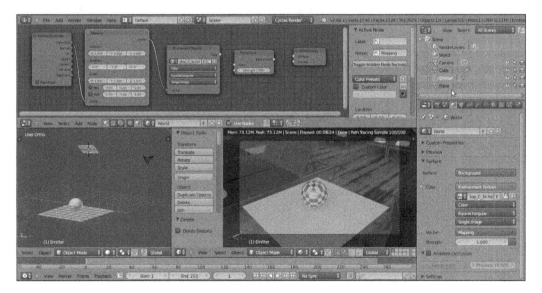

10. Save the file as `start_09.blend`.

How to do it...

1. Select the **Emitter** plane and click on the little cube icon on the header of the **Node Editor** window.

2. Click on the **New** button in the header and rename the material as **Emitter**.

3. In the **Properties** panel, go to the **Material** window and under the **Surface** tab, click on the **Surface** button to switch the **Diffuse BSDF** shader with an **Emission** shader. Leave the default color unchanged (RGB 0.800) and set the **Strength** slider to **35.000**.

4. Save the file.

5. In the 3D view, scale the **Emitter** plane five times bigger (press *S*, digit *5*, and hit *Enter*), then set the **Strength** slider to **3.500**.

6. Save the file as `start_10.blend`.

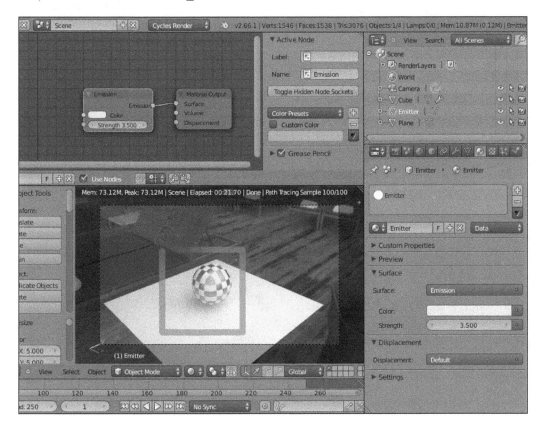

7. Now let's scale the **Emitter** plane a lot smaller (press *S*, digit *0.05*, and hit *Enter*) and set the **Strength** slider to **350.000**.

8. Save the file as `start_11.blend`.

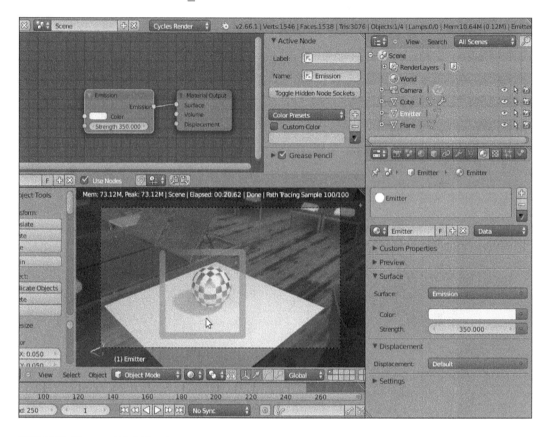

How it works...

From step 5 to step 7, we saw how a mesh-light can be scaled bigger or smaller to obtain a softer (in the first case) or a sharper (in the second case) shadow. The **Strength** value must be adjusted for the light intensity to remain consistent, or the mesh-light must be moved closer or more distant from the scene.

Scaling the mesh-light basically is the same as setting the size value for a lamp. For lamps, the softness of the shadows can be set by the **Size** value on the left of the **Cast Shadow** option in the **Lamp** window under the **Properties** panel (by default, the **Size** value is set to **1.000**). At a value of **0.000**, the shadow is at its maximum crispness, or sharpness. By increasing the **Size** value, the softness of the shadow increases too.

Differently from the mesh-light, varying the **Size** value of a lamp doesn't require us to adjust the **Strength** value to keep the same light intensity.

There's more...

In several cases, you would want the emitters to not appear in your render. There are node arrangements to accomplish this (by using the **Light Path** node in a very similar way to the *Setting the World material* recipe we have seen before), but the easiest way to do this is as follows:

1. Start with the last saved blend (`start_11.blend`) with the 3D window on the left also set to the **Rendered** mode, to see the scene out of the **Camera** view (so the **Emitter** plane is rendered too).

2. With the **Emitter** plane still selected, go to the **Object** window under the **Properties** panel.

3. Look in the **Ray Visibility** tab (usually, at the bottom of the **Properties** window), where there are five items: **Camera**, **Diffuse**, **Glossy**, **Transmission**, and **Shadows** with corresponding checked boxes.

4. Uncheck the **Camera** item and watch the **Emitter** plane disappear in the rendered 3D window, but the scene still lit by it, as shown in the following screenshot:

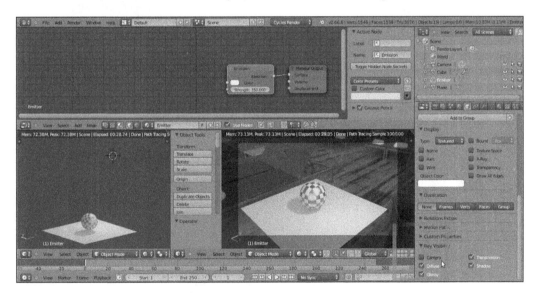

By checking any one of the items, the corresponding property won't take part in the rendering. In our case, by unchecking the **Camera** box, the mesh won't be rendered, although still emitting light. Be careful that, at this moment, the **Emitter** plane is not renderable but, because all the other items in the tab are still checked, it can be reflected, and if this is the case, can cast its own shadow on the other objects.

5. Now reselect the spheroid (remember that, unless you have renamed it, its name in the **Outliner** still shows as **Cube**). Next, from the **Ray Visibility** tab in the **Object** window under the **Properties** panel, uncheck the **Camera** item as well.

   Now the spheroid has disappeared, but it's still casting its shadow on the plane, as shown in the following screenshot:

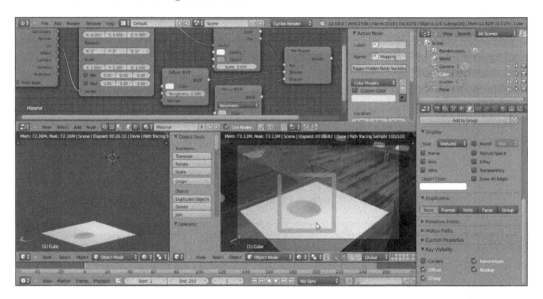

6. Now uncheck the **Camera** and the **Shadow** checkboxes. In this case, the spheroid is visible again but is not casting any shadow, as shown here:

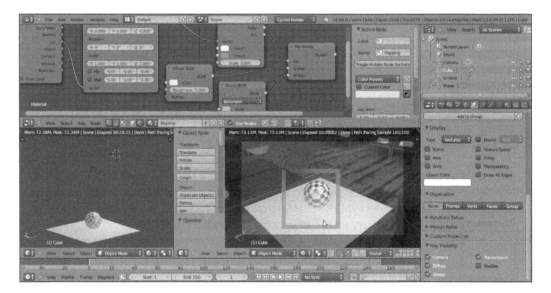

7. Save the file as `start_12.blend`. Let's try tweaking this a little.

8. Check the **Shadow** box for the spheroid and select the bottom plane.

9. In the **Material** window under the **Properties** panel, switch the **Diffuse BSDF** shader with a **Glossy BSDF** shader. The bottom plane is now acting as a perfect mirror, reflecting the spheroid and the `.hdr` image, which we had formerly set in the **World** material.

10. Go back to the **Object** window and reselect the spheroid. In the **Ray Visibility** tab, uncheck the **Glossy** item and watch the spheroid still rendered but no more reflected by the mirroring plane, as shown here:

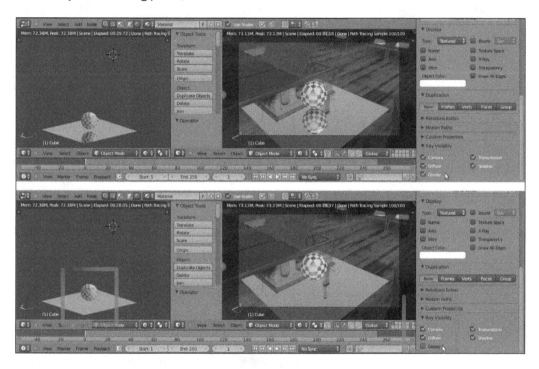

11. Save the file as `start_13.blend`.

The **Ray Visibility** trick we've just seen, of course, is not needed for lamps, because a lamp cannot be rendered in any case. At the moment, only **Point**, **Spot**, **Area**, and **Sun** lamps are supported inside Cycles; **Hemi** lamps are rendered as **Sun** lamps.

Both lamps and mesh-lights can use textures to, for example, project colored lights on the scene, but only a mesh-light can be unwrapped and UV mapped with an image map.

More, it seems that mesh-lights work better than lamps in Cycles, that is, the light casting and diffusion looks better and more realistic with an emitting plane. It's not clear if this is just a technical lamp limitation or if it will be improved in the future.

One advantage lamps have on mesh-lights is that they are easily made unidirectional, that is, apart from **Point** lamps, they cast light in only one direction, as shown in the following screenshot:

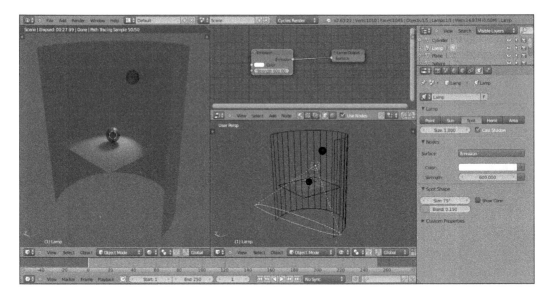

In the preceding screenshot, you can see that only the plane and the sphere in front are lit by the **Spot** lamp. With a mesh-light plane replacing the **Spot** lamp, instead, both the sphere and the cylindrical green wall behind are lit, as shown here:

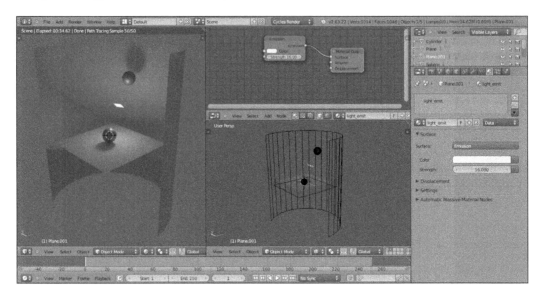

So what if we want to only light the object in one direction (plane and sphere in front) with a mesh-light? Is there a way to make a light-emitting plane to emit it only from one side and not the opposite one? Yes, of course, there is:

1. Open the `1301OS_01_meshlight.blend` file, which has a prepared scene similar to the one used for the preceding screenshots, and set the bottom 3D window to the **Rendered** mode by clicking on the **Viewport Shading** button in the header and selecting the upper item.

2. Left-click the **Emitter** item in the **Outliner** and put the mouse pointer in the **Node Editor** window. Add a **Mix Shader** node (press *Shift + A* and go to **Shader | Mix Shader**) and move it to the link connecting the **Emission** node to the **Material Output** node to paste it in between.

3. Add a **Geometry** node (press *Shift + A* and go to **Input | Geometry**) and connect its **Backfacing** output to the **Fac** input socket of the **Mix Shader** node.

4. Switch the **Emission** node output from the first **Shader** input socket of the **Mix Shader** node to the second one, as shown in the following screenshot:

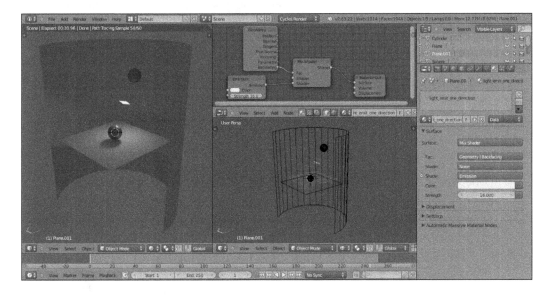

5. Save the file as `1301OS_01_meshlight_final.blend`.

The plane is now emitting light only in one direction.

How it works...

We have already seen that in a **Mix Shader** node the first (upper) green **Shader** input socket is considered equal to a 0 value, while the second one to a 1 value. So, the **Backfacing** output of the **Geometry** node is stating Cycles to make the plane emit light only in the face-normal direction, and to keep black and non-emitting (just like a blank shader) the opposite "backfacing" side of the plane.

By switching the **Emission** node connection to the first **Mix Shader** input sockets, it's obviously possible to invert the direction of the light emission.

Using displacement (aka bump)

To obtain both bumps and displacement effect in Cycles, there are a few options.

The simplest way to have bumps on our material's surface is by connecting the **Color** or the **Fac** output of a texture node to the **Displacement** input socket of the **Material Output** node. Despite the fact that the socket's name is **Displacement**, the effect I'm writing at the moment is just a simple bump effect (by the way, a very good one), affecting as a whole the total result of the sum of the material's nodes.

How to do it...

Just as we did for color textures, the bump textures can also be mapped on the object with the **Mapping** and **Texture Coordinate** nodes. There is naturally also a way to set the amount (the strength) of bumpiness of the texture on the object's surface:

1. Open the `start_02.blend` file and set the 3D view to the **Rendered** mode.

2. Put the mouse pointer in the **Node Editor** window and press *Shift + A* to bring up the **Add** menu and select a **Math** node from the **Convertor** item (press *Shift + A* and go to **Convertor | Math**).

3. Connect the **Fac** output of the **Wave Texture** node, already connected to the **Roughness** input socket of the **Glossy BSDF** shader node, to the first upper gray **Value** input socket of the **Math** node. Connect the **Math** node output to the **Displacement** input socket of the **Material Output** node.

4. Set the operation mode of the **Math** node to **Multiply**. By sliding the second **Math** node **Value**, we can set the influence, the strength, of the bumping. Try, for example, to set it to **3.000**, as shown in the following screenshot:

5. Save the file as `start_14.blend`.

How it works...

Put simply, the gray-scale values of the texture are multiplied for the value we put in the second slider of the **Math** node. For example, if we set a value of `0.500`, the intensity of the effect will be the half of the default one (1.000 x 0.500 = 0.500). With a value of `3.000`, the effect will be three times the default one. Similar to Blender Internal, the value can also be set as negative (`-3.000` in this case), thereby inverting the direction of the bump effect.

Note that there is an evident problem at the terminator of the spheroid (that is, at the limit of the lit surface with the self-shadowed one) that seems as a general limit of path tracers. To get rid of it, you can try to subdivide the mesh by a higher value (a little impractical method, honestly), but this not always is enough. A different way is to modify the **Size** value of the lamp (or the scale if you are using a mesh-light). Select the lamp in the **Outliner**, and in the **Size** button under the **Type of Lamp** row in the **Object Data** window, set **Size** to **1.000**. The terminator looks a lot smoother now (along with also, obviously, the projected shadow on the plane):

There is more...

From Blender 2.65 onwards, a **Normal** input socket has been added to all the appropriate shader nodes, to input values for the bump of each shader node itself. This input socket must be fed by a **Bump** node (press *Shift + A* and go to **Vector | Bump**). This is how we do so:

1. Starting from the `start_14.blend` file, select the **Math** node in the **Node Editor** window and delete it (press *X*).

2. Put the mouse pointer in the **Node Editor** window and press *Shift + A* to add a **Bump** node (press *Shift + A* and go to **Vector | Bump**).

3. Connect the **Fac** output of the **Wave Texture** node to the **Height** input socket of the **Bump** node and the output of the latter to the **Normal** input socket of the **Diffuse BSDF shader** node. Set the **Strength** value to `0.050`.

4. Add a **Voronoi Texture** node (press *Shift + A* and go to **Texture | Voronoi Texture**) and a new **Bump** node (press *Shift + A* and go to **Vector | Bump**). Connect the **Fac** output of the **Voronoi Texture** node to the **Height** socket of the new **Bump** node and connect the latter to the **Normal** input socket of the **Glossy BSDF** shader node:

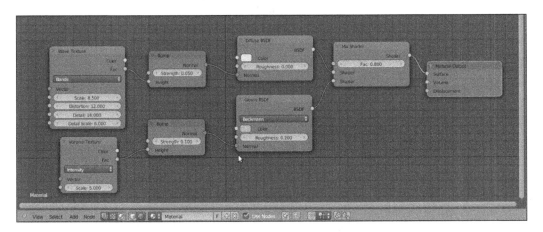

5. Save the file as `start_15.blend`.

As you can see in the preceding image, it's now also possible to have the bump effect *per node*. That is, every shader node can have a different bump with different strength (note that it's no more needed to connect anything to the **Displacement** input socket of the **Material Output** node). This way, we can have a certain bump effect only on an established component of the shader (the diffuse shader), and a different bump on the other components (the glossy shader), as shown here:

As far as displacement is concerned, we can use the **Displace Modifier** option in the **Object Modifiers** panel, using a texture to be set in the **Textures** tab under the **Properties** panel. It seems no Cycles texture can be used for this at the moment, but only the old Blender Internal textures at disposal from a menu. In this case, the displacement is not behaving any differently from the displacement we have in BI. The mesh must be subdivided (usually the **Subdivision Surface** modifier is used, but also the **Multiresolution** modifier can be used) and then displaced. In short, there is nothing as a "micro-polygon displacement rendering" yet.

By the way, by enabling **Experimental** in the **Feature Set** tab under **Render** in the **Render** window, it's possible to have access to a (still incomplete) displacement feature:

1. Go to the **Render** window under the **Properties** panel. In the **Render** tab click on the **Feature Set** button, by default labeled with **Supported**, and select **Experimental**.

2. Go to the **Object Data** window to find a new tab named **Displacement**, where we can choose between three options: **Bump**, **True**, or **Both** (the **Use Subdivision** and **Dicing Rate** buttons don't seem to work yet).

> **Bump** will give us the average bump effect, which is the same as connecting the texture output in the **Displacement** input of the **Material Output** node (that we'll have to do in any case).
>
> By setting the method to **True**, we can have a displacement effect not different from the **Displace Modifier** output, and the mesh must be subdivided.
>
> **Both** will use the texture gray-scale values' information for a displacement and the bump effect together.

3. Select **True**.

4. Reselect the spheroid. Go in the **Material** window under the **Properties** panel, and in the **Displacement** tab click on the blue **Value** button labeled **Wave Texture** to select an **Image Texture** node from the pop-up menu.

5. Click on the **Open** button, browse to the `textures` folder, and load the `quads.png` image.

6. Just under the **Open** button, click on the **Color Space** button to set it to **Non-Color Data**.

7. Split the bottom 3D window to open a **UV/Image Editor** window. Press *Tab* to go in edit mode and then press *U* with the mouse pointer in the 3D window. In the **UV Mapping** menu, select **Smart UV Project**, then press *Tab* again to go out of edit mode (this is a quicker way of unwrapping the spheroid which, remember, at its lower level of subdivision is still a cube. If you want, you can do a better unwrapping by placing seams to unfold it and by selecting a normal **Unwrap** from the menu).

8. Go to the **Object Modifiers** window and raise the **Subdivisions** levels for both **View** and **Render** to 6:

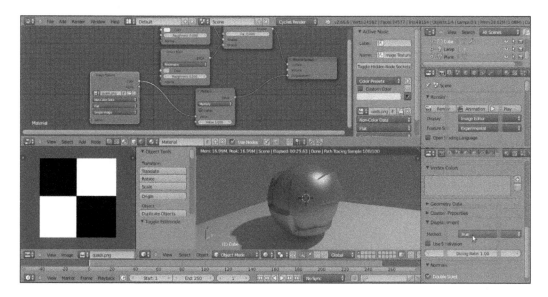

In any case, this is just for a temporary demonstration, the feature is still incomplete and at the moment seems to work (quite) properly only if the texture is mapped with UV coordinates. This is definitely going to change in the future.

2
Managing Cycles Materials

In this chapter, we will cover:

- Preparing an ideal Cycles interface for material creation
- Naming materials and textures
- Creating node groups
- Linking materials

Introduction

As with Blender Internal materials, Cycles materials can (and should) be organized to optimize not only your workflow but also Blender memory management.

Material nodes can easily grow quite complex in Cycles so it's sometimes a good idea to split and label the different parts of a shader's network, just to make the meaning of the different sections more clear (even to yourself; maybe at a certain point of your workflow, you forget how exactly you organized the 120 nodes of material you made a couple of months before working). Moreover, organized materials can be easily reused in other files, projects, or as parts of bigger and different materials.

The organization of the materials basically is made by grouping them and/or giving them proper names and defined locations, so as to be easily found on the hard disk.

Preparing an ideal Cycles interface for material creation

Before starting with the actual organization, it's a good idea to prepare a material creation screen to be saved in your Blender preferences.

It is possible, in fact, to prepare a basic scene setup including the elements and the settings we need to do the job in the best way.

In any case, just take this paragraph with a pinch of salt; that is, more as a suggestion or as a starting point that you can eventually modify to better agree with your needs.

How to do it...

1. Start Blender and in the upper menu (**Engine to use for rendering** button) switch to **Cycles Render**.

2. Split the 3D view into two horizontal rows: move the mouse cursor onto the edge of the window; the cursor changes to a double arrow icon, right-click, and from the context menu select **Split Area**.

3. Change the upper window into a **Node Editor** by selecting the item from the **Editor type** button in the left-hand corner of the bottom bar.

4. Select the default cube in the scene and press *Tab* to go in edit mode.

5. Press *W* on the keyboard; in the **Specials** pop-up menu select **Subdivide Smooth**. Do it three times; the cube is now a Spheroid made by 386 vertexes.

6. Go out of edit mode and set the cube's **Shading** mode to Smooth using the **Object Tools** panel on the left.

7. Move the cube two units upward on the **Z** axis (*G* | *Z* | *2* | *Enter*).

8. Being careful that the cursor is still at the center of the scene (if not, press *Shift + C* to center it), press *Shift + A* | **Mesh** | **Plane** to add a plane.

9. Still with the plane in edit mode, scale it four times bigger.

10. Split the bottom row into two parts, put the mouse cursor in the 3D window on the right and press *O* in the numpad of the keyboard to go in Camera view; then press *T* to close the **Object Tools** panel on the left.

The following screenshot shows where we are so far:

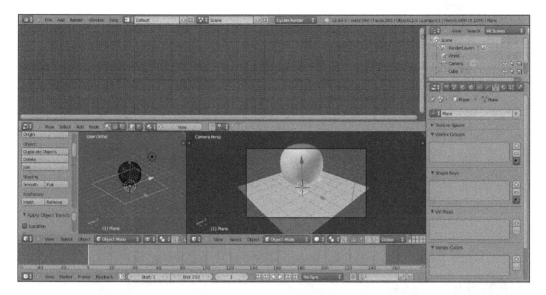

11. In the **Editor type** button in the left-hand corner of the bottom bar, of the left 3D window, select **UV/Image Editor**.

12. Put the mouse in the Camera view and press *Shift + F* to enter fly mode (a viewfinder appears to show the center of the camera field); by slightly moving the mouse upward (scroll wheel to go forward or backward) adjust the Camera view to better fit the cube, then hit *Enter* or left-click to confirm:

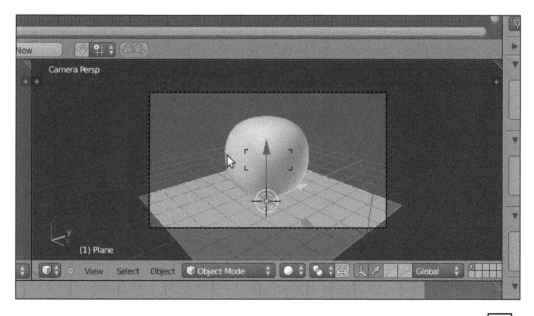

13. Select the plane and press **New** in the **Node Editor** header to assign a new material, rename it **Plane**, and let all the settings be as they are.

14. Select the cube and press **Use Nodes** in the **Material** window under the **Properties** panel or in the **Node Editor** header.

15. Under the **Surface** tab in the **Material** window, switch the **Diffuse BSDF** shader with a **Mix Shader**, then click in the first slot to select a **Diffuse BSDF**, and in the second slot for a **Glossy BSDF** shader.

16. In the **Node Editor** adjust the position of the nodes to make them more easily readable:

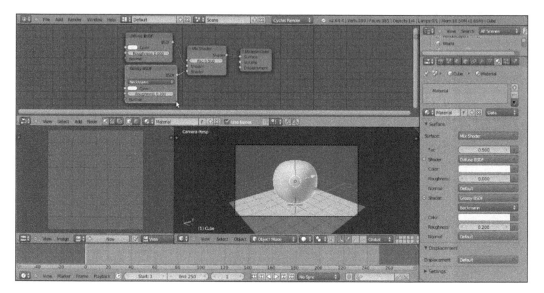

17. Set the Camera view to **Rendered** mode by clicking on the **Viewport Shading** button on the window header and selecting the upper item. Then go in the **Render** window under the **Properties** panel on the right, and under the **Sampling** tab, set **Clamp** to **1.00**, and both **Render** and **Preview** to **50** samples:

18. Set the Percentage scale for **render resolution** under **Dimensions** to **25**%.

19. Under the **Performance** tab, set the **Acceleration** structure to **Static BVH** and check both **Use Spatial Splits** and **Cache BVH** (this is probably not really useful for a simple Spheroid but just in case you want to render a more complex object).

20. Now select the lamp and delete it (press *X* on the keyboard); go to the **World** window and click on **Use Nodes** for the material.

21. Click on **Color** and set the RGB values to 0.100 and the **Strength** to **0.100**; set the **Ambient Occlusion** (**AO**) to **0.30** but let it be unchecked (it's a low value ready in case we want to use the AO, but it's usually better not to have it activated by default).

22. Now press *Shift + A* and add a new plane; out of edit mode, press *N* in the Camera view and in the **Transform** tab on the right of the 3D window set these values: **Location X** as **145.00**, **Y** as **-65.00**, and **Z** as **110.00**; **Rotation X** as **-16°**, **Y** as **-126°**, and **Z** as **-4°**; **Scale X**, **Y**, and **Z** as **12**.

23. Go into the **Material** window and assign a new material; switch the **Diffuse BSDF** shader with an **Emission** one, set the **Color** to pure white, and the **Strength** to **120.000**; change the material's name in **Emitter**:

24. Press *N* to close the Camera view **Properties** panel.

Optionally, other things that you can do: increase the scale of the floor plane, in the Outliner set the mode to **Visible Layers**, and click on the arrows of the two planes (floor and emitter) to make them non-selectable; select the cube and in the **Object Modifiers** window assign a **Subdivision Surface** modifier to make it look more smoothed.

25. Go back to the **Material** window. Press *Ctrl + U* to save the setting as user default (**Save Startup File**). Done.

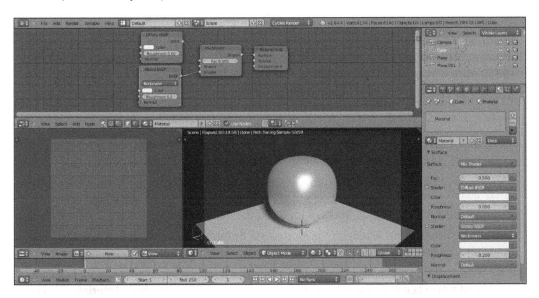

How it works...

We set a very low **World** global illumination, keeping it gray so as not to affect the color of the material. For the same reason we added a quite powerful mesh-light emitting pure white light, scaling it big and moving it quite distant from the center of the scene to obtain clear shadows. The floor plane is to have bouncing light on the shadowed parts of the object.

We prepared the **Rendered** viewport as a Camera view to have a better feedback for the final rendered image, which will show at 25 percent of the established size in the **UV/Image Editor** window on the bottom left-hand side of the screen.

By setting the **Clamp** value to **1.00** we reduced the fireflies produced by the **Glossy** shader and by increasing the **Render** and **Preview** samples to **50** we reduced the noise, keeping at the same time the rendering times reasonable even with a not very powerful workstation.

The **Acceleration structure** set to **Static BVH** and the **Use Spatial Splits** and **Cache BVH** options are useful to reduce the calculation time for the bounding volume hierarchy of the mesh that Cycles has to calculate every time it starts a rendering. Anyway, this is useful only if the mesh doesn't get any modification between renderings.

There's more...

The layout and the settings we just saved as default are what we are going to see at first from now on every time we start Blender.

But maybe we don't want to have a Cycles material interface every time to start with, and we prefer to have it as an option to be used only if there is the need.

Here is a simple way to do this:

1. Start Blender with the factory settings (**File | Load Factory Setting**) and look at the top of the screen, in the main header on the side of the **Blender Render** button: there are two more buttons labeled **Default** and **Scene**.

2. By clicking on the **Default** button we can set a different interface layout (there are already nine, each one studied for a different task, and their names are perfectly explicative); clicking on **Scene** shows just the current scene.

3. By clicking on the **+** icon on the side of the **Default** button, add a new screen layout, and rename it **Materials**.

4. Then click on the **+** icon on the side of the **Scene** button and, by choosing **Full Copy**, add a new scene to the file and rename it something like **Cycles_Materials**. This new scene is a full copy of the default one, coexisting but independent.

At this point we can start with all the instructions already seen in the *How to do it...* section of this recipe, that is switching to **Cycles Render**, splitting the 3D window, subdividing the cube, and so on.

When done, just click on the screens button and switch back to **Default**, then save the user preferences (*Ctrl + U*). Now our material creation interface is saved as a screen option in a different scene; every time we need to access it, we simply select the layout **Materials** from the screens button.

Naming materials and textures

It is known that one of the most important things to do (working in every workflow with every 3D package) is to give all the assets proper and explicative names; that is, in our case, to the materials and to the textures.

How to do it...

1. Start Blender, go to the **File** menu in the top-left corner of the screen, and choose **Load Factory Setting** (this is just to be sure to start with the default **Blender/Cycles** settings):

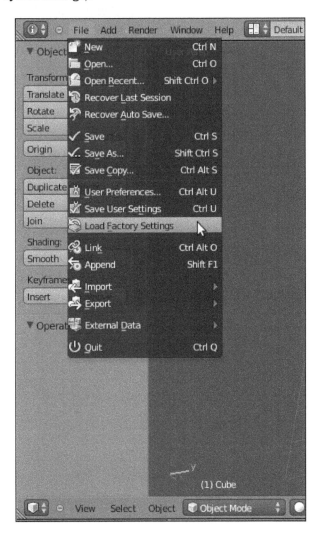

2. Now, if you are in Blender Internal mode, switch to **Cycles Render**.

3. Select the default Cube and go to the **Material** window in the **Properties** panel: the default cube already has a material assigned. This material has already been named by Blender itself, yes, **Material**:

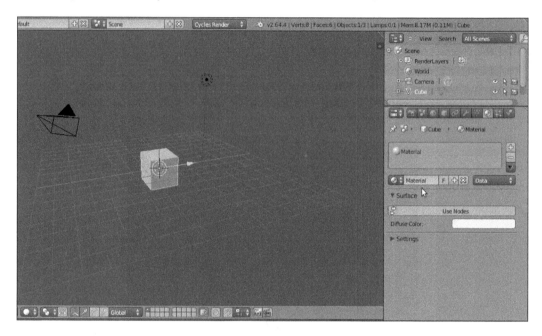

4. When you create a new material, for example by clicking on the **+** symbol on the side of the material data block (Add a new material) under the **Properties** panel, Blender automatically assigns a new name to this material, usually something like **Material.001**, **Material.002**, **Material.003**, and so on:

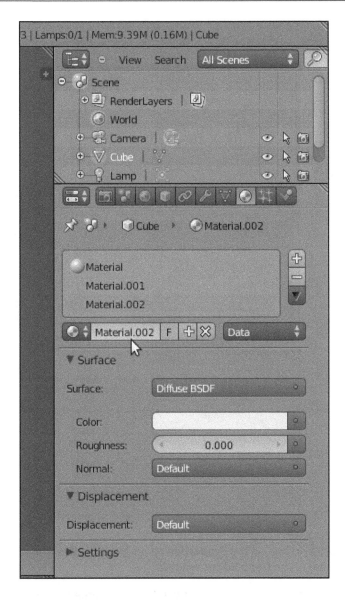

To have an automatic nomenclature can be handy in most cases but can become really confusing as a scene grows in complexity or if you have to reuse some of the materials in other situations. If this is the case then we'd better rename all our materials with significant names.

5. To rename a material it's enough to click with the left mouse button in the material name data block and define a new name, then press *Enter* to confirm:

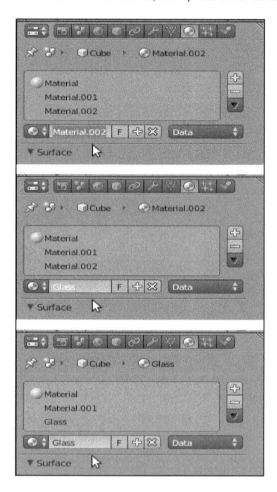

6. This can be done both in the **Properties** panel as in the **Material** data block button on the header of the **Node Editor** window.

   Things are a little different for textures; in Cycles textures are no more data blocks but nodes, so every time we add a texture node to a material network it gets automatically named accordingly to the kind of texture we added. That is, if we add a **Voronoi Texture**, the texture node is named **Voronoi Texture** and actually there should be no reason to change it.

   But it is always possible to find a reason to rename it; in this case:

   ❑ Put the mouse in the **Node Editor** and press *N* on the keyboard, a new panel appears on its right side. The first two slot in this panel, **Label** and **Name**, are meant exactly for this purpose.

- By clicking in the texture name in the **Textures** window under the **Properties** panel, we see that a second **Voronoi** texture we just added has been automatically renamed by Blender as **Voronoi Texture.001**.

- At least at the moment this isn't reflected in the **Node Editor** but only in the **Active Node** panel on its right. If we need a different name for that texture we can change it by clicking in the **Name** slot and by entering a new name, then confirmed by pressing *Enter*.

The same goes for the **Label** slot, but this time the label name gets reflected only in the **Node Editor**, exactly as a label applied to the node.

Creating node groups

The single nodes (shaders, textures, input, or whatever) can be grouped together and this is probably one of the best optimizations we can use to organize our workflow.

Thanks to node groups it's easy to store complex materials in ready-to-use libraries. It's possible to share or reuse them in other files or they can also be used to build handy shader interfaces, for easier tweaking of a material properties.

How to do it...

1. Start Blender and open the file `1301OS_02_09_basicshader.blend`:

2. It's a sphere leaning on a floor plane and with four little cubes at the plane's corners; as you can see in the **Node Editor**, the sphere (the already selected object) has a simple material composed by a **Diffuse** and a **Glossy** shaders mixed via the **Mix Shader** node.

3. Now box select (mouse cursor in the **Node Editor**, press *B* and drag a box to include the nodes) the **Diffuse** and the **Glossy** nodes.

4. Press *Ctrl + G* on the keyboard, a pop up appears; left-click with the mouse to confirm that you want to create a group of the selected nodes.

5. The two shaders get wrapped inside a box, that actually is the node group in edit mode; that is, the node group is open and editable, and we can access and modify its content.

6. Because the two shaders were already connected to the **Mix Shader** (that in this case we left out of the group on purpose), both the **Diffuse** and the **Glossy** outputs are now connected to two **BSDF** sockets automatically created on the right side of the node group.

7. As for every edit mode in Blender, by pressing the *Tab* key we go out of edit mode, closing the node group:

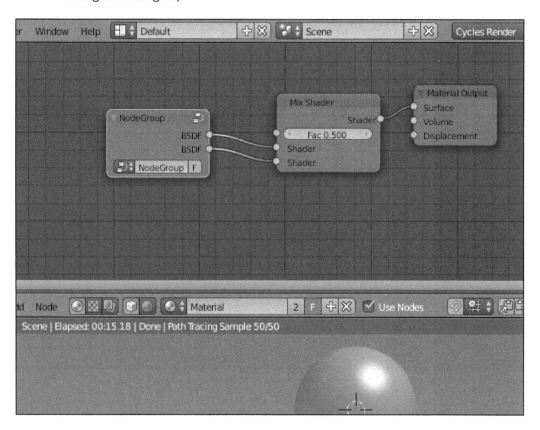

The node group is still showing the two **BSDF** outputs (actually connected to the input sockets of the **Mix Shader** node), the name data block and the **Fake User** button; this last one is the same as in Blender Internal, it prevents the user count from ever becoming zero and therefore any non-assigned material to be deleted when you close Blender or the file. By assigning the **Fake User** to a material you are sure that it will not be deleted. Particularly handy when you build your material library.

8. Now press *Tab* to enter edit mode again, click in the name data block, and change the default name NodeGroup to something else; I wrote **BasicShader**.

9. Left click on the **Roughness** input socket of the **Glossy** shader and drag the mouse to the left side of the node group; a new link appears:

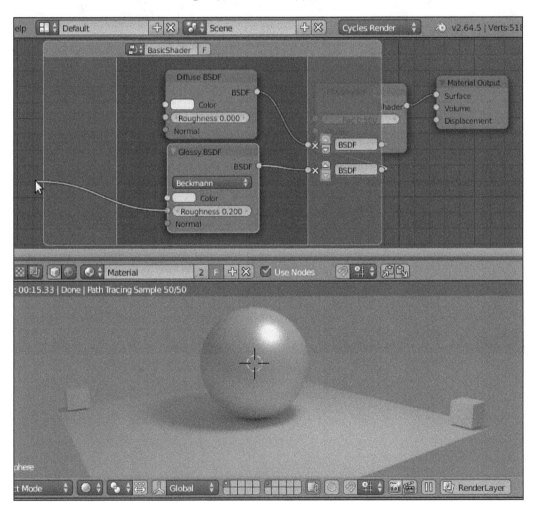

10. Release the mouse button, and a new input socket for the **Roughness** value will be created on the left side of the node group:

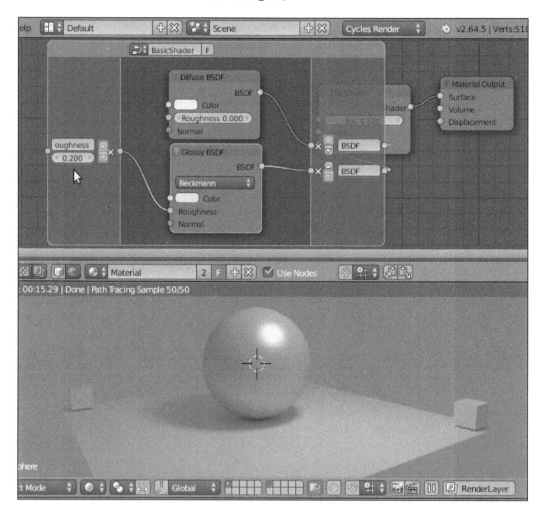

11. Do the same for the input socket of the color box of the **Diffuse** shader; new sockets are created in vertical order:

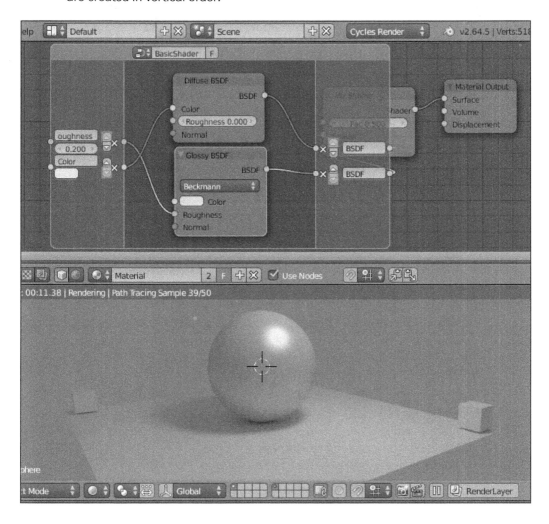

12. Look at the little arrows on the side of the group sockets:

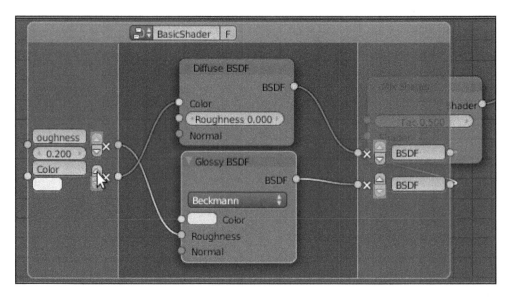

13. Click on the upper arrow to move the color socket upward.

14. Do the same things for the color box of the **Glossy** shader and for the **Normal** sockets of both the shaders (it's enough to create one and then connect to it the other **Normal** socket, because in this case we want just one single input driving the **Normal** sockets of both the shaders).

15. Click on the names of the new sockets to rename them as **DiffuseColor**, **SpecColor**, and **Bump**.

16. Now press *Tab* on the keyboard to go out of edit mode and here it is: a simple interface for the node group **BasicShader**:

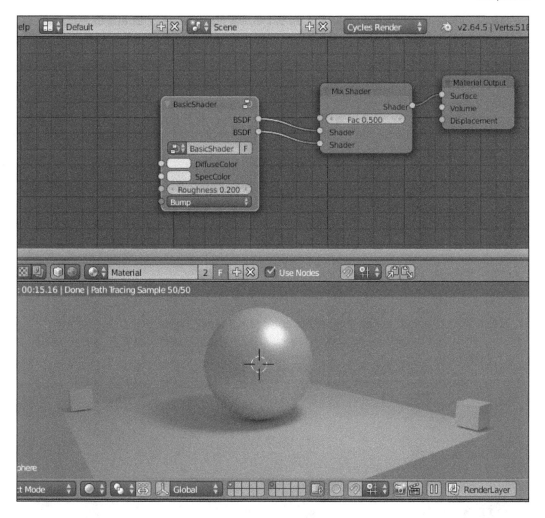

17. Press *Tab* again to go back in edit mode; put the mouse cursor inside the node and press *Shift + A* to add a **Mix Shader** node inside the group.

18. Connect the **Diffuse** and the **Glossy** to the new **Mix Shader** node and its output to one of the **BSDF** sockets; delete the other one by clicking on the **X** icon:

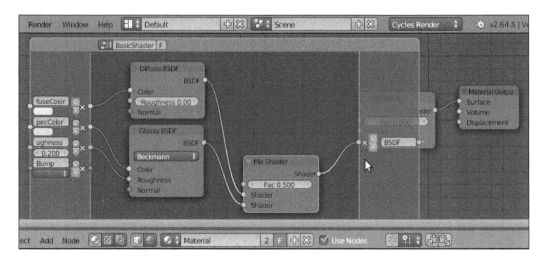

19. Go out of edit mode and select the outer **Mix Shader**; press *Alt + D* (this shortcut removes a node from a network leaving the connection untouched) to disconnect it. Delete it.

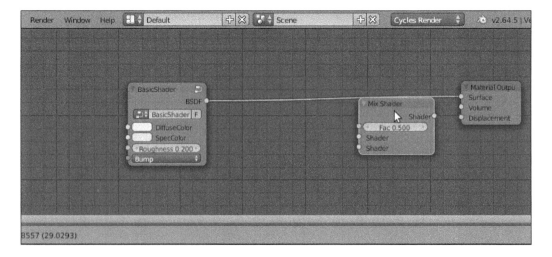

How it works...

I think you get the picture: basically any input or output socket of the nodes wrapped in a group can be piped to the outside of the node group itself to be tweaked; for example, we could also have made an input socket for the **Diffuse** roughness, or better, an input for the **Fac** of the inner **Mix Shader**, to change the reflectivity of the shader.

Another good thing about a node group is that you can make (*Shift + D*) instances of that node. Note that as you modify the inner structure of a node group, the modifications get reflected in all the group instances; conversely, the outer (exposed) values on the node group interface are local to each instance and can be individually tweaked.

Every newly created node group is available both in the *Shift + A* | **Add** menu and in the slots in the **Material** window of the **Properties** panel as well, under the voice Group, to be added to the network on-the-fly.

To remove a node group select it and press *Alt + G*; this will break the node envelope, keeping the content intact and connected.

Linking materials

Exactly as for Blender Internal, Cycles materials can be linked from libraries. Every blend file containing linkable assets can be a library.

Linking materials is really a useful practice: let's say you have 20 different blend files with objects using an iron shader, and that at a certain point of your workflow you need to modify this iron material in all the files; by having this material linked in all the 20 files from a single blend is possible to update all of them at once by modifying just one shader in one file.

How to do it...

1. Just go to the **File** menu in the left part of the main header and select **Link**:

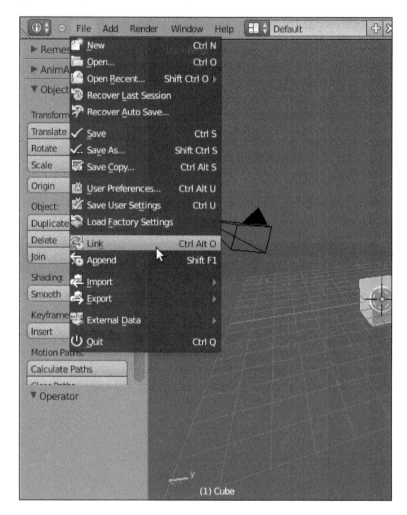

2. Browse to the directory where you store your library files and select the blend file you want to link the material from (for example, try the file `1301OS_02_library.blend`).

3. Browse inside the blend structure, where the linkable assets are divided into subdirectories (shown as folders named as `Scene`, `Mesh`, `Material`, `NodeTree`, `Object`, and so on; note that the various folders appear only if inside the blend file the corresponding asset to be linked actually exists).

4. Click on the `Material` subdirectory. Once inside, select the material you want to link (for example, `Material_04`) and press *Enter* to confirm (or click on the **Link/Append from Library** button on the top right).

5. Now click on the **Material** data block button on the header of the **Node Editor** window and select the name of the linked material, the one labeled with a **LF** prefix, L is for Linked and F is for Fake User.

6. This because, in the library file, we assigned the Fake User to the material by clicking on the **F** icon on the side of the **Material** name data block. If not assigned to any Fake User, the prefix of the linked material would have been L0, that is Linked and 0 Fake Users inside this blend file (for example, `Material_05`, which is simply assigned to the object but has no Fake User).

7. The name of the material is grayed out to show that is a linked one; on the side of the name a new icon has appeared, a little arrow, and the users number has been updated to **2** (the Fake User and the object we assigned the linked material to).

From now on, every modification we make to the material in the library will be reflected in the linked material at the moment we load the file.

Not only can materials be linked, but also node groups: in this case, instead of the `Material` subdirectory to link from, choose the `NodeTree` subdirectory, and then select one or more node groups you want to link.

The data block name of a linked node group is grayed as well; you can modify the exposed values and colors but if you try to enter edit mode a pop up asks if you want to make the group local; if you confirm, the node group becomes editable but, of course, local and no longer linked from the library file.

3
Creating Natural Materials in Cycles

In this chapter, we will cover:

- ▶ Creating a rock material using image maps
- ▶ Creating a rock material using procedural textures
- ▶ Creating a sand material using procedural textures
- ▶ Creating a simple ground material using procedural textures
- ▶ Creating a snow material using procedural textures
- ▶ Creating an ice material using procedural textures
- ▶ Creating a clean running water material

Introduction

Replicating "nature" can be quite a difficult task. Natural materials are usually the most difficult to recreate in a satisfying way using computers, mainly because the "orderly chaos" of nature is not the best fit for the "orderly logic" of an electronic machine.

Too often we see even cubes that look obviously computer generated because of the neatness add regularity of their shapes or surfaces. Actually, in reproducing true-to-life natural objects (or material as well), we have to start from the absolute regularity of the computer simulation and then, step by step, blemish it in a controlled way, to reach a more natural look.

Creating a rock material using image maps

In this recipe, we will create a realistic rock material similar to the one shown in the following screenshot:

The best way to start this task is by using image maps. Image maps are particularly useful for several reasons: they already have the necessary color information of a natural surface ready to use. They can be easily edited in any image editor to obtain different information as, for example, high levels for the bump maps. They are processed faster than procedurals by the software (procedural textures must be calculated every time). Moreover, they can be easily found for free on the Web in several sizes and resolutions.

Just remember to make any image you are going to use "tileable" using your preferred image editor. In Gimp, this job is automatically done by a plugin under **Filter** | **Map** | **Make Tileable**.

Getting ready

Open the `1301OS_03_start.blend` file, which is a simple layout ready for material creation:

▶ On layer **1** there are a smooth-subdivided "spheroid" cube and a modified plane, with extruded and curved vertical walls working as a backdrop and a default white material assigned.

▸ On layer **6** there is a mesh-light, a big plane, with a white emission material set to an intensity of 6.000.

▸ There is also a dark gray World, set to an intensity of 0.100 and with an **Ambient Occlusion** set to a **Factor** of 0.10 but left unchecked.

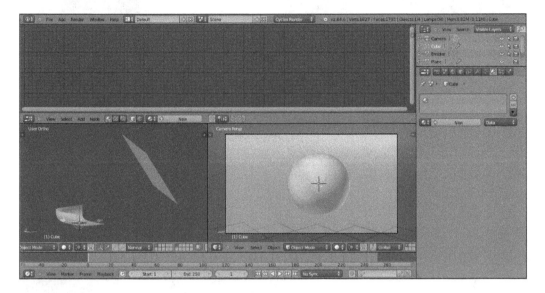

How to do it...

Carry out the following steps to create a rock material:

1. Select the subdivided cube and, for the purposes of this exercise, delete it by pressing *X* from the keyboard.

2. With the mouse pointer in the 3D window, press *Shift + A* to pop up the **Add** menu and add a new **Cube** primitive (press *Shift + A* and go to **Mesh | Cube**). Press *Tab* to go out of edit mode if needed.

3. Click on **New** in the **Material** window on the right, under the **Properties** panel, or in the header of the **Node Editor** window.

4. Put the mouse in the **Node Editor** window and add an **Image Texture** node (press *Shift + A* and go to **Texture | Image Texture**), then add a **Mapping** node (press *Shift + A* and go to **Vector | Mapping**) and a **Texture Coordinate** node (press *Shift + A* and go to **Input | Texture Coordinate**).

5. Connect the **Texture Coordinate** node's **Generated** output socket to the **Vector** input socket of the **Mapping** node, then its **Vector** output to the **Vector** input of the **Image Texture** node. Also connect the **Image Texture** node's **Color** output to the **Color** input of the **Diffuse BSDF** shader.

6. Set the mode of the **Camera** view to **Rendered**. The rendered cube turns pink because there isn't any image texture loaded yet, as shown here:

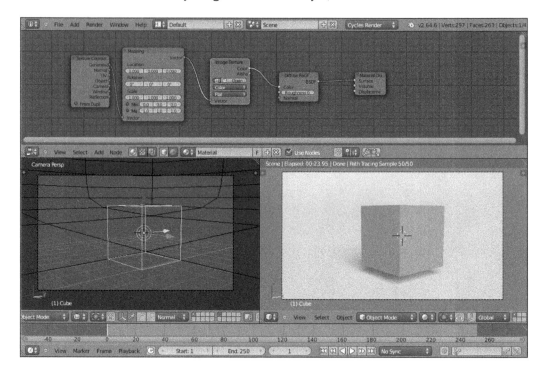

7. Click on the **Open** button in the **Image Texture** node. Browse to the `textures` folder and select the `rockcolor_tileable_low.png` image (this is just for the sake of this exercise, obviously you can use any other image you wish).

8. As we selected **Generated** as mapping mode, the image is mapped flat on the cube from the z axis and it appears stretched on the sides of the cube. Disconnect the **Generated** output of the **Texture Coordinate** node and connect instead the **Object** node instead. Click on the **Flat** button on the **Image Texture** node to select **Box**. The image now looks correctly mapped on each face of the cube.

9. Go to the **Object Modifiers** window and assign a **Subdivision Surface** modifier to the cube. Set the subdivision levels for both **View** and **Render** to 4.

10. Although the image map we used is tileable, there are visible seams on the corners of the subdivided cube. In the **Image Texture** node, set the **Blend** factor to 0.500, to soften the corners (this factor is to blend the faces of the cube which, remember, although it is a subdivided spheroid now, at its lower level it is still a six-faced cube):

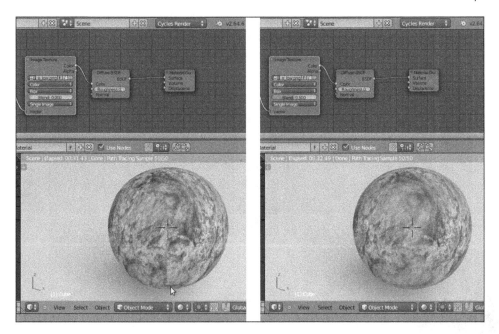

11. Now add a **ColorRamp** node (press *Shift + A* and go to **Convertor | ColorRamp**) between the **Image Texture** node and the **Diffuse** shader. Set the interpolation to **Ease**, move the marker of the black color to the middle of the slider and the white marker to a quarter on the left of the slider:

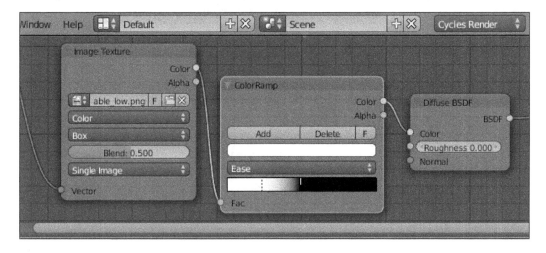

12. Add a **Bump** node (press *Shift + A* and go to **Vector | Bump**), connect the **Color** output of the **ColorRamp** node to the **Height** input of the **Bump** node and the **Normal** output of the latter to the **Normal** input of the **Diffuse** shader. Detach the **Color** link from the **Color** input of the **Diffuse** shader and set the **Bump** strength to 0.500.

13. Add a **Mix Shader** node and a **Glossy BSDF** shader and connect them to be mixed with the **Diffuse** shader. Set the **Glossy** shader's **Roughness** value to 0.400 and the **Mix Shader** factor to 0.300. Connect the **Normal** output of the **Bump** node to the **Normal** socket of the **Glossy** shader:

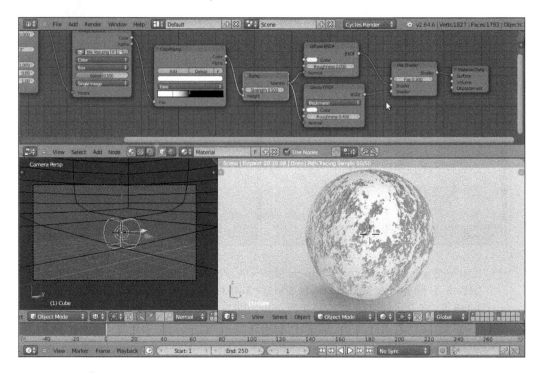

14. Add a **RGB** node (press *Shift + A* and go to **Input | RGB**). Add a **Mix** node (press *Shift + A* and go to **Color | Mix**). Connect both the **Color** outputs of the **RGB** and **Image Texture** nodes to the **Color1** and **Color2** input sockets of the **Mix** node. Connect the **Color** output of the **Mix** node to the **Color** input sockets of the **Diffuse** and **Glossy** shaders.

15. Click on the color slider of the **RGB** node and set these values: **R 0.407**, **G 0.323**, and **B 0.293**. Connect the **Color** output of the **ColorRamp** node to the **Fac** input of the **Mix** node.

16. In the **Texture Coordinate** node, set the **Y** rotation angle to **20°** and set the scale for all the three axes to **0.500**:

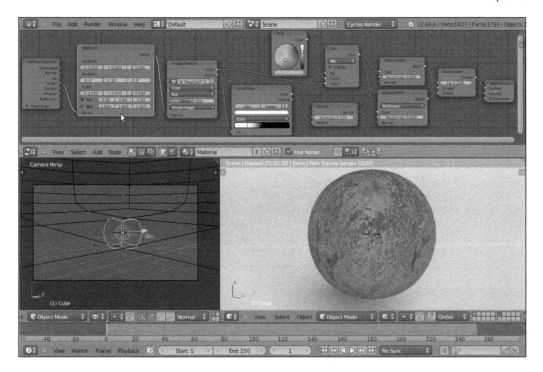

17. As a last step (which is optional, but can improve the material), add a new **Mix** node (press *Shift + A* and go to **Color | Mix**). Set the **Blend Type** to **Difference** and drag it to be pasted between the **ColorRamp** and the first **Mix** node.

18. Switch the **ColorRamp** output from the **Color1** input to the **Fac** input of the **Difference** node, connect the **RGB** node output to the empty **Color1** input and the **Image Texture** color output to the **Color2** input.

19. Change the **Mix** node **Blend Type** to **Color**, switch the **Diffuse** node output from the **Fac** to the **Color2** input of the **Color** node and connect the color output of the **Image Texture** node to the **Color1** input of the same **Color** node. You can let the **Fac** value of the **Color** node to `0.500`. The more you increase this value, even to the maximum value of `1.000`, the more the color of the **RGB** node will influence the final result.

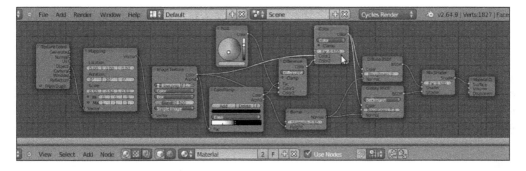

20. Rename the material as `Rock_01` (the numeration is because I assume that you are going to experiment with the several values producing more and different kind of rock materials). If you wish, model a very quick rock mesh, by sculpting or deforming the subdivided cube in proportional edit mode, and assign to it the `Rock_01` material:

How it works...

We have mapped a color rock image with the **Box** option available in the **Image Texture** node (developed by the Mango Team for the "Tears Of Steel" production to quickly map objects without the need to unwrap them) and set the **Blend** factor to `0.500` to have smooth transitions at the corners.

First, we have applied the image map to the cube as color, to have a quick feedback. Thanks to the **ColorRamp** node, we have obtained the following goals:

▶ We have converted the color image to a gray-scale image, which is to be used for the bump

▶ By moving the color markers, we have remapped this value to reverse and increase the contrast (we could have obtained the same result by processing the color map in Gimp, for example, by desaturating it and playing with the Curve Tool).

This contrasted result has been applied as a bump map both on the **Diffuse** as well as on the **Glossy** shaders.

Then, we have mixed a brownish color (the **RGB** node) with the color output of the rock image. The contrasted values of the **ColorRamp** node have been used as a factor for the mixing of the colors, thereby giving more and nicer variations to the surface.

In the last optional step, we added more variations to the coloration by also calculating the "difference" between the image and the **RGB** color, with the contrasted gray-scale output of the **ColorRamp** node as blending factor, and we added it to the final result using the **Color** node.

There's more...

We can also improve the "rocky" effect by adding displacement to the geometry. Unlike bump or normal effects on the mesh surface, which are just optical illusions giving the impression of a perturbed mesh surface, displacement is an actual deformation of the mesh based on the gray-scale values of a texture.

At least in this case, there is no need for a precise correspondence between the already textured surface and the displacement, because it would be barely noticeable, so we can use object modifiers to obtain a fast but effective result:

1. Starting from the `Rock_01` file we just created, select the cube and go to the **Object Modifier** panel. In the **Subdivision Surface** modifier already assigned, set the **Subdivisions** levels for both **View** and **Render** to 3.

2. Add a new **Subdivision Surface** modifier and set its levels to 4.

3. Now add a **Displace** modifier and click on the **Show textures in texture tab** button, the last button to the right of the **Texture** slot. This switches the **Textures** window on from where we can click on **New** and then change the default **Clouds** texture with a **Voronoi** texture. Set the **Size** value to 2.00 and let the rest be unchanged. Go back to the **Object Modifier** window and set the modifier strength to 0.300.

4. Add a new **Displace** modifier. Switch to the **Textures** window and assign a new texture. We will use the default **Clouds** texture now, but just change the **Size** value to 0.50 and **Depth** value to 8. Now, back at the modifiers, set the **Strength** value to 0.350.

5. Add a last **Displace** modifier. In the **Textures** window, select a **Noise** texture and set the **Strength** value to 0.005. The following is what we come up with:

Of course, these are just basic values. However, you can change them and also play with different kinds of procedural textures to obtain several different rock shapes.

Creating a rock material using procedural textures

In this recipe, we will create a rock material using procedural textures. We will create something similar to the following:

Getting ready

Open the `1301OS_03_start.blend` file and set the **Camera** view to the **Rendered** mode.

How to do it...

Now, this is how we are going to create the rock material:

1. Select the spheroid (the subdivided cube) and click on **New** in the **Material** window under the **Properties** panel or in the **Node Editor** header. Rename the material as `Rock_procedural_01`.

2. Add a **Voronoi** texture, a **Musgrave** texture, and a **Noise** texture (press *Shift + A* and navigate to **Texture**) in the **Node Editor** window. Press *Shift + D* to duplicate the **Voronoi** texture and adjust them in a column.

3. Add **Texture Coordinate** (press *Shift + A* and go to **Input | Texture Coordinate**) and a **Mapping** node (press *Shift + A* and go to **Vector | Mapping**). Connect the **Object** output of the **Texture Coordinate** node to the **Vector** blue input of the **Mapping** node. Now, connect the **Mapping** node's **Vector** output to the **Vector** input sockets of the four texture nodes.

4. Add a **Mix** node (press *Shift + A* and go to **Color | Mix**) and connect the first two **Voronoi** and **Fac** outputs to the **Color1** and **Color2** inputs of the **Mix** node. Set the **Mix** node **Blend Type** to **Screen** and set the **Fac** value to 1.00.

5. Connect the **Mix** node output to the color input of the **Diffuse** shader.

6. In the **Voronoi** textures, switch **Coloring** from **Intensity** to **Cells**. In the first **Voronoi** texture, set **Scale** to 2.700, and in the second to 16.000.

7. Select the **Screen** node and press *Shift + D* to duplicate it. Drag it to the link connecting the **Screen** node and the **Diffuse** shader to paste it in between. Set its **Blend Type** to **Multiply** and the **Fac** value to 0.950. Connect the **Color** output of the **Musgrave** texture to the **Color2** input of the **Multiply** node.

8. Set the **Musgrave** scale to 2.776, **Detail** to 3.500, **Dimension** to 0.100, and **Lacunarity** to 1.796.

9. Select the **Multiply** node and press *Shift + D* to duplicate it. Paste it on the link connecting the first **Multiply** node with the **Diffuse** shader. Set its **Fac** value to 0.300 and then connect the **Fac** output of the **Noise** texture to the **Color2** input.

10. Set the **Noise** texture's **Scale** value to 7.980, **Detail** to 16.000, and **Distortion** to 2.380.

11. Add a **Bump** node (press *Shift + A* and go to **Vector | Bump**) and connect its **Vector** output to the **Vector** input of the **Diffuse** shader. Then, connect the second **Multiply** output to the **Height** input socket of the **Bump** node. Disconnect the link to the shader color input.

12. Add four **ColorRamp** nodes (press *Shift + A* and go to **Convertor | ColorRamp**, then press *Shift + D*) and paste them, one for each texture node, on the four links to the **Mix** nodes. Set their interpolation to **B-Spline**. In the first two (connected to the **Voronoi** nodes) links, move the black color marker to the middle of the slider. You can actually edit only the first **ColorRamp** slider, then put the mouse cursor on the slider. Press *Crtl + C* to copy it and, with the mouse cursor in the slider of the second one, press *Crtl + V* to paste it.

13. In the third **ColorRamp** (connected to the **Musgrave** texture) node, move the black marker only one-fourth to the right. In the fourth node (connected to the **Noise** texture), move the black marker to the middle and the white marker almost one-fourth to the left.

14. Set the **Bump** strength value to 1.000.

15. Add a **Hue Saturation Value** node (press *Shift + A* and go to **Color | Hue Saturation Value**) and paste it between the **Screen** node and the **Color1** input of the first **Multiply** node. Set **Value** to 10.000.

16. Add a **Bright/Contrast** node (press *Shift + A* and go to **Color | Bright/Contrast**) and paste it between the third (**Musgrave**) **ColorRamp** node and the **Color2** input of the first **Multiply** node. Set **Contrast** to -0.700.

17. Add a **Frame** (press *Shift* + *A* and go to **Layout | Frame**). Press *Shift* to multiselect the four texture nodes, the four **ColorRamp** nodes, the three **Mix** nodes, the **Bright/contrast** node, and **Hue Saturation Value** nodes and, last, the just added **Frame**. Press *Crtl* + *P* to parent all the selected elements to the **Frame**. Press *N* in the **Node Editor** window to bring out the **Active Node** panel and rename the **Frame** as **1st Bump**. If you want, provide a background color to it (by checking the **Custom Color** box).

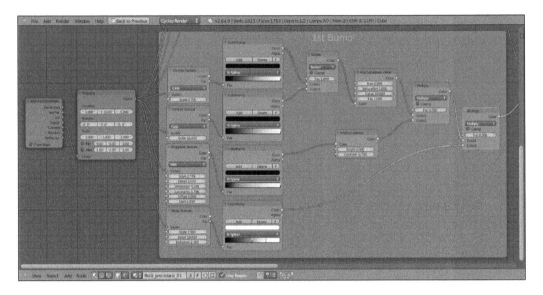

18. Add a **Voronoi** texture, two **Musgrave** textures, one **Noise** texture (press *Shift* + *A* | **Texture**), and one **ColorRamp** node (Press *Shift* + *A* and go to **Convertor | ColorRamp**). Move them above and adjust the textures in a column with the **ColorRamp** node to their side. Connect the second **Musgrave** color output to the **Fac** input of the **ColorRamp** node.

19. Set the **ColorRamp** node's interpolation to **B-Spline** and move the white marker three-fourths to the left. Switch the **Voronoi** texture's coloring from **Intensity** to **Cell** and set the **Scale** value to 8.000. Set both the **Musgrave** texture's type to **Hetero Terrain**. Set the first texture's **Scale** to 3.696 and the second's **Scale** to 2.192. Also, for both the textures, set **Detail** to 3.500, **Dimension** to 0.300, and **Lacunarity** to 3.000. In the **Noise** texture, set the **Scale** value to 15.000, **Detail** to 16.000, and **Distortion** to 0.400.

20. Select the **Mapping** node and (press *Shift*) one texture node, and then press *F* to automatically connect the **Vector** output of the **Mapping** node to the **Vector** input of the texture. Do this for all the new texture nodes, one at a time.

21. Add three **Mix** nodes (press **Shift** + **A** and go to **Color | Mix**, then press *Shift* + *D*) and move them above as well. Change their blend types to **Screen**, **Multiply**, and **Divide** respectively.

22. Connect the first top **Voronoi** texture's **Fac** output to the **Color1** input of the **Screen** node and the color output of the first **Musgrave** texture to the **Color2** input of the **Screen** node, then connect its output to the **Color1** input of the **Multiply** node. Connect the color output of the **ColorRamp** node to the **Color2** input of the **Multiply** node. Connect the output of the **Multiply** node to the **Color1** input socket of the **Divide** node and the **Fac** output of the **Noise** texture to the **Color2** input of the **Divide** node.

23. Add an **Invert** node (press *Shift + A* and go to **Color | Invert**) and connect the output of the **Divide** node to the input of the **Invert** node. Add a new **Frame** and parent all these new nodes to the **Frame**. Rename it as **2nd Bump**.

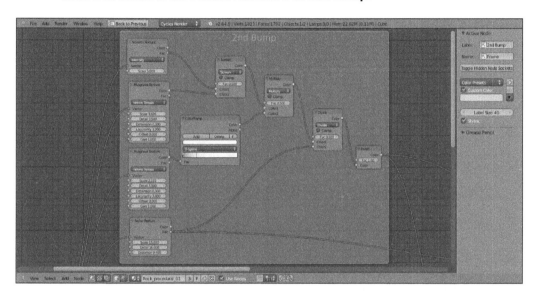

24. Finally, add a **Mix** node (press *Shift + A* and go to **Color | Mix**) and drag it to be pasted just before the **Bump** node. Change its **Blend Type** to **Multiply** and increase the **Fac** value to 1.000. Connect the output of the **Invert** node to the **Color1** input socket of this **Mix** node.

25. Now select the **Diffuse** shader and press *Shift + D* to duplicate it. Then, add a **Mix Shader** node (press *Shift + A* and go to **Shader | Mix Shader**) and paste it between the first **Diffuse** shader and the **Material Output** node. Connect the second **Diffuse** shader to the empty **Shader** input socket of the **Mix Shader** node.

26. Change the color of the first **Diffuse** shader to **R 0.365, G 0.379, B 0.400**, set the **Roughness** value to 1.000. Change the color of the second **Diffuse** shader to **R 0.130, G 0.092, B 0.075** and set the **Roughness** value to 1.000.

27. Select and press *Shift + D* to duplicate the **Mix Shader** node. Set its **Fac** value to 0.300 and paste the duplicate between the original one and the **Material Output** node. Add a **Glossy BSDF** shader (press *Shift + A* to go to| **Shader | Glossy BSDF**) and connect its output to the second **Shader** input of the duplicated **Mix Shader** node.

28. Set the **Glossy** shader color to **R 0.560**, **G 0.742**, **B 0.800** and its **Roughness** value to 0.400.

29. Add a **Mix** node (press *Shift + A* and go to **Color | Mix**) and change the **Blend Type** to **Burn**. Connect the **Fac** output of the **Noise** texture of the second bump to the **Color1** input and the **Invert** node output to the **Color2** input socket.

30. Add a **ColorRamp** node (press *Shift + A* and go to **Convertor | ColorRamp**) and change its interpolation to **Ease** and move the white marker three-fourth to the left. Connect the output of the **Burn** node to the **Fac** input of the **ColorRamp** node and its color output to the **Fac** input of the first **Mix Shader** node, as shown in the following screenshot:

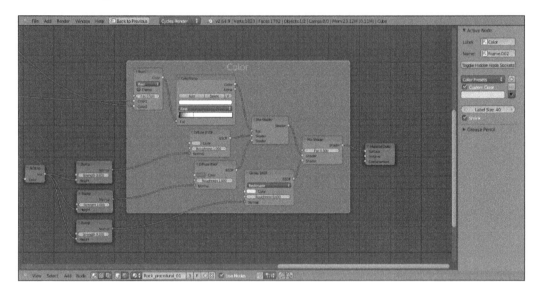

31. Add a **RGB to BW** node (press *Shift + A* and go to **Convertor | RGB to BW**) and paste it between the **Bump** node and the **Multiply** one.

32. Select the **Bump** node and press *Shift + D* to duplicate it twice. Connect the **RGB to BW** output to their **Height** inputs and then connect the **Normal** output of the second **Bump** node to the **Normal** input of the second **Diffuse** shader, and the **Normal** output of the third **Bump** node to the **Normal** input of the **Glossy** shader.

33. Decrease the **Strength** value of the first **Bump** node to `0.600` and the **Strength** value of the third **Bump** node to `0.200`. Finally, we are done! This is what we have achieved:

How it works...

Even if at first glance, this material can look quite complex, basically we just mixed, with different blend types and iterations, three procedural textures. This process is better understood if it's divided into four separate stages, which are as follows:

- ▸ The first stage, from step 2 to step 16, in which we built a "first bump" pattern.

- ▸ The second stage, from step 18 to step 23, where we added a second bump pattern to increase the detail in the material, and then (step 23) where we multiplied it to the first bump.

- ▸ The third stage, from step 25 to step 30, where we built a color pattern by mixing two differently colored **Diffuse** shaders on the ground of the bump output as factor for the blending, in addition to building a **Glossy** shader to add specularity.

> ▸ In the last three steps, we just added an **RGB to BW** converter to transform the colored data to black and white data, which is more suitable for bump effects, and we then classified the bump effects as per their shader, to give different strength values to each one.

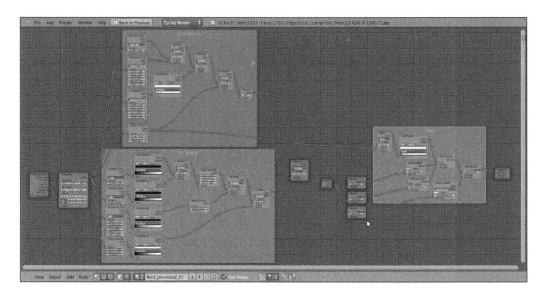

Creating a sand material using procedural textures

In this recipe, we will create a sand material, good for close objects as for distant ones:

Getting ready

To get ready, start Blender and switch to Cycles. Delete the default cube and add a plane. In the edit mode, scale it nine times bigger (18 units per side).

1. Go to the **World** window and click on **Use Nodes**, then click on the little square with a dot on the right-hand side of the color slot. From the menu, select **Sky Texture**. Set the **Strength** value to 0.300.

2. Select the lamp and go to the lamp's **Object Data** window and click on **Use Nodes**. Then change the **Lamp** type to **Sun** and set the **Size** value to 0.100 and the **Strength** value to 2.000. Change the light's color to **R 1.000**, **G 0.782**, **B 0.310**. In an orthogonal top view, rotate the **Sun** lamp to **45°**.

3. Place the camera to have a nice angle on the plane and switch the 3D view to a **Camera** view (press 0 from numpad).

4. Add a cube and a UV Sphere to the scene and place them leaning on the plane.

5. Select the cube and in the **Object Modifiers** window add a **Bevel** modifier. Set the **Width** value to 0.0600. Assign a **Subdivision Surface** modifier and set both the levels to **2**. Assign a **Smooth** modifier and set the **Factor** value to 1.000 and **Repeat** to 25. Press *T* to call the **Object Tools** panel on the left, and under **Shading** select **Smooth**.

6. Split the 3D window to two horizontal rows and change the upper one to a **Node Editor** window and set the **Camera** view mode to **Rendered**.

We are now ready to go and make this:

How to do it...

After you have prepared the scene, let's start with creation of the material:

1. Select the plane and click on **New** in the **Material** window under the **Properties** panel, or in the **Node Editor** window's header. Rename the material as Sand_01.

2. Press *Shift* and select the UV Sphere, the cube, and the plane (because it's the active object of the multiselection). Press *Crtl + L* and from the **Make Links** pop-up menu, select **Material** to assign the same material to the other two objects. The Sand_01 material is now assigned to all three objects.

3. In the **Material** window under the **Properties** panel on the right, switch the **Diffuse** shader with a **Mix Shader** node. In both the two **Shader** slots, assign a **Diffuse BSDF** shader.

4. Change the color of the first **Diffuse** shader to **R 0.800, G 0.659, B 0.504**. Change the color of the second **Diffuse** shader to **R 0.521, G 0.513, B 0.335**.

5. Add a **Noise Texture** node (press *Shift + A* and go to **Texture | Noise Texture**), add a **Texture Coordinate** node (press *Shift + A* and go to **Input | Texture Coordinate**), and a **Mapping** node (press *Shift + A* and go to **Vector | Mapping**).

6. Connect the **Object** output of the **Texture Coordinate** node to the **Vector** input of the **Mapping** node, and then the **Vector** output to the **Vector** input of the **Noise** texture.

7. Connect the **Fac** output of the **Noise** texture to the **Fac** input of the **Mix Shader** node. Increase the **Detail** value of the **Noise** texture to **5.000**, as shown here:

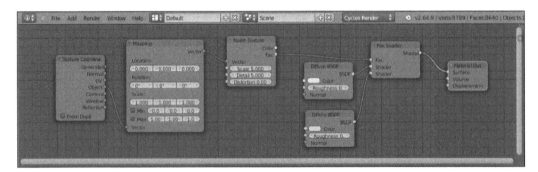

8. Add a **Frame** (press *Shift + A* and go to **Layout | Frame**). Press *Shift* to multi-select the **Noise** texture, the two **Diffuse** shaders, the **Mix Shader** node, and the **Frame**. Press *Crtl + P* to parent them. In the **Active Node** panel (Press *N* in the **Node Editor** window), rename the **Frame** as **Sand Color**.

9. Add a new **Noise** texture and a **Wave Texture** node (press *Shift + A* and go to **Texture | Wave Texture**). Select both these textures and press *Shift + D* to duplicate them. Adjust them in a column in this order: **Wave**, **Noise**, **Noise**, and **Wave**. Connect the **Mapping** output to their corresponding **Vector** inputs.

10. Set the first **Wave** texture's **Scale** value to 3.000, **Distortion** to 25.000, and **Detail** to 10.000. Set the first **Noise** texture's **Detail** value to 10.000 and **Distortion** to 0.500. Set the second **Noise** texture's **Detail** value to 10.000. Set the last **Wave** node's **Scale** value to 25.000, **Distortion** to 15.000, and **Detail Scale** to 5.000.

11. Add a **Mix** node (press *Shift + A* and go to **Color | Mix**) and connect the first **Wave** color output to the **Color1** input, and the second **Noise** texture color output to the **Color2** input.

12. Select the **Mix** node and press *Shift + D* to duplicate it. Connect the color output of the first **Mix** node to the **Color1** input of the second **Mix** node, and the last **Wave** texture color output to its **Color2** input.

13. Connect the color output of the third **Noise** texture to the **Fac** input socket of the second **Mix** node.

14. Select a **Mix** node and press *Shift + D* to duplicate it. Change the **Blend Type** to **Multiply**. Connect the output of the second **Mix** node to the **Color1** input socket of the **Multiply** node. Set its **Fac** value to 0.300 and connect its output to the **Displacement** input socket of the **Material Output** node.

15. Add a **Hue Saturation Value** node (press *Shift + A* and go to **Color | Hue Saturation Value**) and drag it to the link connecting the second **Noise** texture to the first **Mix** node to paste it in between. Set **Value** to 10.000.

16. Press *Shift + D* to duplicate it and drag it to the link connecting the last **Wave** texture to the second **Mix** node. Set **Value** to 0.100.

17. Press *Shift + D* to duplicate it again and drag it between the second **Mix** node and the **Multiply** node. Set **Value** to 0.350.

18. Add a **Bright/Contrast** node (press *Shift + A* and go to **Color | Bright/Contrast**) and drag it to be pasted between the second **Noise** texture and the second **Mix** factor input. Set the **Bright** value to **-0.250** and the **Contrast** value to **1.000**, as shown in the following screenshot:

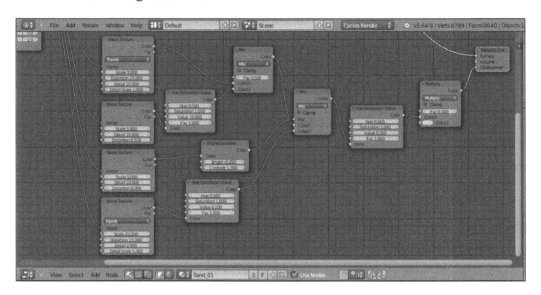

19. Add a **Frame**, select these last 11 nodes and the **Frame**, and then press *Crtl + P* to parent them. Rename the **Frame** as **Sand Bump**.

20. Select the last **Wave** texture and press *Shift + D* to duplicate it twice (press *Alt + P* unparent it, if after the duplication, the node is still parented to the **Frame**). Do the same with the **Bright/Contrast** node. Connect the **Mapping** output to their **Vector** input. Select a **Mix** node and press *Shift + D* to duplicate it. Set the **Blend Type** to **Divide** and the factor to 1.000.

21. Connect each **Color** output of the two textures to the respective **Color** input of the **Bright/Contrast** nodes. Then, connect their color outputs to the **Color1** and **Color2** inputs of the **Divide** node.

22. In the first **Wave** texture, set the **Scale** value to 0.500, **Distortion** to 25.000, **Detail** to 10.000, and **Detail Scale** to 1.000. In the **Bright/Contrast** node, set the **Bright** value to 0.000 and the **Contrast** value to -0.800. In the second **Wave** texture, set the **Scale** value to 1.000, **Distortion** to 10.000, **Detail** to 5.000, and **Detail Scale** to 1.000. In the respective **Bright/Contrast** node again set the **Bright** value to 0.000 and the **Contrast** value to -0.800.

23. Add a **Math** node (press *Shift + A* and go to **Convertor | Math**). Set the operation to **Multiply** and the first **Value** the same as the **Scale** value of the first **Wave** texture (0.500). Set the second **Value** to 1.000. Connect the **Value** output to the **Scale** input of the first **Wave** texture node.

24. Press *Shift + D* to duplicate the **Math** node, move it on the side of the second **Wave** texture, and set the first **Value** the same as the **Scale** value of the second **Wave** texture (1.000). Connect the **Value** output to the **Scale** input.

25. Add a **Value** node (press *Shift* and go to **Input | Value**) and connect the output to both the second **Value** input sockets of the **Math** nodes, as shown here:

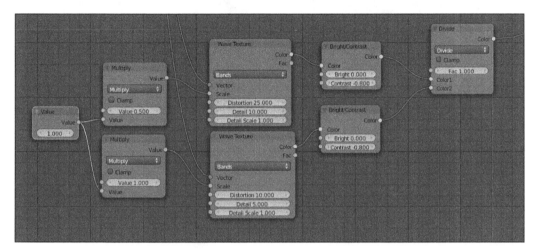

26. Add a **Frame**, parent and rename the **Frame** as **Big Waves**.

27. Duplicate a **Multiply** node and drag it to the link between the **Sand Bump** frame's **Multiply** node output and the **Material Output** node. Connect the **Divide** node output of **Big Waves** to the **Color2** input of this last **Multiply** node.

28. Duplicate a **Noise** texture, a **Bright/Contrast** node, and a **Multiply** node. Connect the **Mapping** output to the **Vector** input of the texture node, then connect the **Noise** color output to the **Bright/Color** color input and its output to the **Color1** input of the **Multiply** node.

29. Set the **Noise** texture's **Scale** value to 200.000, **Detail** to 1.000, and **Distortion** to 0.000. Set the **Bright/Contrast** node's **Bright** value to 0.000 and the **Contrast** value to 0.200. Set the **Multiply** factor value to 0.050.

30. Duplicate a **Multiply** node and paste it between the **Multiply** node and the **Material Output** node. Connect the **Multiply** output of the **Granularity** to its **Color2** input and set the **Fac** value to **1.000**:

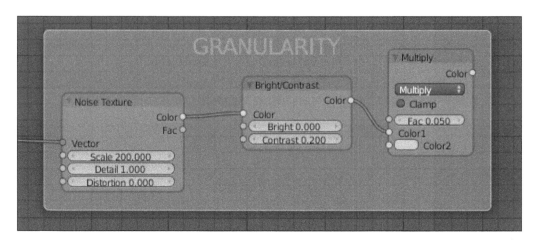

31. Add a **Math** node (press *Shift + A* and go to **Convertor | Math**) and a **RGB to BW** node (press *Shift + A* and go to **Convertor | RGB to BW**). Paste the **Math** node between the last **Multiply** node and the **Material Output** node, then paste the **RGB to BW** node just before the **Math** node.

32. Set the **Math** node's operation to **Multiply** and the second **Value** to **1.500**, as shown in the following screenshot:

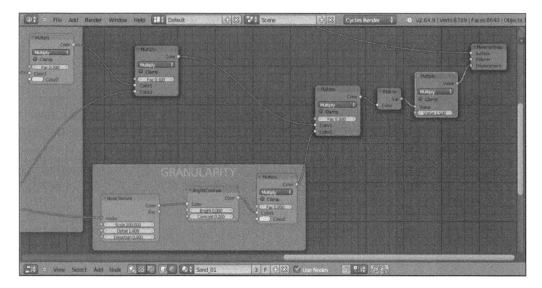

33. Add a **Frame** and parent the **RGB to BW** node and the **last Math** nodes. Rename the frame as **Total Bump Strength**. For better visibility, give different colors to the frames, as shown here:

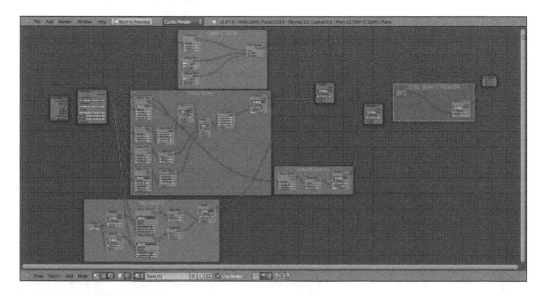

How it works...

The concept behind the structure of this material is basically the same as for the procedural rock and can be subdivided in stages as well:

- ▶ From step 1 to step 7, we built the color part of the shader, blending two differently colored **Diffuse** shaders on the ground of a **Noise** texture factor.

- ▶ From step 9 to step 18, we built the main bump effect, this time piped directly as a whole in the **Displacement** input of the **Material Output** node rather than to the per shader **Normal** inputs.

- ▶ From step 20 to step 25, we built a supplementary bump effect, this time to simulate the big waves you can usually see on the desert sand dunes. This effect is left apart from the main bump to be easily reduced or eliminated if the case, and we added two **Math** nodes set to **Multiply** and driven by a **Value** node to automatically set the size of the sand big waves (actually, this is more of a "repeating" effect, that is, the bigger the value, the smaller and closer the waves).

- ▶ In steps 28 and 29, we built a last bump effect to add, if necessary, the sand grain, for example, for objects very close to the camera. From step 31 to step 33, we summed all the bump effects as a whole, to be driven by the **Math** node value.

Every stage has been "framed" and labeled to make it more easily readable in the **Node Editor** window.

There's more...

One more thing we can do to improve this material is to combine everything in a "group" node, leaving, at the same time, the fundamental values exposed to be tweaked from the interface.

1. Put the mouse cursor in the **Node Editor** window and press *B*. Horizontal and vertical lines now appear at the mouse cursor's location, left-click and drag the mouse to encompass the framed nodes, leaving outside only the **Texture Coordinate**, the **Mapping**, and the **Material Output** nodes. After the mouse button is released, everything you encompassed is now selected.

2. Press *Crtl + G* and confirm by clicking on the **Make Group | New** pop-up and create the group:

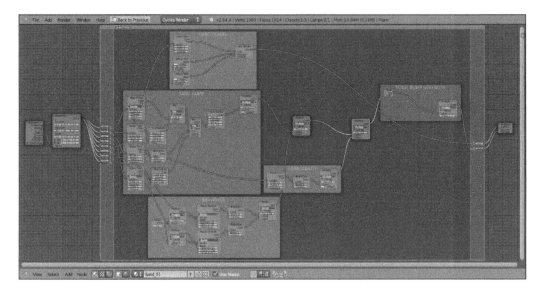

3. As you can see, all the links to the external nodes have been created on the left and right sides of the group interface. Rename the group (in the little window on the top-left of the interface) as **Sand_group**.

4. All the mapping coordinates for the texture nodes are **Object**, so one **Vector** input is enough. Replace all the connections to the texture nodes with the first input and then delete the unnecessary empty sockets, as shown here:

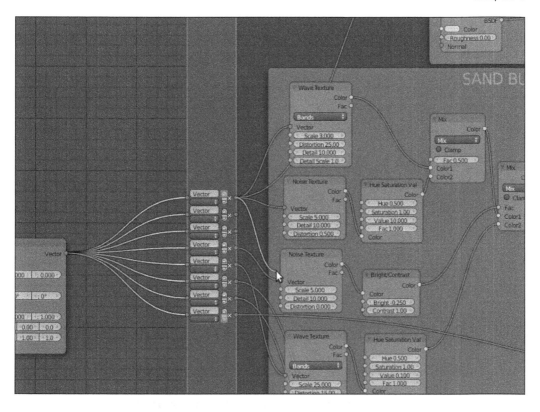

5. Now we need to expose the values to modify the material from the interface. From the **Fac** input of the first **Multiply** node, click and drag a link to the left border of the group. In the newly appeared input socket name, enter `Big waves strength`. This value actually drives the strength (the multiplication value) of the **Big Waves** bump summed to the main **Sand Bump**.

6. Do the same with the second **Multiply** node and rename the input as **Granularity**. Again, this value will drive the amount of multiplication of the sand grain to the rest of the bump effect.

7. Now click on the **Value** node inside the **Big Waves** frame and press *X* to delete it. Click and drag to the border around the second **Value** socket of the first **Wave** node and rename the exposed new socket as **Big waves repeat**. Also, Click and drag a link also from the second **Value** socket of the second **Wave** node and connect it to the **Big waves repeat** socket. By clicking on the upper little arrow on the socket side, move it up just before the **Granularity** frame.

8. We also need to expose the **Multiply** node inside the **Total Bump Strength** frame, by dragging the second **Value** socket. Rename the new socket on the interface as **Bump strength**. This is, in fact, the value for the overall bump of the material.

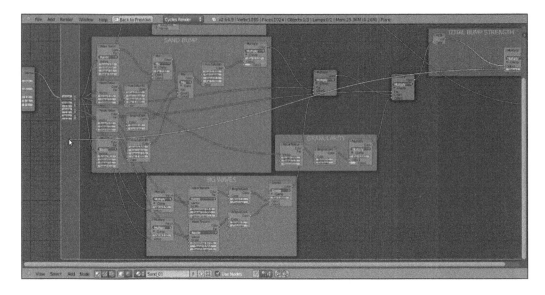

9. Press *Tab* to close the group. On the interface we have the controls to increase or decrease the overall bump effect, the sand grain, and the waves' strength and scale/repetition. We can have exposed even more values, for example, also the first bump amount for more finer tweaking, and the two color inputs in the **Sand Color** frame.

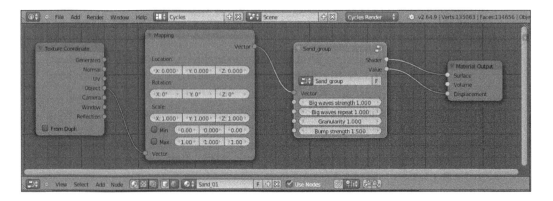

The group is now available under the **Add** menu by using a shortcut (press *Shift + A* and go to **Group | Sand_group**), and can be easily re-used for other materials in the same scene and also with different interface values; or linked/appended from a library in other blend files.

Creating a simple ground material using procedural textures

In this recipe, we will create a basic raw ground material.

Getting ready

The first step is to start Blender and switch to Cycles. Delete the default cube and add a plane. In edit mode, scale it nine times bigger (18 units per side) and then follow these steps:

1. Go in the **Object Modifiers** window and assign a **Subdivision Surface** modifier to the plane. Switch from **Catmull-Clark** to **Simple** and set the levels of **Subdivisions** for both **View** and **Render** to 2.

2. Assign a second **Subdivision Surface** modifier. Again, switch to **Simple** and set the levels of **Subdivisions** for both **View** and **Render** to 4.

3. Assign two **Displace** modifiers. In the first one, assign a **Voronoi** texture, increase the **Size** value to 1.80, and set the displacement strength to 0.400. In the second one, assign the default **Clouds** texture, increase the **Size** value to 0.75 and the **Depth** value to 5, set the displacement strength to 0.400 as well.

4. In the **Object Tool** panel, under **Shading**, set the plane smooth.

5. Go to the **World** window and click on **Use Nodes**, then click on the little square with a dot to the right-hand side of the color slot. From the menu, select **Sky Texture**. Set the **Strength** value to 0.250.

6. Select the lamp, go to the lamp's **Object Data** window and click on **Use Nodes**. Then, change the **Lamp** type to **Sun**, set the **Size** value to 0.100, and the **Strength** value to 1.400. Change the light color to **R 1.000, G 0.935, B 0.810**. In orthogonal top view, rotate the **Sun** lamp to a degree of 90°.

7. Place the camera to have a nice angle on the plane and switch the 3D view to a **Camera** view (press *0* from numpad).

8. Split the 3D window to two horizontal rows and change the upper one to a **Node Editor** window.

9. Set the **Camera** view mode to **Rendered**.

We are now ready to create this:

How to do it...

1. Select the plane and click on **New** in the **Material** window under the **Properties** panel, or in the **Node Editor** window's header.

2. In the **Node Editor** window, add a **Texture Coordinate** node (press *Shift + A* and go to **Input | Texture Coordinate**), a **Mapping** node (press *Shift + A* and go to **Vector | Mapping**), and a **Musgrave Texture** node (press *Shift + A* and go to **Texture | Musgrave Texture**).

3. Connect the **Object** output of the **Texture Coordinate** node to the **Vector** input of the **Mapping** node and the **Vector** output of the latter to the **Vector** input of the **Musgrave Texture** node.

4. Connect the **Color** output of the **Musgrave Texture** node to the **Color** input of the **Diffuse** shader. Set the **Scale** value of the **Musgrave Texture** node to 0.500.

5. Add a **Wave Texture** node (press *Shift + A* and go to **Texture | Wave Texture**) and a **Mix** node (press *Shift + A* and go to **Color | Mix**). Connect the **Wave** color output to the **Color2** input of the **Mix** node, and then connect the **Color** output of the **Musgrave** node to the **Color1** input.

6. Connect the **Mix** node output to the **Color** input of the **Diffuse** shader. Set the **Mix** node's **Blend Type** to **Subtract**. Connect the **Mapping** output to the **Wave** texture's **Vector** input.

7. Set the **Wave** node's **Scale** value to 0.200, **Distortion** to 20.000, **Detail** to 16.000, and **Detail Scale** to 5.000.

8. Add a **ColorRamp** node (press *Shift + A* and go to **Convertor | ColorRamp**) and drag it to the link connecting the **Wave** node to the **Mix** node to paste it in between. Change the interpolation mode to **B-Spline** and move the black marker nearly one-fourth of the slider length to the right.

9. Add two **Noise** texture nodes (press *Shift + A* and go to **Texture | Noise Texture** and then press *Shift + D*) and connect them to the **Mapping** node. Select the **Subtract** node and press *Shift + D* to duplicate it twice. Change their blend types to **Multiply** and connect the **Color** output of the **Subtract** node to the **Color1** input of the first **Multiply** node, and also connect the **Color** output of the first **Noise** texture to the **Color2** input.

10. Then, connect the **Color** output of the first **Multiply** node to the **Color1** input of the second **Multiply** node and the **Color** output of the second **Noise** texture to the **Color2** input.

11. Connect the second **Multiply** output to the color input of the **Diffuse** shader. Set the first **Noise** texture's **Scale** value to 10.000, **Detail** to 5.000, and **Distortion** to 0.300. For the second **Noise** texture, set **Scale** to 35.000, **Detail** to 5.000, and **Distortion** to 1.000.

12. Add a **Bright/Contrast** node (press *Shift + A* and go to **Color | Bright/Contrast**), drag it to be pasted between the **Subtract** node and the first **Multiply** node. Set the contrast to -0.800.

13. Press *Shift + D* to duplicate the **Bright/Contrast** node and drag it to be pasted between the first **Noise** texture and the first **Multiply** node. Also, set the contrast to -0.400.

14. Press *Shift + D* to duplicate the **Bright/Contrast** node again and drag it to be pasted between the second **Noise** texture and the second **Multiply** node. Also, set the contrast to -0.500.

15. Add a **Bump** node (press *Shift + A* and go to **Vector | Bump**) and paste it between the second **Multiply** node and the **Diffuse** shader. Switch the input connection from **Strength** to **Height** and the **Normal** output from the **Color** input of the **Diffuse** to the **Normal** input, as shown in the following screenshot:

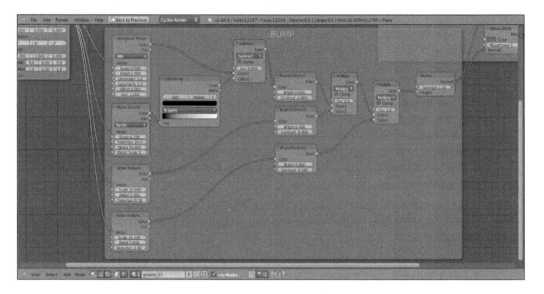

16. Add a **Mix Shader** node (press *Shift + A* and go to **Shader | Mix Shader**) and a second **Diffuse BSDF** shader (press *Shift + A* and go to **Shader | Diffuse BSDF**). Paste the **Mix Shader** node between the first **Diffuse** shader and the **Material Output** node and connect the second **Diffuse** shader to the second **Shader** input socket.

17. Connect the **Bump** output to the second **Diffuse** shader's **Normal** input. Set the **Bump** strength to 1.000.

18. Change the first **Diffuse** shader's color to **R 0.593, G 0.479, B 0.242**. Change the second **Diffuse** shader's color to **R 0.106, G 0.067, B 0.053** and the set **Roughness** value to 1.000.

19. Add one more **Noise** texture node (press *Shift + A* and go to **Texture | Noise Texture**) and a new ColorRamp node (press *Shift + A* and go to **Convertor | ColorRamp**). Connect the **Mapping** node output to the **Noise** vector input and the texture **Color** output to the **Fac** input of the **ColorRamp** node. Then, connect the **ColorRamp** node's **Color** output to the **Fac** input socket of the **Mix Shader** node.

20. Set the **Noise** node's **Scale** value to 1.000 and the **Detail** value to 5.000. Switch the **ColorRamp** node's interpolation to **B-Spline** and move the black marker one-third to the right, the white marker one-third to the left, and click on the **Add** button to add a new marker. Set its color to black and move it very close to the first black marker, as shown in the following screenshot:

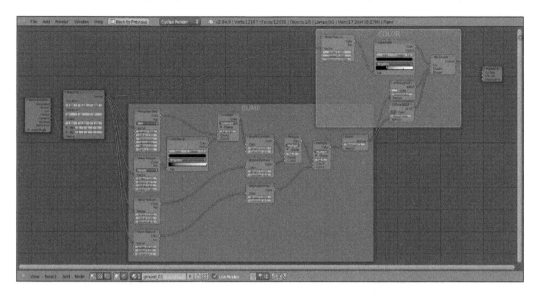

How it works...

The way this material works is very similar to the sand material:

▶ We mixed two slightly different colors using a **Noise** texture as a stencil factor

▶ We created the ground roughness by an ensemble of procedural textures whose total sum has been then connected to the **Normal** input sockets of the **Diffuse** shader nodes

Creating a snow material using procedural textures

In this recipe, we will create a snow material and also fake a slight Sub Surface Scattering effect.

Getting ready

Start Blender and open the 1301OS_03_start.blend file.

How to do it...

Now we are going to create the material:

1. Select the cube and click on **New** in the **Material** window, under the **Properties** panel, or in the **Node Editor** window's header. Rename the material to **Snow**.

2. Set the **Camera** view to **Rendered**.

3. In the **Material** window on the right, under **Surface**, switch the **Diffuse** shader with a **Mix Shader** node. In the first **Shader** slot, select a **Diffuse BSDF** shader and in the second slot a **Glossy BSDF** shader.

4. Set the **Roughness** value of the **Glossy** shader to 0.300.

5. Add a **Fresnel** node (press *Shift + A* and go to **Input | Fresnel**) and a **Math** node (press *Shift + A* and go to **Convertor | Math**). Set the **IOR** value of the **Fresnel** node to 1.300, and then connect the **Fac** output to the first **Value** socket of the **Math** node. Set the second **Value** to 10.000, the operation mode to **Divide**, and finally connect its **Value** output to the **Fac** input socket of the **Mix Shader** node.

6. Add a **Translucent BSDF** node (press *Shift + A* and go to **Shader | Translucent**) and set its color to **R 0.598**, **G 0.721**, **B 1.000**.

7. Select the **Mix Shader** node and press *Shift + D* to duplicate it. Set the **Fac** value of this duplicate to 0.300 and then connect the first **Mix Shader** node output to its first input socket, and set the **Translucent** output to the second input socket. Connect the output of the second **Mix Shader** node to the **Surface** input of the **Material Output** node.

8. Add a **Noise Texture** node (press *Shift + A* and go to **Texture | Noise Texture**) and press *Shift + D* to duplicate it.

9. Add a **Texture Coordinate** node (press *Shift + A* and go to **Input | Texture Coordinate**) and a **Mapping** node (press *Shift + A* and go to **Vector | Mapping**). Connect the **Object** output of the **Texture Coordinate** node to the **Vector** input of the **Mapping** node, then its **Vector** output to both the **Vector** input sockets of the **Noise Texture** nodes.

10. Add a **Math** node (press *Shift + A* and go to **Convertor | Math**). Press *Shift + D* to duplicate it thrice (so, now you have obtained a total of four **Math** nodes). Connect the first **Noise Texture** node's **Fac** output (the gray one) to the first **Value** input of the first **Math** node and set the second **Value** to 2.000. Also, set the operator to **Multiply**.

11. Connect the second **Noise Texture** node's **Fac** output to the first **Value** input of the second **Math** node and let its second **Value** be set to the default of 0.500. Again set the operator to **Multiply**.

12. Now connect the outputs of the two **Math** nodes to the input **Value** sockets of the third **Math** node. Let the operator be set to **Add**.

13. Connect the output of the third **Math** node to the first **Value** input of the fourth **Math** node, set its operator to **Multiply**, and let the second **Value** to the default value of 0.500.

14. Connect the fourth **Math** node output to the **Displacement** input socket of the **Material Output** node.

15. Now go to the second **Noise Texture** node and change the **Scale** value to 15.000. Let the other values, also for the first texture node, unchanged (that is, set **Scale** to 5.000, **Detail** to 2.000, and **Distortion** to 0.000).

16. Optionally, in the **Mapping** node set the **Scale** value to `0.500` for all the three axes, as shown here:

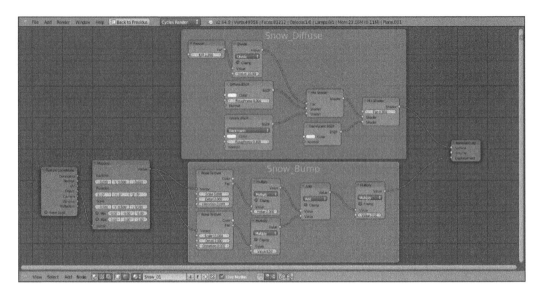

How it works...

As usual, to better understand this recipe, we can divide this material creation in two stages: the first one for the general color and consistency of the snow and the second one to add bumpiness to the surface.

> ▶ **First stage**: We just made a basic shader by mixing **Diffuse** and **Glossy** shaders by the **Index Of Refraction** of the **Fresnel** node. This **Fresnel** value is divided by the **Math** node to obtain a softer transition (try changing this value from `10.000` to `1.000` to see a totally different effect). We then also mixed in a bluish **Translucent** shader, but giving predominance to the basic shader by setting the factor value in the second **Mix Shader** node to `0.300`. The **Translucent** shader gives the appearance of the light seeping through the snow and showing in the shadowed areas of the object.

> ▶ **Second stage**: Here, we added two **Noise Texture** nodes with different scale values to simulate the soft snow bumpiness. The first two **Multiply** math nodes separately set the influence of each noise. These values get merged by the **Add** node and finally piped in one more **Math** node, which is set to **Multiply** as well, to establish the overall weight of the bump effect that, being directly connected to the **Displacement** input in the **Material Output** node, affects together all the shaders in the network.

Creating an ice material using procedural textures

In this recipe, we will create a semi-transparent ice material.

Getting ready

Start Blender and load the usual blend file `1301OS_03_start.blend`.

1. Delete the subdivided cube and add a new cube primitive.

2. In the **Camera** view, press *Shift + F* and by using the middle mouse button zoom the camera to better frame the cube.

3. Select the background plane and delete it. Add a new plane, being still in edit mode, scale it eight times bigger. Go out of edit mode and move it one unit down on the z axis. Assign the **Plane** material to it.

4. Set the **World** color to black.

5. Select the cube, go in edit mode, and press *W*. In the **Specials** pop-up, select **Subdivide**. Press *T* and in the bottom of the **Mesh Tools** panel set the **Number of Cuts** value to 2. Go out of edit mode and press *T* again to hide the **Mesh Tools** panel.

6. Go to the **Object Modifier** panel and add a **Subdivision Surface** modifier. Switch from **Catmull-Clark** to **Simple** and set the **Subdivision** levels to 5.

7. Add a **Displace** modifier and in the **Textures** window click on **New** and select a **Voronoi** texture; set the **Size** value to 1.20. Back to the **Object Modifiers** window, set the displacement strength to 0.050.

8. Add a new **Displace** modifier, assign a **Voronoi** texture again but this time set the **Size** value to 0.80. Set the **Displace** strength to 0.075.

9. Add a third **Displace** modifier, assign a **Voronoi** texture, and let the default size (0.25) unchanged. Set the displacement strength to 0.020.

10. Switch the **Camera** view to **Rendered**.

How to do it...

After the scene preparation, now we are going to create the material itself:

1. Select the cube and click on **New** in the **Material** window under the **Properties** panel, or in the **Node Editor** window's header. Rename the material as `Ice_01`.

2. In the **Material** window on the right, under **Surface**, switch the **Diffuse** shader with a **Mix Shader** node. In the first **Shader** slot, select a **Glass BSDF** shader and in the second slot a **Transparent BSDF** shader.

3. Set the **Glass** shader's color totally white and the **IOR** value to `1.309`.
   Set the **Transparent** shader's color to **R 0.448**, **G 0.813**, **B 1.000**.

4. Add a **Fresnel** node (press *Shift + A* and go to **Input | Fresnel**) to the **Fac** input socket of the **Mix Shader** node and set the **IOR** value to `1.309` as well.

5. Add a **Glossy BSDF** shader (press *Shift + A* and go to **Shader | Glossy BSDF**), set the color to pure white and the **Roughness** value to `0.050`.

6. Select the **Mix Shader** node and press *Shift + D* to duplicate it. Connect the other **Mix Shader** output to the first **Shader** input socket and the **Glossy** shader output to the second one. Add a **Layer Weight** node (press *Shift + A* and go to **Input | Layer Weight**) and connect the **Facing** output to the **Fac** socket of the second **Mix Shader** node.

7. Add a **Voronoi Texture** node (press *Shift + A* and go to **Texture | Voronoi Texture**), set to **Cells** and **Scale** to `50.000`.

8. Add a **Noise Texture** node (press *Shift + A* and go to **Texture | Noise Texture**), set only the **Scale** value to `50.000`.

9. Add a **Math** node (press *Shift + A* and go to **Convertor | Math**) and set the operator to **Maximum**. Connect the **Fac** outputs of the **Voronoi** and **Noise** texture nodes to the first and second **Value** input of the **Math** node.

10. Add a **Bump** node (press *Shift + A* and go to **Vector | Bump**), connect the **Math** node output to the **Height** input of the **Bump** node and its **Normal** output to the **Normal** input sockets of the **Glass** and the **Glossy** shaders.

11. Set the **Strength** value of the **Bump** node to `0.005`.

12. Add a **Texture Coordinate** (press *Shift + A* and go to **Input | Texture Coordinate**) and a Mapping (press *Shift + A* and go to **Vector | Mapping**) nodes, connect the **Object** output of the first to the **Vector** input of the second one, and then connect the **Vector** output of the **Mapping** node to the **Vector** input sockets of both the **Voronoi** and **Noise** textures.

So, finally, this is our result:

And this is the nodes network as seen in the **Node Editor** window:

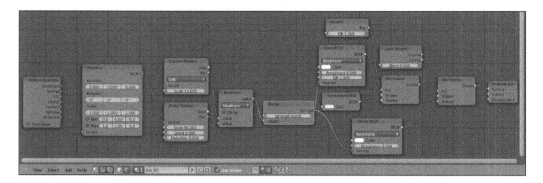

How it works...

This time we started by mixing a **Glass BSDF** shader and a **Transparent** shader node, modulated by a **Fresnel** node, and we set the **Index Of Refraction** of both the Fresnel and the glass to the value of ice. We also added a **Glossy BSDF** shader to provide specularity, mixed by a **Layer Weight** node set on **Facing** (that is, the more a mesh normal is facing the point of view, the more evident is the specular effect).

Then, by using mixed procedurals textures we created the bump effect to perturb the object's surface (and note that the bump is also actually affecting the material's refraction).

Creating a clean running water material

The simpler way to make a water shader is by using a glass node and setting the **IOR** value (**Index Of Refraction**, a number specifying the capacity of a medium to refract the light passing through it) to 1.33, and actually, this should be enough; by the way, although physically correct, this does not work well in every light condition or particular situation. A better approach is to use the glass shader mixed with another "specularity" node and, in some cases, also with the aid of a texture.

Getting ready

1. Start Blender and switch to the Cycles rendering engine. Select the cube and scale it at least six units on the z axis (press *S* followed by *Z*, digit *3*, and hit *Enter*; the default cube is already of 2 units, so 2 X 3 = 6). Then scale down to the half its width (press *S* followed by *Shift* + *Z*, digit *0.500*, and hit *Enter*).

2. Go in edit mode, and press *Crtl* + *R* and scroll the middle mouse wheel to add four horizontal cuts to the cube.

3. Select the upper and the bottom faces and delete them (press *X* and go to *Faces*). Go out of edit mode and set the cube smooth (press *T* to bring up the **Object Tools** panel on the left and press the **Smooth** button under **Shading**).

4. Press *Crtl* + *A* and select **Scale** to apply the new size of the cube as original.

5. Go to the **Object Modifiers** window and assign a **Subdivision Surface** modifier, set the **Subdivision** levels to 6.

6. Add a **Displace** modifier. Click on the **Show textures in texture tab** button, the last to the right of the **Texture** slot; this switches to the **Textures** window. Click on **New** and then change the **Size** value of the default **Clouds** texture to 0.50. Back to the **Object Modifiers** window, set the displacement strength to 0.500.

7. Go to the **World** window, click on **Use Nodes** and change the color to **R 0.118, G 0.129, B 0.142**.

8. Go in the **Render** window and, under **Sampling**, change the samples to 100 both for **Render** and **Preview**. Also, increase the **Clamp** value to 1.00.

9. Split the 3D window to two horizontal windows and change the upper one to a **Node Editor** window.

10. Set the 3D window as a **Camera** view and in **Rendered** mode.

11. In the **Outliner**, select the lamp, click on **Use Nodes** and set the **Strength** value to 1000.000.

How to do it...

And now, let's jump straight to the material creation:

1. Select the cube and click on **Use Nodes** in the **Material** window, under **Surface** in the **Properties** panel, or in the **Node Editor** window's header. Rename the material as Running_water.

2. In the **Material** window on the right, under **Surface**, switch the **Diffuse** shader with a **Mix Shader** node. In the first **Shader** slot, select a **Glass BSDF** shader and in the second slot a **Glossy BSDF** shader.

3. Set the **Glass** shader's **IOR** value to `1.330` and the color of both the **Glass** and **Glossy** shaders to pure white. Set the **Roughness** value of the **Glossy** shader to `0.010`.

4. Add a **Fresnel** node (press *Shift + A* and go to **Input | Fresnel**) and connect its output to the **Fac** socket of the **Mix Shader** node; set the **IOR** value to `1.330`.

5. Add a **Musgrave Texture** node (press *Shift + A* and go to **Texture | Musgrave Texture**) and a **Bump** node (press Shift + A and go to **Vector | Bump**). Connect the **Musgrave** node's **Fac** output to the **Height** input of the **Bump** node, then its **Normal** output to the **Normal** sockets of the **Glass** and **Glossy** shaders.

6. Add a Texture Coordinate node (press *Shift + A* and go to **Input | Texture Coordinate**) and a **Mapping** (press *Shift + A* and go to **Vector | Mapping**) node. Connect the **Object** output of the first to the **Vector** input of the second one, and then connect the **Vector** output of the **Mapping** node to the **Vector** input socket of the **Musgrave Texture** node.

7. In the **Mapping** node, set the **Scale** value for the z axes to **0.200**, as shown here:

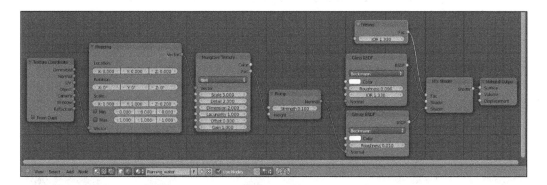

How it works...

The water material is very simple: it is a **Glass BSDF** shader mixed with a **Glossy BSDF** to provide a better reflection of the environment. Note that the **Roughness** value of the **Glossy** shader is set really low, at `0.010`, to provide almost the most of reflection, and that the index of refraction for both the **Glass** shader and the **Fresnel** node is `1.330`.

The **Musgrave** texture is there just to add "pattern" to the **Running_water** shader. The only difference between the **Running_water** shader and the **Water_calm** shader in the containers lies in the **Musgrave** texture and, of course, the displacement, replaced in the **Water_calm** case by a **Wave** modifier to provide some "life".

There's more...

Both the displacement and the **Musgrave** texture assigned to our running water are, at the moment, static. Of course, it's possible to animate them; just follow these steps:

1. Add an **Empty** (press *Shift + A* and go to **Empty** with the mouse in the 3D window) to the scene, possibly at the origin pivot point of the cube. Reselect the cube and go to the **Object Modifiers** window. Now, in the **Displace** modifier, under **Texture Coordinates**, switch from **Local** to **Object**; in the just appeared **Object** new slot, click to select the name of the **Empty**. Now the displacement is mapped on the position of this **Empty**.

2. Looking in the **Timeline** at the bottom of the screen, be sure to be at frame **1**. Select the **Empty** and press *I* and go to **Location**. This sets a position key for the **Empty** at frame **1**.

3. Now, in the **Timeline**, go at frame **25**; move the **Empty** 10 units down on the z axis and again press *I* and go to **Location**, to set a second position key for the **Empty**.

4. In the **Screen lay-out** button at the top, switch from **Default** to **Animation**. In the **Graph Editor** window, press *T* and go to **Linear** and press *Shift + E* and go to **Linear Extrapolation** to make the twenty-fifth frame's **Empty** animation constant and continuous.

5. Switch back to the **Default** screen, go at frame **1**, and select the cube. In the **Node Editor** window, zoom on the **Mapping** node. Put the mouse on the **Location** values and press *I*; the values turn yellow, to show that a key has been assigned.

6. Go to frame **25**, change the **Z Location** value to `-10.000` and press *I* again.

7. Switch to the **Animation** screen, again press *T* and go to **Linear** and press *Shift + E* and go to **Linear Extrapolation** in the **Graph Editor** window.

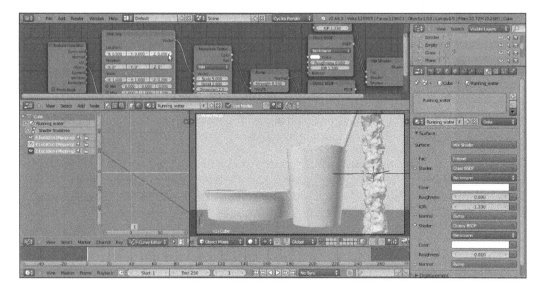

4

Creating Man-made Materials in Cycles

In this chapter, we will cover:

- ▸ Creating a generic plastic material
- ▸ Creating a bakelite material
- ▸ Creating an expanded polystyrene material
- ▸ Creating a clear (glassy) polystyrene material
- ▸ Creating a rubber material
- ▸ Creating an antique bronze material with procedurals
- ▸ Creating a multipurpose metal group node
- ▸ Creating a worn metal material with procedurals
- ▸ Creating a rusty metal material with procedurals
- ▸ Creating a wood material with procedurals

Introduction

For the most part, artificial materials are quite easy to recreate in Cycles. In the previous chapters we discussed the mechanics of building, for the most part with procedural materials using the Cycles render engine. In the following section we'll go on to discuss some example materials, in particular those that are typically used; namely artificial materials, starting with one or two examples of simple materials, progressing on to more complex ones. We'll also have a look at the decayed material shaders, as worn or rusty metals.

Just a note: by default, in Cycles it would not actually be necessary to add the nodes for the texture mapping coordinates in any shader network; this because if not specified, Cycles use the **Generated** mapping coordinates for the procedural textures and any existing UV coordinate layer for the image textures.

I think it's a good habit to add the **Texture Coordinate** and the **Mapping** nodes to all the materials, in order to permit an easy reutilization of the shaders on different objects with different mapping options, scale, and location.

Creating a generic plastic material

In this recipe we will create a generic plastic shader, adding a slight granularity to the surface:

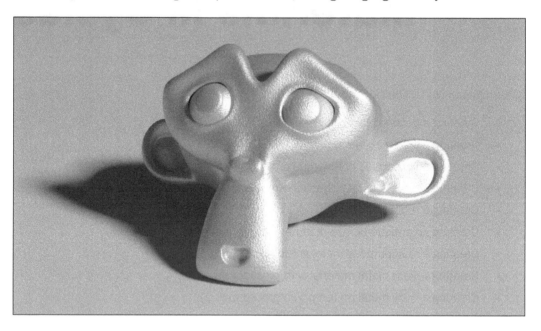

Getting ready

Start Blender and load the file `1301OS_04_start.blend`. It's a prepared scene with Suzanne (the monkey head primitive that is also Blender's mascot) leaning on a plane, a Camera, a Mesh light and an already set low intensity gray World.

How to do it...

Now, straight to the material creation:

1. If not already, select Suzanne and click on **New** in the **Material** window under the **Properties** panel or in the **Node Editor** header. Rename the material `Plastic_green_soft`.

2. Set **Viewport Shading** of the **Camera** view to **Rendered**.

3. Switch the **Diffuse** shader with a **Mix Shader** node. In the first **Shader** slot select a **Diffuse BSDF** shader, in the second **Shader** slot select a **Glossy BSDF**.

4. Change the **Diffuse** color to a bright green (R 0.040, G 0.800, B 0.190) and the **Glossy** shader color to pure white; set the Roughness value of the **Glossy** shader to **0.300**.

5. Add a **Noise Texture** node (press *Shift + A* and go to **Texture | Noise Texture**), then add a **Texture Coordinate** node (press *Shift + A* and go to **Input | Texture Coordinate**) and a **Mapping** node (press *Shift + A* and go to **Vector | Mapping**).

6. Connect the **Object** output of the **Texture Coordinate** node to the **Vector** input of the **Mapping** node and the output of this one to the input of the **Noise Texture** node.

7. Set the **Noise Texture** scale to `50.000`. Add an **RGB to BW** node (press *Shift + A* and go to **Convertor | RGB to BW**) and a **Math** node (press *Shift + A* and go to **Convertor | Math**); connect the **Noise Texture** node's **Color** output to **RGB to BW** and the **RGB to BW** node's **Val** output to the first **Value** input of the **Math** node.

8. Set the **Math** node operation to **Multiply** and the second **Value** to `0.100`; connect its **Value** output to the **Displacement** input socket of the **Material Output** node.

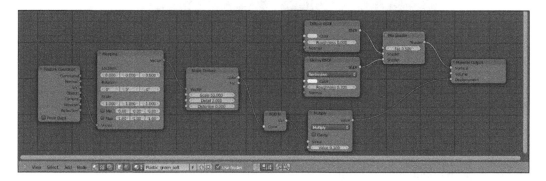

How it works...

This is one of the simplest materials you can build in Cycles; it consists of a colored **Diffuse** component mixed at 50% with a white **Glossy** shader. A tiny **Noise Texture**, connected directly to the **Displacement** input of the **Material Output** node, adds a slight dotted bump effect to the whole material; this effect actually is optional, the shader is already very plastic-looking without the bump.

Creating a bakelite material

Bakelite is a very common type of plastic and can be found in a lot of different colorations and patterns. In this recipe we will create the black type that was once commonly used for, among other things, the classic home telephone.

Getting ready

1. Start Blender and load again the file `1301OS_04_start.blend`.

2. Select the Suzanne mesh and press *T*; in the **Object Tools** panel on the left, select **Flat** from the **Shading** option; press *T* again to get rid of the **Object Tools** panel.

3. Go to the **Object Modifiers** window in the **Properties** panel and set the **Subdivision Surface** modifier levels both for **View** and **Render** to 1.

How to do it...

Now we are going to create the material:

1. Go to the **Material** window and click on **New** (or do it, as usual, in the **Node Editor** header). Rename the material `Plastic_bakelite_black`.

2. Set **Viewport Shading** of the **Camera** view to **Rendered**.

3. Switch the **Diffuse** shader with a **Mix Shader** node. In the first **Shader** slot select a **Diffuse BSDF** shader, in the second **Shader** slot select **Glossy BSDF**.

4. Change the **Diffuse** shader color to a pure black and the **Glossy** shader color to a light gray (RGB 0.253); set the **Roughness** value of the **Glossy** shader to `0.100` and the **Factor** value of the **Mix Shader** node to `0.800`.

5. Press *Shift + D* to duplicate the **Mix Shader** node and paste it between the **Glossy** shader and the first **Mix Shader** node.

6. Place the mouse cursor in the **Node Editor** window and press *N*; select the first **Mix Shader** node and in the **Active Node** panel on the right, and in the **Label** slot, write `Mix Shader1`; select the second one and in the **Label** slot, write `Mix Shader2`.

7. Add an **Anisotropic BSDF** shader (press *Shift + A* and go to **Shader | Anisotropic BSDF**) and connect its output to the second input socket of the **Mix Shader** (2) node.

8. Set the **Mix Shader** (2) factor value to `0.500`. Set the **Anisotropic** color to the same light gray as for the **Glossy** shader (that is, RGB 0.253), the **Roughness** to `0.100` and the **Rotation** to `0.500`.

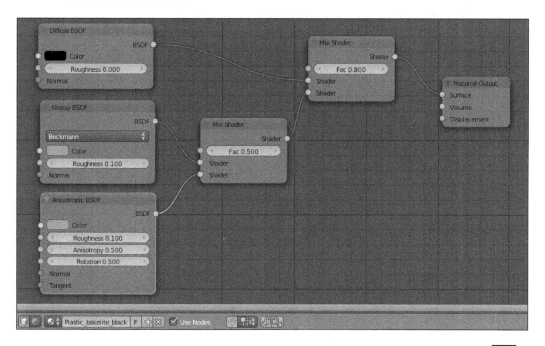

How it works...

Basically we made the same kind of material as the former green plastic, but this time we enhanced the reflectivity (mirror) by lowering the **Roughness** value. We also added an **Anisotropic** specularity effect with the same **Roughness** value and color as for the **Glossy** shader.

 Anisotropy is a method for enhancing the image quality of textures on surfaces that are far away and steeply angled with respect to the point of view; an anisotropic surface will change in appearance as it's rotated about its geometric normal.

The **Rotation** value of the **Anisotropic** shader set the flow of the highlights on the mesh, the direction of the specularity rotates as this value increases from 0.000 to 1.000.

There's more...

Let's try now, starting from the black one, to make a differently processed kind of bakelite material:

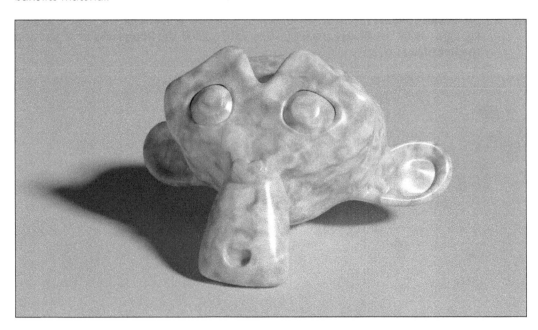

1. Select the **Diffuse**, **Glossy**, **Anisotropic**, and the second **Mix Shader** nodes and press *Ctrl* + G to make a group; rename it `Bakelite`.

2. Click and drag the **Diffuse** shader's **Color** socket to expose it; drag also the **Fac** socket of the **Mix Shader2** node and rename it as Aniso. This will drive the influence of the **Anisotropic** shader on the **Glossy** one. Click and drag also the **Fac** socket of the **Mix Shader1** and rename it Spec: this will drive up the amount of final specularity of the shader. Press *Tab* to close the group.

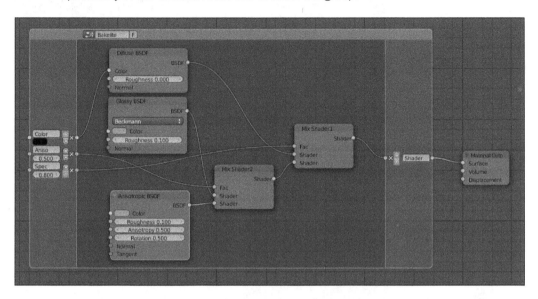

3. Now add: a **Texture Coordinate** node (press *Shift + A* and go to **Input | Texture Coordinate**); a **Mapping** node (*Shift + A* and go to **Vector | Mapping**); a **Noise Texture** node (press *Shift + A* and go to **Texture | Noise Texture**); a **ColorRamp** node (press *Shift + A* and go to **Converter | ColorRamp**); and a **Mix** node (press *Shift + A* and go to **Color | Mix**).

4. Connect the **Object** output of the **Texture Coordinate** node to the **Vector** input of the **Mapping** node, then connect the output of this to the **Noise Texture** node input. Connect the **Color** output of the **Noise Texture** to the **ColorRamp** input socket, **Fac** and the **Color** output of the latter one to the **Color1** input socket of the **Mix** node. Connect the **Color** output of the **Mix** node to the **Color** input of the **Bakelite** node group.

5. Set the **Noise Texture** node **Scale** to 4.000, **Detail** to 4.200 and **Distortion** to 1.700.

6. Set the **ColorRamp** node interpolation to **B-Spline**, moving the black color marker one-fourth to the right and the white color marker one-fourth to the left.

7. Set the **Mix** node's **Blend Type** to **Divide** (but experiment also with others types), the **Fac** value to 0.600 and the **Color2** value to R 0.799, G 0.442, and B 0.220.

8. In the **Bakelite** node group interface, set the **Spec** value to 0.300.

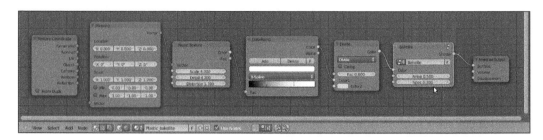

9. Optionally, smooth the Suzanne mesh in the **Object Tools** panel (*T*) and increase the subdivision levels of the **Subdivision Surface** modifier to 2.

Creating an expanded polystyrene material

In this recipe, we will create the classic white expanded polystyrene material:

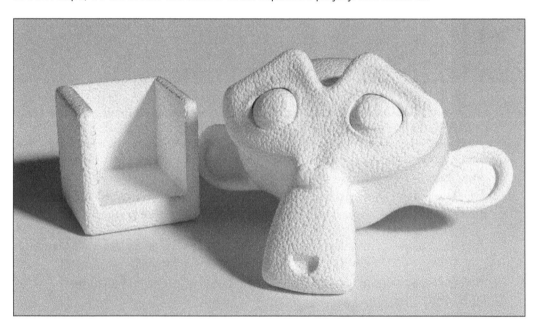

Getting ready

Start Blender and load the file 1301OS_04_start.blend.

How to do it...

Now we are going to create the material:

1. Select Suzanne (or whatever mesh you are going to use) and click on **New** in the **Material** window under the **Properties** panel or in the **Node Editor** header. Rename the material `Plastic_expanded_polystyrene`.

2. Switch the **Diffuse** shader with a **Mix Shader** node. In the first **Shader** slot select a **Diffuse BSDF** shader, in the second **Shader** slot select a **Glossy BSDF**.

3. Set the **Diffuse** shader **Color** and the **Glossy** shader **Color** to pure white; set the **Roughness** value of the **Glossy** shader to `0.600`. Add a **Fresnel** node (press *Shift + A* and then go to **Input | Fresnel**) and connect its output to the **Fac** input socket of the **Mix Shader** node; set the **IOR** value to `1.550`.

4. Add a **Voronoi Texture** node (press *Shift + A* and go to **Texture | Voronoi Texture**), then add a **Texture Coordinate** node (press *Shift + A* and go to **Input | Texture Coordinate**) and a **Mapping** node (press *Shift + A* and go to **Vector | Mapping**).

5. Connect the **Object** output of the **Texture Coordinate** node to the **Vector** input of the **Mapping** node, then the output of this one to the **Vector** input of the **Voronoi Texture** node.

6. Set the **Voronoi Texture** node **Scale** to `25.000`. Add an **RGB to BW** node (press *Shift + A* and go to **Convertor | RGB to BW**) and a **Math** node (*Shift + A* and go to **Convertor | Math**); connect the **Voronoi Texture** node's **Color** output to the **RGB to BW** node and this one to the first **Value** input of the **Math** node.

7. Set the **Math** node operation to **Multiply** and the second **Value** to `-0.150`; connect its **Value** output to the **Displacement** input socket of the **Material Output** node.

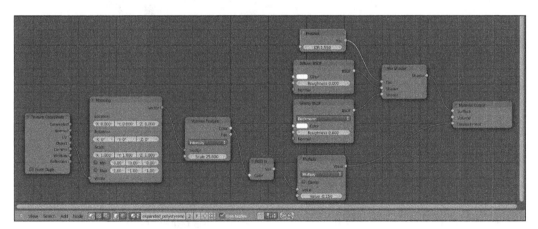

How it works...

You have probably noticed that this recipe is simply a variation of the generic plastic shader. We changed the **Color** to white and, instead of the **Noise Texture** node, we used a **Voronoi Texture** node with a different **Scale** to add the typical polystyrene pattern; then, by increasing the **Roughness** value of the **Glossy** shader, we made the specularity more diffused.

Creating a clear (glassy) polystyrene material

In this recipe, we will create a glassy polystyrene plastic material; the type you can find on the body of ballpoint pens:

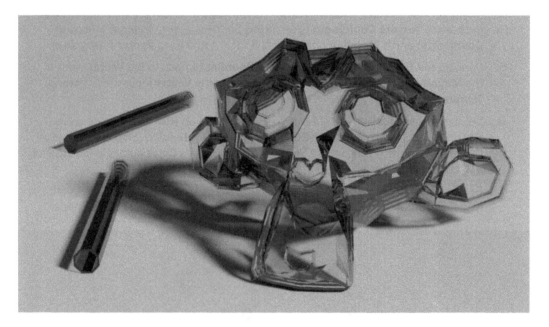

Getting ready

1. Start Blender and load the usual file `13010S_04_start.blend`.

2. Select the **Suzanne mesh** and press *T*. In the **Object Tools** panel on the left select **Flat** from the **Shading** option, press *T* again to get rid of the **Object Tools** panel.

3. Go to the **Object Modifiers** window in the **Properties** panel and delete the **Subdivision Surface** modifier. Add a **Solidify** modifier and set **Thickness** to 0.0350. Add a **Bevel** modifier and set **Width** to 0.0025.

How to do it...

Now we are going to create the material:

1. Go to the **Material** window and click on **New** (or do it, as usual, in the **Node Editor** header). Rename the material `Plastic_clear_polystyrene`.

2. Set **Viewport Shading** of the **Camera** view to **Rendered**.

3. Switch the **Diffuse** shader with a **Mix Shader** node and in the first **Shader** slot select a **Mix Shader** node again, in the second **Shader** slot select a **Glass BSDF** node; set its **IOR** value to `1.460` and the **Color** value to R `0.688`, G `0.758`, and B `0.758`.

4. Go to the second **Mix Shader** node and in its first **Shader** slot select a **Transparent BSDF**, in the second a **Glossy BSDF**; set the **Glossy** node's **Color** to R `0.688`, G `0.758`, and B `0.758`, and **Roughness** to `0.010`.

5. Add a **Fresnel** node (press *Shift + A* and go to **Input | Fresnel**) and connect it to the **Fac** input sockets of both the **Mix Shader** nodes; set the **IOR** value to `1.460` as well.

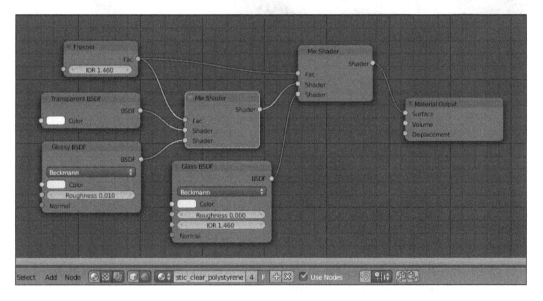

Creating a rubber material

In this recipe we will create a generic rubber shader:

Getting ready

Start Blender and load the file 1301OS_04_start.blend.

How to do it...

Now we are going to create the material:

1. Click on **New** in the **Material** window under the **Properties** panel or in the **Node Editor** header. Rename the material Rubber.

2. Switch the **Diffuse** shader with a **Mix Shader** node. In the second **Shader** slot select **Glossy BSDF**; in the first **Shader** slot select a new **Mix Shader** node. Set the **Glossy** node's **Roughness** value to 0.350.

3. Go to the second **Mix Shader** node. In the first **Shader** slot select a **Diffuse BSDF** node and in the second, a **Velvet BSDF** node. Set the **Velvet** shader's **Sigma** value to 0.600.

4. Add a **Fresnel** node (press *Shift + A* and go to **Input | Fresnel**) and connect it to the **Fac** inputs of both the **Mix Shader** nodes. Set the **IOR** value to 1.519.

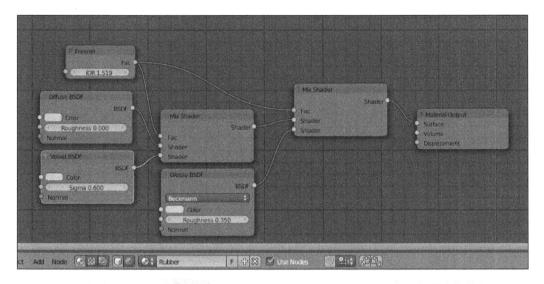

5. Add a **Texture Coordinate** node (press *Shift + A* and go to **Input | Texture Coordinate**), a **Mapping** node (*Shift + A* and go to **Vector | Mapping**), a **Voronoi Texture** node, and a **Noise Texture** node (*Shift + A* and go to **Texture | Noise Texture**).

6. Connect the **Object** output of the **Texture Coordinate** node to the **Vector** input of the **Mapping** node and this latter's output to the **Vector** input sockets of the two texture nodes.

7. Set the **Voronoi** node's **Coloring** to **Cells** and the **Scale** to 350.000. Set the **Noise** node's **Scale** to 450.000 and the **Detail** value to 5.000.

8. Add two **Math** nodes (*Shift + A* and go to **Convertor | Math**), set the operation of the second to **Multiply**; connect the **Fac** output of the **Voronoi** node to the first **Value** input socket of the **Add** math node, and the **Fac** output of the **Noise** node to the second **Value** input socket.

9. Connect the **Add** node output to the first **Value** input socket of the **Multiply** node; set the second **Value** of **Multiply** node to 0.060 and connect the output to the **Displacement** node input socket of the **Material Output** node.

10. Add a **Mix** node (press *Shift + A* and go to **Color | Mix**) and move it close to the **Voronoi Texture** node. Set the **Blend Type** to **Multiply** and connect the **Voronoi** node's **Color** output to the **Color2** input socket of the **Multiply** node, then connect the **Color** output to the **Color** input sockets of the three shaders—**Diffuse**, **Velvet**, and **Glossy**.

11. Add an **RGB** node (*Shift + A* and go to **Input | RGB**) and connect it to the **Color1** input socket of the **Multiply** node.

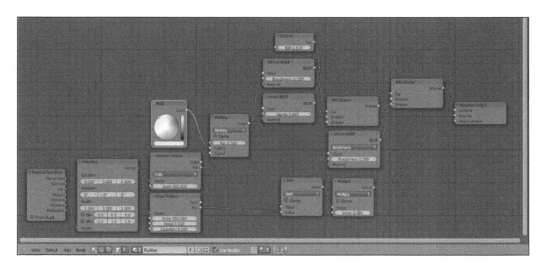

Creating an antique bronze material with procedurals

In this recipe we will create a bronze shader similar to a ruined antique statue:

Getting ready

1. Start Blender and load the file `1301OS_04_start.blend`.

2. With Suzanne selected, click on the **Mode** button in the **Camera** view header and choose **Vertex Paint**; Suzanne turns a shadeless white color.

3. Place the mouse cursor on the **Paint** item at the left of the **Mode** button, click and select **Dirty Vertex Colors**, then press *T* and in the bottom window of the **Object Tools** panel set **Blur Strength** to `0.01`, **Dirt Angle** to `90`, and check the **Dirt Only** option.

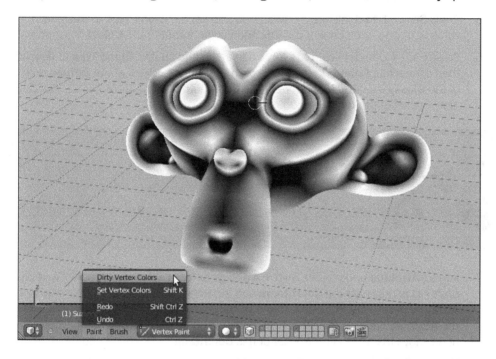

4. Go to the **Object Data** window under the **Properties** panel. In the **Name** slot under the **Vertex Colors** subpanel, rename the vertex color layer as `V_col`.

5. Return to **Object Mode** and press *T* to get rid of the **Object Tools** panel.

How to do it...

And now we are going to create the material:

1. Click on **New** in the **Material** window under the **Properties** panel or in the **Node Editor** header. Rename the material as `Bronze_antique`.

2. Switch the **Diffuse** shader with a **Mix Shader** node. In the first **Shader** slot select a **Diffuse BSDF** shader, in the second **Shader** slot select a **Glossy BSDF**. Set the **Diffuse** shader **Roughness** to `1.000` and the **Glossy** shader **Roughness** value to `0.300`.

3. Now add a **Layer Weight** node (press *Shift + A* and go to **Input | Layer Weight**), a **ColorRamp** node (press *Shift + A* and go to **Convertor | ColorRamp**), and a **Mix** node (press *Shift + A* and go to **Color | Mix**). Connect the **Facing** output of the **Layer Weight** node to the **Fac** input of the **ColorRamp** and its **Color** output to the **Fac** input socket of the **Mix** node.

4. Add an **Invert** node (press *Shift + A* and go to **Color | Invert**) and paste it between the **ColorRamp** node and the **Mix** node. Set the **ColorRamp** interpolation mode to **B-Spline** and the **Color1** value of the **Mix** node to R `0.187`, G `0.319`, and B `1.000`; set the **Color2** value to R `0.000`, G `0.880`, and B `0.222`.

5. Press *Shift + D* to duplicate the **Mix** node and set the **Blend Type** to **Burn**; set the **Fac** value to `0.200` and connect the **Mix** node color output to the **Color1** input socket.

6. Press *Shift + D* to duplicate the **Mix** node again and set the **Blend Type** to **Overlay**, then connect its **Color** output to both the **Color** input sockets of the **Diffuse** node and of the **Glossy** shaders. Now connect the **Color** output of the **Burn** node to the **Color1** input socket of the **Overlay** node.

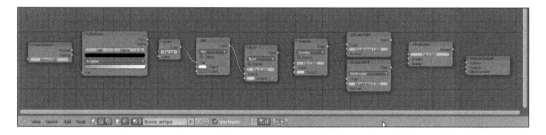

7. Add an **Attribute** node (press *Shift + A* and go to **Input | Attribute**); select and press *Shift + D* to duplicate the **ColorRamp** and the **Invert** nodes, move them closer to the **Attribute** node. Write the name of the vertex color layer (`V_col`) in the **Name** slot of the **Attribute** node, then connect the **Color** output to the **Fac** input of the **ColorRamp** node. Move the white color marker of this **ColorRamp** node to the middle of the slider.

8. Connect the **Color** output of the second **Invert** node to the **Fac** input socket of the **Mix Shader** node.

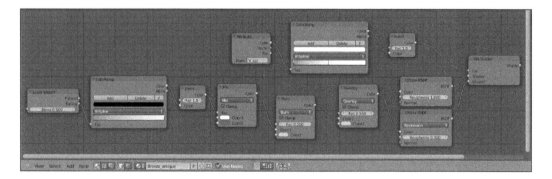

9. Add a **Texture Coordinate** node (press *Shift + A* and go to **Input | Texture Coordinate**), a **Mapping** node (press *Shift + A* and go to **Vector | Mapping**), two **Noise Texture** nodes (press *Shift + A* and go to **Textures | Noise Texture**), and two **Musgrave Textures** (press *Shift + A* and go to **Textures | Musgrave Texture**).

10. Connect the **Object** output of the **Texture Coordinate** node to the **Vector** input of the **Mapping** node, then connect the **Vector** output of this one to the **Vector** inputs of all four texture nodes.

11. For the first **Noise** node, set **Scale** to 22.100, **Detail** to 12.000, and **Distortion** to 3.000; for the second **Noise**, set **Scale** to 3.500 and **Detail** to 5.800.

12. For the first **Musgrave**, just set the **Scale** value to 8.500. For the second one change the type to **Multifractal** and set **Scale** to 8.500, **Detail** to 2.600, **Dimension** to 0.800, and **Lacunarity** to 0.400.

13. Add a **Mix** node (press *Shift + A* and go to **Color | Mix**); set the **Blend Type** to **Difference** and the **Color2** value to pure white. Connect the **Color** output of the first **Musgrave** node to the **Color1** input socket, and the **Fac** output of the second **Noise Texture** node to the **Fac** input socket of the same **Mix** node.

14. Press *Shift + D* to duplicate the **Mix** node, set the **Blend Type** to **Subtract** and connect the **color** output of the **Difference** node to the **Color2** input of the **Subtract** node, and the **Color** output of the first **Noise Texture** to its **Color1** input socket.

15. Connect the **Color** output of the first **Noise Texture** node to the **Color2** input socket of the **Burn** node that we made in step 5.

16. Add a **Math** node (*Shift + A* and go to **Convertor | Math**) and set the operation to **Multiply**. Connect the **Subtract** node output to the first **Value** input of the **Math** node, then connect the **Math** node output to the **Displacement** input socket of the **Material Output** node. Set the second **Value** to 0.200.

17. Add a **ColorRamp** node (*Shift + A* and go to **Convertor | ColorRamp**) and paste it between the **Subtract** node and the **Math** node. Set the interpolation to **Ease** and move the color white marker three-fourths to the left of the slider.

18. Add a **Mix** node (*Shift + A* and go to **Color | Mix**) and paste it just after this last **ColorRamp** node. Connect the first **Noise Texture** node's **Color** output to the **Color2** input socket of the **Mix** node, and the **ColorRamp** node's **Color** output also to the **Color2** input socket of the **Overlay** node we made in step 6.

19. Add a last **ColorRamp** (*Shift + A* and go to **Convertor | ColorRamp**); set its interpolation to **Ease**, move the black color marker one-third to the right and the white color marker one-third to the left. Connect the **Fac** output of the fourth **Musgrave Texture** node to the **Fac** input of this last **ColorRamp** node.

20. Add a **Math** node (*Shift + A* and go to **Convertor | Math**) and paste it between the **Mix** node and the last **Math** node (the one set to **Multiply**).

21. Connect the **ColorRamp** node's **Color** output to the second **Value** input of the just added **Math** node.

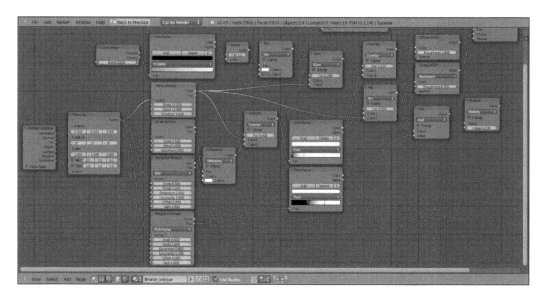

How it works...

We are using the vertex color layer set in the *Getting ready* section as a stencil map to distribute both the colored **Diffuse** and the **Glossy** shaders, driven also by the **Facing** option of the **Layer Weight** input node.

For the rest, the bulk of the effect is in the bump obtained by the **Noise** and **Musgrave** textures mixed and clamped in several ways by the **ColorRamp** nodes.

As usual, the last **Math** node set to **Multiply** establishes the strength of the bump.

Creating a multipurpose metal group node

In this recipe we will build a generic node group shader applicable, by setting different values, to the most part of different metal materials:

Getting ready

Start Blender and load the file `1301OS_04_start.blend`.

How to do it...

Now we are going to create the node group:

1. Click on **New** in the **Material** window under the **Properties** panel or in the **Node Editor** header.

2. Switch the **Diffuse** shader with a **Mix Shader** node. In the first **Shader** slot select a **Glossy BSDF** shader, in the second **Shader** slot select an **Anisotropic BSDF**.

3. Press *Shift + D* to duplicate the **Mix Shader** node and paste it just after the first **Mix Shader** node. Add a **Diffuse** shader (press *Shift + A* and go to **Shader | Diffuse BSDF**) and connect it to the second **Shader** input of the second **Mix Shader** node.

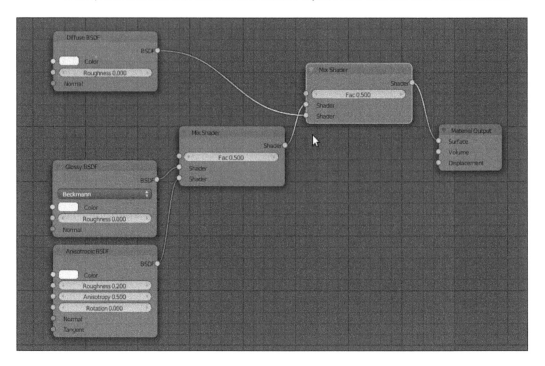

4. Add a **Fresnel** node (press *Shift + A* and go to **Input | Fresnel**) and connect it to the **Fac** input of the second **Mix Shader** node.

5. Add a **Mix** node (press *Shift + A* and go to **Color | Mix**), set the **Blend Type** to **Add** and connect the **Color** output to the **Color** input sockets of the **Diffuse, Glossy**, and **Anisotropic** shader nodes.

6. Add a **Bump** node (press *Shift + A* and go to **Vector | Bump**) and connect its **Normal** output to the **Normal** input sockets of the **Diffuse, Glossy**, and **Anisotropic** shader nodes.

7. Select all the nodes except for the **Material Output** node and press *Ctrl + G* to create a group; rename the group `Metal`.

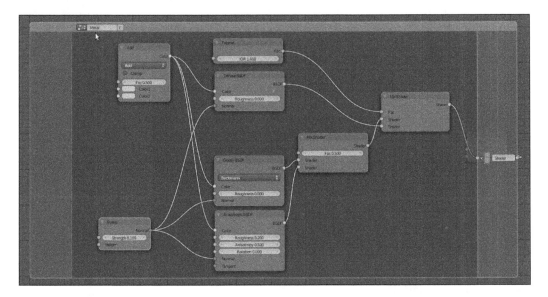

Now we must expose all the values necessary to tweak the node group for different types of metals.

8. Click and drag the **IOR** input socket of the **Fresnel** node to the extreme left border of the group envelope.

9. Do the same with the **Color1** input socket of the **Add** node, renaming the newly appeared slot, `Color`; also drag the **Color2** socket of the **Add** node to the same **Color** interface socket.

10. Drag the **Roughness** input socket of the **Glossy** shader to the same interface socket, then do the same with the **Roughness** socket of the **Anisotropic** shader.

11. Click and drag the **Fac** socket of the first **Mix Shader** node to the envelope border, rename it `Aniso_Amount`.

12. Click and drag the **Anisotropy** socket of the **Anisotropic** shader.

13. Repeat the same for the **Rotation** input socket.

14. Now click and drag the **Height** socket of the **Bump** node, renaming it `Bump`.

15. Do the same for the **Strength** socket, renaming it `Bump_Strength`.

16. Lastly, click and drag the **Tangent** input socket of the **Anisotropic** shader.

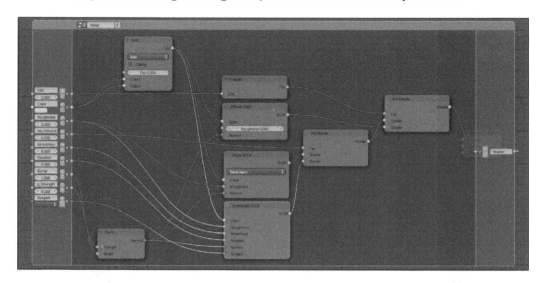

How it works...

The effect of this node group is mainly based on the **IOR** value, which is usually quite different for the different metals.

 Index Of Refraction: The refractive index of a material is a number that describes how light propagates through that material.

In the node, the exposed **IOR** value drives the amount of blending of the **Diffuse** component with the **mirror** component, made by the **Glossy** and **Anisotropic** shaders combined together but which in turn can be mutually blended accordingly to the `Aniso_Amount` value.

The **Anisotropy** and **Rotation** values of the **Anisotropic** shader are exposed as well, and the same for the **Tangent** input—in case a particular mapping option must be used (for example, a UV coordinates layer).

The **Bump** socket is the input socket to connect any texture and the **Bump_Strength** interface socket establishes the amount of bump influence.

 The **Bump** node output is piped to all the three **Normal** input of the **Diffuse**, **Glossy**, and **Anisotropic** shaders, to keep a consistent effect among all the components.

Similarly, both the **Glossy** and **Anisotropic** shaders' **Roughness** values are driven by a single interface input.

Finally, the same is true for the color of the metal, shared among all the three components of the shader; the **Add** node in between is to enhance it (optionally you could also expose its **Fac** value for further tweaking).

For a quite exhaustive list of IOR of materials, you can have a look at the following addresses:

▸   http://refractiveindex.info/

▸   http://www.robinwood.com/Catalog/Technical/Gen3DTuts/
    Gen3DPages/RefractionIndexList.html

▸   http://forums.cgsociety.org/archive/index.php/t-513458.html

Note that for some material (especially metals), different lists report different IOR values.

Creating a worn metal material with procedurals

In this recipe we will create a worn metallic shader:

Getting ready

1. Start Blender and load the file `13010S_04_start.blend`.

2. With Suzanne selected, click on the **Mode** button in the **Camera** view header and choose **Vertex Paint**—Suzanne turns a shadeless white color.

3. Place the mouse cursor on the **Paint** option at the left of the **Mode** button, click and select **Dirty Vertex Colors**, then press *T* and in the bottom window of the **Object Tools** panel, set **Blur Strength** to `0.01`, **Dirt Angle** to `90`, and check the **Dirt Only** option.

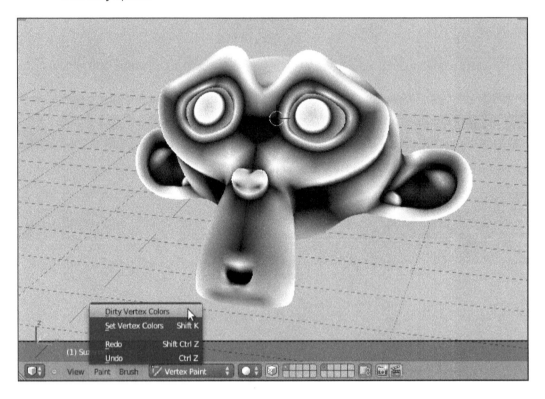

4. Go to the **Object Data** window below the **Properties** panel, and in the **Name** slot below the **Vertex Colors** subpanel, rename the vertex color layer `Col_vp`.

5. Return to **Object Mode** and press *T* to get rid of the **Object Tools** panel. In the **Properties** panel go back to the **Material** window.

How to do it...

Now let's create the material:

1. From **13010S_04_metal.blend | NodeTree**, append the node group **Metal**.

2. Click on **New** in the **Material** window under the **Properties** panel or in the **Node Editor** header. Rename the material `Worn_Metal`.

3. Switch the **Diffuse** shader with a **Mix Shader** node and in the first **Shader** slot select, under **Group**, the **Metal** node group. Do the same for the second **Shade** slot; now you have two instances of the **Metal** node group connected to the two input sockets of the **Mix Shader** node:

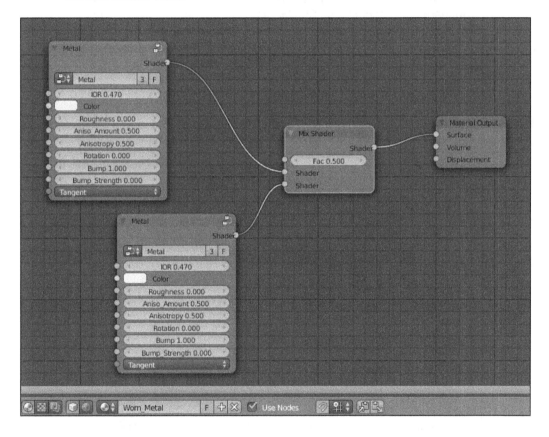

4. Add an **Attribute** node (press *Shift + A* and go to **Input | Attribute**) and a **ColorRamp** (press *Shift + A* and go to **Convertor | ColorRamp**); in the **Name** slot of the **Attribute** node write the name of the vertex color layer, `Col_vp`, and connect the node's **Color** output to the **Fac** input socket of the **ColorRamp**.

5. Connect the **Color** output of the **ColorRamp** node to the **Fac** input socket of the **Mix Shader** node. Set the **ColorRamp** node interpolation to **B-Spline** and move the white color marker three-fourths to the left side of the slider.

6. Add a frame (press *Shift + A* and go to **Layout | Frame**), select the **Attribute** and **ColorRamp** nodes, then the frame itself and press *Ctrl + P* to parent them. Rename the frame VERTEX_COLOR_STENCIL.

7. Now go to the first **Metal** group and set **IOR** to 0.870, **Color** to R 0.229, G 0.307, and B 0.299, and **Roughness** to 0.200. In the second **Metal** group set **IOR** to 1.000, **Color** to R 0.584, G 0.786, and B 0.765, **Roughness** to 1.000, and **Aniso_Amount** to 0.100.

8. Add a **Texture Coordinate** node (press *Shift + A* and go to **Input | Texture Coordinate**), then connect the **Object** output to the **Tangent** input of both the **Metal** group instances.

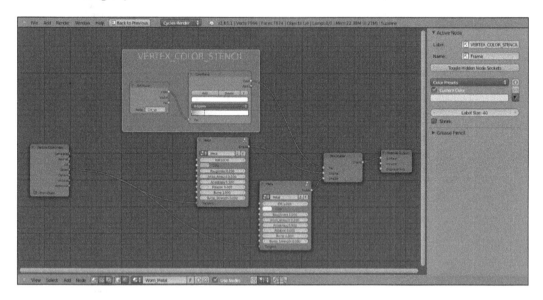

So far the shader looks really simple. Now we are going to build the bump complex to be piped in the **Bump** input socket of the second **Metal** group.

9. Add a **Mapping** node (press *Shift + A* and go to **Vector | Mapping**), a **Wave Texture** node (press *Shift + A* and go to **Texture | Wave Texture**), a **Musgrave Texture** node (press *Shift + A* and go to **Texture | Musgrave Texture**), a **Mix** node (press *Shift + A* and go to **Color | Mix**), and a **ColorRamp** node (press *Shift + A* and go to **Convertor | ColorRamp**).

10. Press *Shift + D* to duplicate the **Mapping** node, then connect the **Object** output of the **Texture Coordinate** node to the **Vector** input sockets of both the **Mapping** nodes. In the second **Mapping** node set the **Location** to 0.010 for all three axes.

11. In the **Wave Texture** set the **Wave Type** value to **Rings**, **Scale** to 27.000, **Distortion** to 11.800, and **Detail** to 16.000. Press *Shift + D* to duplicate the node and move it just under the first one. Also, move the **Musgrave** node under this second **Wave**.

12. Connect the first **Mapping** node's **Vector** output to the first **Wave Texture** node's **Vector** input socket; connect the second **Mapping** node's **Vector** output to the **Vector** input sockets of the second **Wave** and of the **Musgrave Texture** node.

13. Set the **Musgrave** type to **Ridged Multifractal**, **Scale** to 27.000, **Detail** to 5.700, and **Offset** to 0.500.

14. Connect the input **Color** outputs of the two **Wave Texture** nodes to the **Color1** and **Color2** sockets of the **Mix** node. Set the **Mix** node's **Fac** value to 1.000 and the **Blend Type** to **Difference**. In the **Active Node** panel (N in the **Node Editor** window), in the **Label** slot, rename it Difference1. Connect the **Difference1** node's **Color** output to the **Fac** input of the **ColorRamp** node; move the white color marker to the middle of the slider and the black color marker one-fourths to the right.

15. Press *Shift + D* to duplicate the **ColorRamp** node and move it under the first one; connect the **Color** output of the **Musgrave Texture** node to the **Fac** input socket of the duplicated **ColorRamp**. Move the white color marker to the far left of the slider.

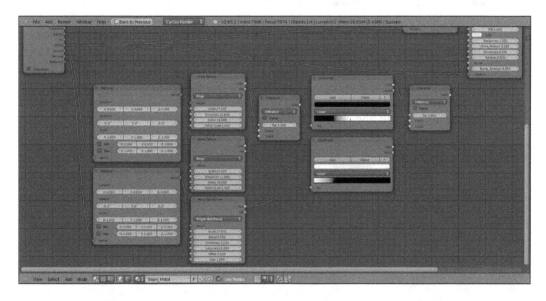

16. Press *Shift + D* to duplicate the **Difference** node, rename it Difference2 and connect the **Color** outputs of the two **ColorRamp** nodes to its **Color1** and **Color2** input sockets. Connect the **Color** output of the **Difference2** node to the **Bump** input socket of the second **Metal** node group; set its **Bump_Strength** to 0.050.

17. Press *Shift + D* to duplicate the second **Mapping** node plus the connected **Wave Texture**, **Musgrave Texture**, and **ColorRamp** nodes; move them further down. Connect the **Object** output of the **Texture Coordinate** node to the **Vector** input of this last **Mapping** node, and restore its **Location** to 0.000 for all three axes (we could use the first **Mapping** node output as well, but this is just to make more readable the graphic appearance in the **Node Editor** window).

18. Press *Shift + D* to duplicate one of the **Difference** nodes, move it down aside the duplicated **ColorRamp** node and rename it as Difference3. Connect the **ColorRamp** node's **Color** output to the **Color2** input socket and the duplicated **Wave Texture** node's **Color** output to the **Color1** input socket, setting the **Fac** value to 0.500. In the **ColorRamp** node set the interpolation to **B-Spline** and move the black color marker a bit to the left (under the n letter of the word **B-Spline**, to be precise) and the white color marker to the right one-third of the total length of the slider.

19. In the duplicated **Wave Texture** node set the **Scale** value to 0.500, and in the duplicated **Musgrave** node set **Scale** to 10.000, **Dimension** to 1.000, **Lacunarity** to 0.200, and **Offset** to 0.600.

20. Add a new **ColorRamp** node (press *Shift + A* and go to **Convertor | ColorRamp**), set the interpolation to **Ease** and move the white color marker one-third to the left; change the black color marker to RGB 0.500 and click on the **Add** button. Set the **Color** of the new marker to pure black. Connect the **Color** output of the **Difference3** node to the **Fac** value of the **ColorRamp** node.

21. Add a **Mix** node (press *Shift + A* | **Color | Mix**) and paste it between the **Difference2** node and the second **Metal** group; connect the last **ColorRamp** node's **Color** output to the **Color2** input socket of the **Mix** node; set the **Mix** node **Blend Type** to **Add**, the **Fac** value to 1.000 and check the **Clamp** option.

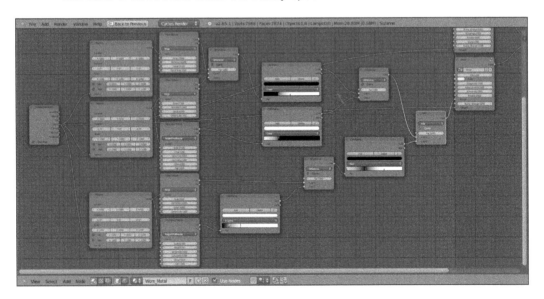

How it works...

As with the bronze material recipe, we used the **Dirty Vertex Colors** layer as stencil factor, this time to mix two instances of the same **Metal** node group; the first one with average metal settings and a polished surface, the second one set as a lot less reflective surface with bump scratches obtained by the texture nodes.

There's more...

Obviously, it's not just the **Dirty Vertex Colors** layer that can be modified and improved by vertex painting the mesh, but we could also use, instead, a gray-scale image map, painted for example in The Gimp or in Blender itself and then UV mapped on the mesh to obtain more precisely localized or peculiar worn effects.

Creating a rusty metal material with procedurals

In this recipe we will create a rusty shader to be mixed by a stencil factor with a metallic shader:

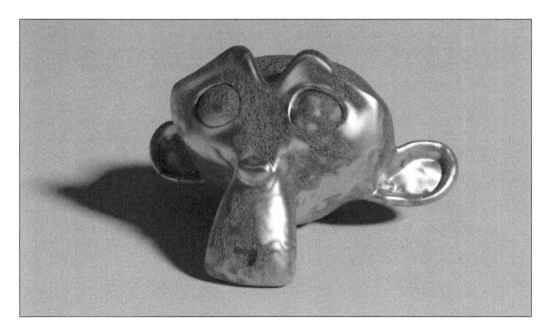

Getting ready

Start Blender and load the file `1301OS_04_start.blend`.

How to do it...

Now we are going to create the shader:

1. From **13010S_04_metal.blend** | **NodeTree**, append the node group **Metal**.

2. Click on **New** in the **Material** window under the **Properties** panel or in the **Node Editor** header. Rename the material `Rusty_Metal`.

3. Switch the **Diffuse** shader with a **Mix Shader** node and in the first **Shader** slot select a **Diffuse BSDF** shader. In the second **Shader** slot load, under **Group**, the appended **Metal** node group.

4. Add a frame (press *Shift + A* and go to **Layout | Frame**), select the **Diffuse** shader, the **Metal** group and the **Mix Shader** node frame and press *Ctrl + P* to parent them. Rename the frame `SHADERS`.

5. Add a **Texture Coordinate** node (press Shift + A and go to **Input | Texture Coordinate**) and connect the **Object** output to the **Tangent** input of the **Metal** group.

6. In the **Metal** group set **IOR** to 1.370, **Color** to R `0.229`, G `0.307`, and B `0.299`, **Roughness** to `0.200`, **Aniso_Amount** to `0.200`, and **Anisotropy** to `0.600`.

7. Add a **Mapping** node (press *Shift + A* and go to **Vector | Mapping**), then connect the **Object** output of the **Texture Coordinate** node to the **Vector** input of the **Mapping** node.

8. Now add a **Musgrave Texture** node (press *Shift + A* and go to **Texture | Musgrave Texture**), a **Noise Texture** node (press *Shift + A* and go to **Texture | Noise Texture**), and a **ColorRamp** node (press *Shift + A* and go to **Convertor | ColorRamp**). Set the **Musgrave** node's **Scale** to `5.400` and **Detail** to `1.300`; set the **Noise** node's **Scale** to `1.400`.

9. Connect the **Vector** output of the **Mapping** node to the **Vector** input sockets of the two texture nodes, then connect the **Fac** output of the **Musgrave Texture** node to the **Detail** and **Distortion** input sockets of the **Noise Texture** node.

10. Connect the **Fac** output of the **Noise Texture** to the **Fac** input of the **ColorRamp**. Set the **ColorRamp** node's interpolation to **Ease** and move the black color marker one-third to the right and the white color marker one-third to left.

11. Add a frame (press *Shift + A* and go to **Layout | Frame**), select the **Musgrave, Noise**, and **ColorRamp** nodes and then the frame and press *Ctrl + P* to parent them. Rename the frame `STENCIL`.

12. Connect the **STENCIL | ColorRamp** node's **Color** output to the **Fac** input socket of the **SHADERS | Mix Shader** node.

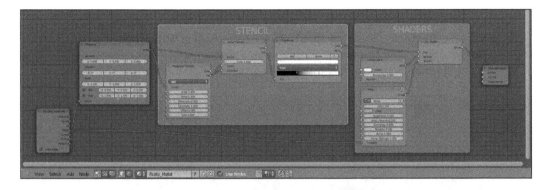

13. Add a **Voronoi Texture** node (press *Shift + A* and go to **Texture | Voronoi Texture**) and a **Wave Texture** node (press *Shift + A* and go to **Texture | Wave Texture**). Press *Shift + D* to duplicate the **Voronoi Texture** node and move it right under the first one. In the first **Voronoi** node set **Coloring** to **Cells** and **Scale** to 20.000; in the second one set **Scale** to 19.000. Set the **Wave Texture** node's **Scale** to 1.000.

14. Connect the **Vector** output of the **Mapping** node to the **Vector** inputs of the three texture nodes.

15. Add a **Mix** node (press *Shift + A* and go to **Color | Mix**), set the **Blend Type** to **Difference** and the **Fac** value to 1.000, then connect the first **Voronoi** node's **Color** output to the **Color1** input socket and the second **Voronoi** node's **Color** output to the **Color2** input socket of the **Difference** node.

16. Press *Shift + D* to duplicate the **Difference** node and connect the **Color** output of the first one to the **Color1** input socket of this duplicated one, then connect the **Color** output of the **Musgrave Texture** node to the **Color2** input socket.

17. Add a **ColorRamp** node (press *Shift + A* and go to **Convertor | ColorRamp**) and connect the output of the second **Difference** node to its **Fac** input socket. Set the **ColorRamp** interpolation to **Ease** and move the black color marker to the middle of the slider.

18. Press *Shift + D* to duplicate the **ColorRamp** node, set the interpolation to **B-Spline** and move back the black color marker to one-third along the total length of the slider. Connect the second **Difference** node's **Color** output to the **Fac** input of this **ColorRamp** too.

19. Press *Shift + D* to duplicate a **Difference** node and move it after the **ColorRamp** nodes; connect the two **ColorRamp** node's **Color** outputs to the **Color1** and **Color2** inputs of the last **Difference** node.

20. Add a frame (press *Shift + A* and go to **Layout | Frame**), select these last nodes and then the frame itself and press *Ctrl + P* to parent them. Rename the frame `RUST_BUMP`.

21. Inside the **SHADERS** frame, add a **Bump** node (press *Shift + A* and go to **Vector | Bump**). Connect the **RUST_BUMP** frame's final **Difference** node's **Color** output to the **Bump** node's **Height** input socket, and its **Normal** output to the **Normal** input socket of the **Diffuse** shader inside the **SHADERS** frame.

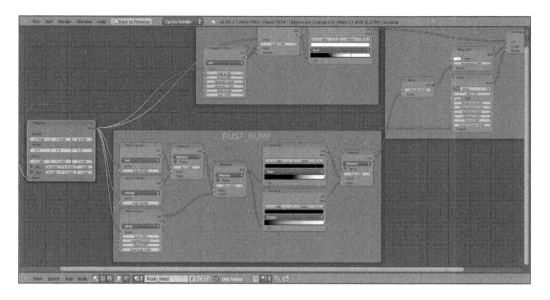

22. Add an **RGB Curves** node (press *Shift + A* and go to **Color | RGB Curves**), a **ColorRamp** node (press *Shift + A* and go to **Convertor | ColorRamp**), a **Noise Texture** node (press *Shift + A* and go to **Texture | Noise Texture**), and a **Mix** node (press *Shift + A* and go to **Color | Mix**).

23. Connect the **Color** output of the **RGB Curves** node to the **Fac** input of the **ColorRamp** node; click on the diagonal line inside the **RGB Curves** to add a control point and in the **X** and **Y** slots on the bottom of the node set **X** to `0.50000` and **Y** to `0.26000`. Click again to add a new control point and set: **X** to `0.51000` and **Y** to `0.75000`.

24. Set the **ColorRamp** node interpolation to **Constant** and set the markers as shown in the following screenshot (basically a stepped graduation from the color R 0.991, G 0.591, and B 0.084 to the color R 0.105, G 0.012, and B 0.009):

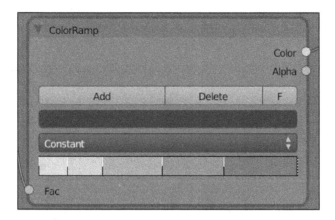

25. Press *Shift + D* to duplicate the **ColorRamp** node and move it above the original. Set the interpolation to **Linear** then connect the **Color** outputs of both the **ColorRamp** nodes to the **Color1** and **Color2** input sockets of the **Mix** node. Set the **Mix** node **Blend Type** to **Dodge** and the **Fac** value to 1.000.

26. Press *Shift + D* to duplicate the **Dodge** node, set the **Blend Type** to **Multiply** and the **Fac** value to 0.500; connect the **Dodge** output to the **Color1** input of the **Multiply** node and the **Color** output of the **Noise Texture** node to the **Color2** input.

27. Set the **Noise Texture** node **Scale** to 16.000, **Detail** to 2.500, and **Distortion** to 0.000; connect the **Object** output of the **Mapping** node to the **Vector** input of the **Noise Texture** node.

28. Add a **Hue Saturation Value** node (Press *Shift + A* and go to **Color | Hue Saturation Value**) and move it to the right of the **Multiply** node; connect the **Multiply** output to the **Color** input socket of the **Hue Saturation Value** node, then set the **Hue** value to 0.465 and the **Saturation** value to 1.050.

29. Press *Shift + D* to duplicate the **Multiply** node and move it close to the **Noise Texture** node; set the **Blend Type** to **Overlay** and the **Fac** value to 0.250. Connect the **Fac** output of the **Noise Texture** to the **Color1** input socket and change the value of **Color2** to pure white. Connect the **Overlay** node output to the **Value** input socket of the **Hue Saturation Value** node.

30. Add a frame (Press *Shift + A* and go to **Layout | Frame**), select these last nodes and then the frame and press *Ctrl + P* to parent them. Rename the frame RUST_COLOR.

31. Connect the output of the **Multiply** node inside the **RUST_COLOR** frame to the **Color** input socket of the **Diffuse** shader inside the **SHADERS** frame, then connect the **Fac** output of the **Noise Texture** node inside the **STENCIL** frame to the **Color** input of the **RGB Curves** node inside the **RUST_COLOR** frame.

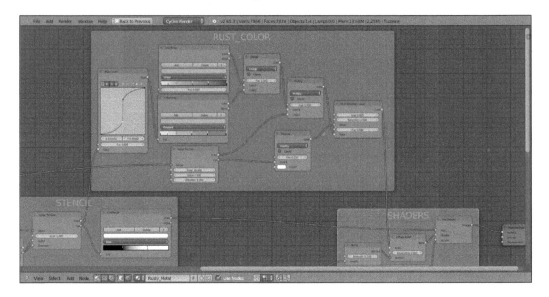

How it works...

From step 1 to step 6 we built the basic shaders arrangement; from step 7 to step 11 we made the **STENCIL** to separate the rust material from the polished metal.

From step 12 to step 20 we built the bump effect for the rust and from step 21 to step 30 the rust color.

Creating a wood material with procedurals

In this recipe we will create a generic wood material; in case you need a particular kind of wood, this shader can be easily adapted:

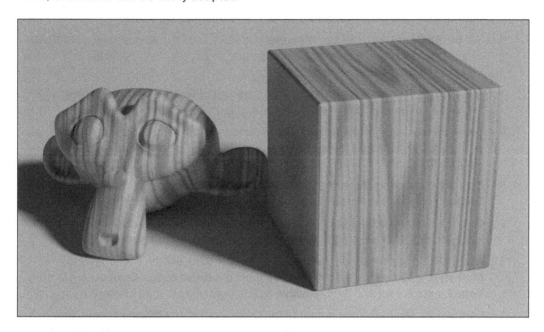

Getting ready

Start Blender and load the file 1301OS_04_start.blend.

How to do it...

Now we are going to create the material:

1. Click on **New** in the **Material** window under the **Properties** panel or in the **Node Editor** header. Rename the material Wood.

2. Switch the **Diffuse** shader with a **Mix Shader** node. In the first **Shader** slot select a **Diffuse BSDF** shader, in the second **Shader** slot select **Glossy BSDF**. Set the **Glossy** node's **Roughness** to 0.300.

3. Add a **Fresnel** node (Press *Shift + A* and go to **Input | Fresnel**) and a **Mix** node (Press *Shift + A* and go to **Color | Mix**). Set the **IOR** value of the **Fresnel** node to 2.000 and connect its output to the **Color1** input socket of the **Mix** node; set the **Mix** node's **Fac** value to 0.900 and the **Blend Type** to **Multiply**. Connect the **Multiply** node output to the **Fac** input socket of the **Mix Shader** node.

4. Add a frame (Press *Shift + A* and go to **Layout | Frame**), select all the nodes and then the frame and press *Ctrl + P* to parent them. Rename the frame as SHADERS.

5. Add one **Texture Coordinate** node (Press *Shift + A* and go to **Input | Texture Coordinate**) and three **Mapping** nodes (Press *Shift + A* and go to **Vector | Mapping**, just add the first and duplicate the others); connect the **Object** output of the **Texture Coordinate** node to the **Vector** inputs of the three **Mapping** nodes.

6. Set the **Scale** value of the first **Mapping** node to 2.000 for all three axes. Set **Scale** only for the x axis of the second **Mapping** node to 20.000. Set the **Scale** only for the x axis of the third **Mapping** node to 15.000.

7. Add a **Noise Texture** node (Press *Shift + A* and go to **Texture | Noise Texture**) and two **Wave Texture** nodes (Press *Shift + A* and go to **Texture | Wave Texture**).

8. Set the **Scale** value of the **Noise Texture** node to 6.000 and the **Detail** value to 0.000; connect the first **Mapping** node output to the **Noise Texture** node's **Vector** input socket.

9. Connect the second **Mapping** node output to the **Vector** input of the first **Wave Texture** node; set the **Wave** node's **Scale** to 0.200 and the **Distortion** to 20.000.

10. Connect the third **Mapping** node output to the second **Wave Texture** node's **Vector** input socket; set **Wave** type to **Rings**, **Scale** to 0.070, and **Distortion** to 44.000.

11. Add a **Mix** node (Press *Shift + A* and go to **Color | Mix**), set the **Blend Type** to **Multiply**, the **Fac** value to 1.000 and connect the **Noise** node's **Color** output to the **Color1** input socket and the first **Wave** node's **Color** output to the **Color2** input socket.

12. Connect the **Multiply** node output to the **Color** input of the **Diffuse** shader. Press *Shift + D* to duplicate it, change the **Blend Type** to **Add** and paste it between the **Multiply** node and the **Diffuse** shader. Connect the second **Wave Texture** node's **Color** output to the **Color2** input socket of the **Add** node.

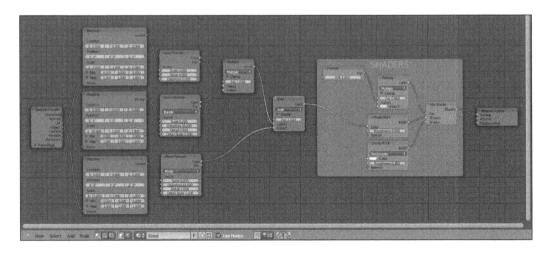

13. Add a **ColorRamp** (Press *Shift + A* and go to **Convertor | ColorRamp**) and paste it right after the **Noise Texture** node; set the interpolation to **B-Spline** and move the black color marker one-third to the right.

14. Press *Shift + D* to duplicate the **ColorRamp** and paste it right after the first **Wave Texture** node; move the black color marker to the middle of the slider and the white color marker just a little bit to the left.

15. Press *Shift + D* to duplicate the **ColorRamp** again and paste it right after the second **Wave Texture** node; move the white color marker to the full left of the slider.

16. Now add a **Mix** node (Press *Shift + A* and go to **Color | Mix**) and connect the **Add** node's **Color** output to to its **Fac** input socket. Set the **Color1** to R 1.000, G 0.500, and B 0.150 and the **Color2** to R 0.694, G 0.205, and B 0.027.

17. Press *Shift + D* on the **Mix** node, pasting the duplicate right next to the original; connect the original's output to the **Color2** input socket too and change the **Blend Type** to **Multiply**.

18. Add a frame (Press *Shift + A* and go to **Layout | Frame**), select the three textures, the three **ColorRamp** nodes and the four **Mix** nodes and then the frame; press *Ctrl + P* to parent them. Rename the frame COLOR.

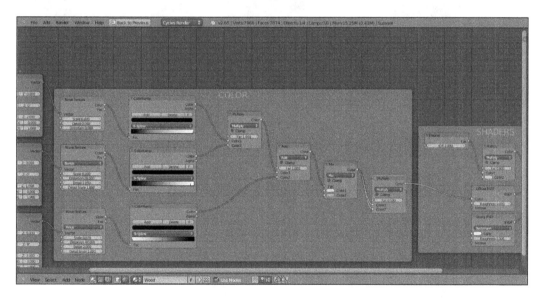

19. Add a new **Noise Texture** node (Press *Shift + A* and go to **Texture | Noise Texture**), a **Math** node (Press *Shift + A* and go to **Convertor | Math**), and a **Bump** node (Press *Shift + A* and go to **Vector | Bump**).

20. Connect the third **Mapping** node output to the **Vector** input socket of the **Noise Texture** node, then connect the **Color** output of the **Noise texture** node to the second **Value** input of the **Math** node. Set its operation to **Add** and connect its output to the **Height** input socket of the **Bump** node.

21. Set the **Bump** node's **Strength** to 0.015 and connect the **Normal** output to the **Normal** inputs of both the **Diffuse** and the **Glossy** shaders inside the **SHADERS** frame. Set the **Noise Texture** node's **Scale** to 43.000 and **Detail** to 16.000.

22. Go to the **Add** node inside the **COLOR** frame, click on the output node and drag it to be connected to the first **Value** input socket of the **Math** node.

23. Add a frame (Press *Shift + A* and go to **Layout | Frame**), select the three nodes and then the frame; press *Ctrl + P* to parent them. Rename the frame BUMP.

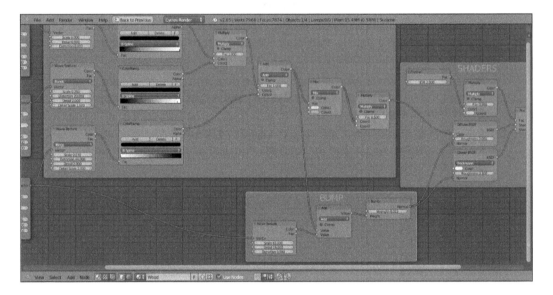

How it works...

From step 1 to step 4 we built the basic shaders, the usual **Diffuse** and **Glossy** nodes mixed by a Fresnel value multiplied by a medium gray color.

From step 5 to step 18 we built the wood veins color, adding three procedurals to be used as splitting factor for the two wood colors set in the penultimate **Mix** node; by the last **Multiply** node we made the color more saturated.

From step 19 to step 23 we built the **Bump** node, made by a noise grain summed to the veins values by the **Add** math node; we set a pretty low value for the **Bump**, **Strength**, but higher values, together with higher **Roughness** values to obtain a less polished surface, are fine for different kinds of woods.

5
Creating Complex Natural Materials in Cycles

In this chapter, we will cover:

- ► Creating an ocean material using procedural textures
- ► Creating underwater environment materials
- ► Creating a snowy mountain landscape with procedurals
- ► Creating a realistic planet Earth as seen from space

Introduction

In *Chapter 3*, *Creating Natural Materials in Cycles*, we have seen some of the simpler natural materials that are possible to build in Cycles, while keeping them out of any landscape context to make them more easily understandable.

Now, it's time to deal with more elaborate natural materials. In this chapter, we will particularly examine the way to mix different basic shaders to mimic the look of complex natural objects and their environments (very often the two things fit together neatly).

Creating an ocean material using procedural textures

In this recipe, we will build an ocean surface material, using the **Ocean** modifier and procedural textures to create the foam and establish a set of nodes to locate it on the higher parts of the waves, as shown here:

Getting ready

Before we start with the shader's creation, let's prepare the ocean scene:

1. Start Blender and switch to the Cycles rendering engine. Select the cube and delete it (press *X*).

2. Add a plane (have your mouse in the 3D window and press *Shift + A* and go to **Mesh | Plane**). In the **Object** mode, scale it to 0.300. Don't apply size.

3. Go to the **Object Modifiers** window and assign an **Ocean** modifier. Set these values: **Geometry** to **Generate**, **Repeat X** and **Repeat Y** to 4, **Spatial Size** to 20, and **Resolution** to 12.

4. Press *N* and in the **Transform** panel set these values for the plane's **Location**: **X -6.90000, Y -7.00000, Z 0.00000**.

5. Be sure to be at frame **1** and place the mouse in the modifier's **Time** slot, press *I* to add a key for the animation. Go at frame **25**, change the **Time** value from 1.00 to 2.00 and press *I* again to set a second key.

6. In the **Screen lay-out** button at the top, switch from **Default** to **Animation**. In the **Graph Editor** window, press *T* and go to **Linear** and press *Shift + E* to go to **Linear Extrapolation** to make the ocean animation constant and continuous.

7. Rename the plane as `Ocean_surface`.

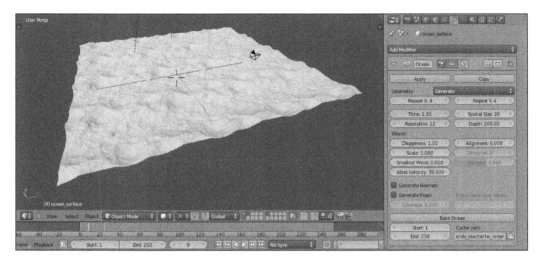

8. Place the Camera to have a nice angle on the ocean and then go in **Camera** view (Press *0* from numpad).

9. Add a cube in the middle of the scene and, if you want, also a UV Sphere in the foreground. Place them around and floating in the air, their only purpose is to be reflected by the ocean's surface.

10. Go to the **World** window, click on **Use Nodes** and then click on the little square with a dot to the right side of the color slot. From the resulting menu, select **Sky Texture**.

11. Select the lamp, click on **Use Nodes** and set a yellowish color for the light (**R 1.000**, **G 0.989, B 0.700**). Turn the lamp to **Sun**, set the **Size** value to `0.010` and the **Strength** value to `2.500`.

12. Go in the **Render** window and under the **Sampling** tab, set the **Clamp** value to `1.00` and the samples for both **Render** and **Preview** to `100`.

All the preceding steps were for the general settings and the ocean surface mesh. Now, because the shader we are going to build is largely transparent, we also need to simulate the water body. This is how it's done:

1. Add a new plane, in edit mode scale it 10 times bigger (20 units per side). Move it to be centered on the ocean **Plane** location and then 1 unit down on the Z axis.

2. In edit mode again, press *W* to subdivide it by the **Specials** menu. Then press *T* to bring out the **Mesh Tools** panel on the left and, under **Number of Cuts**, select **3**.

3. Go in vertex paint mode and paint a very simple gray-scale gradient, going from a medium dark gray at the vertexes close to the **Camera** location to a plain white color at the opposite side. In the **Object Data** window, under the **Vertex Colors** tab, rename the vertex color layer as `Col_emit`.

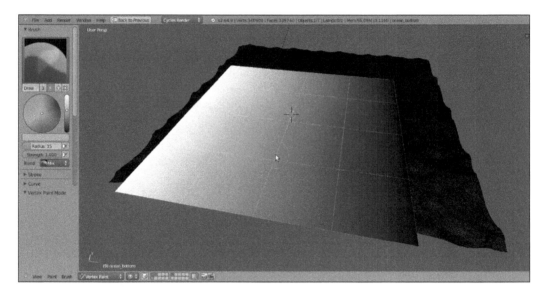

4. Rename the plane as `Ocean_bottom`.

How to do it...

We will be performing this in four parts:

First, creating the water surface and the bottom shaders

And now, let's start with the first material:

1. Split the 3D view to two horizontal rows and change the upper one to a **Node Editor** window.

2. First, give to the cube and to the UV Sphere very simple colored materials; just **Diffuse** shaders are enough.

3. Select **Ocean_bottom** and click on **New** in the **Material** window under the **Properties** panel, or in the **Node Editor** window's header. Rename the new material `Ocean_bottom` as well.

4. Switch the **Diffuse BSDF** shader with a **Mix Shader** node. In the first and second slots, load two **Emission** shaders.

5. Add an **Attribute** node (press *Shift + A* and go to **Input | Attribute**) and connect the **Color** output to the **Fac** input of the **Mix Shader** node. In the **Name** slot of the **Attribute** node, write `Col_emit`, the name of the vertex color layer.

6. Change the color of the first **Emission** node to **R 0.178**, **G 0.150**, **B 0.085** and set the **Strength** value to `1.000`.

7. Change the color of the second **Emission** node to **R 0.213**, **G 0.284**, **B 0.380**, and set the **Strength** value to `2.000`.

   The **Ocean_bottom** material is now ready:

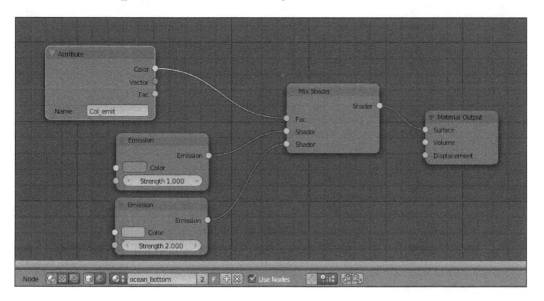

8. Now select the **Ocean_surface** material and again click on **New** in the **Material** window under the **Properties** panel, or in the **Node Editor** window's header. Rename this material as `Ocean_surface`.

9. Replace the **Diffuse** shader with a **Mix Shader** node and in the first **Shader** slot assign a **Transparent BSDF** shader, in the second a **Glass BSDF** shader.

10. Change the **Transparent** color to **R 0.54**, **G 0.124**, **B 0.042** (you can also do this by connecting an **RGB** node to the color input socket). Set the **Glass** shader's **Roughness** value to `0.900` and the **IOR** value to `1.333`.

11. Add a **Layer Weight** node (press *Shift + A* and go to **Input | Layer Weight**), connect the **Facing** output to the **Fac** input of the **Mix Shader** node, and set the blend value to `0.050`.

12. Select the **Mix Shader** node and press *Shift + D* duplicate it. Add a **Glossy** shader and connect it to the second **Shader** input of this duplicated node. Connect the output of the first **Mix Shader** node to the other **Shader** input socket (the first one) and then connect the output to the **Surface** input of the **Material Output** node.

13. Add a **Fresnel** node (press *Shift + A* and go to **Input | Fresnel**), connect it to the **Fac** input of the second **Mix Shader** node and set the **IOR** value to **1.333**, as shown here:

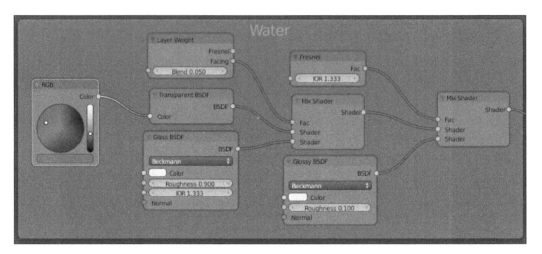

14. Now select all the nodes except for **Material Output** and press *Crtl + G* to make a group. Confirm by clicking on **New** in the pop-up. Rename the group as `Ocean_water` and Press *Tab* to close it.

Second - creating the foam shader

Now let's make the foam shader:

1. Add a **Noise** (press *Shift + A* and go to **Texture | Noise Texture**) and a **Voronoi** (press *Shift + A* and go to **Texture | Voronoi Texture**) nodes, select them and press *Shift + D* to duplicate them.

2. Add four **ColorRamp** nodes (press *Shift + A* and go to **Convertor | ColorRamp** and then press *Shift + D*), move the four texture nodes in a vertical column and put the **ColorRamp** nodes on their side. Now, connect the **Color** output of each texture node to the **Fac** input of the respective **ColorRamp** node.

3. Set the interpolation of the first **ColorRamp** node to **B-Spline**, the second and third to **Ease**, and the fourth to **B-Spline** again.

4. Move the color markers accordingly to the following screenshot:

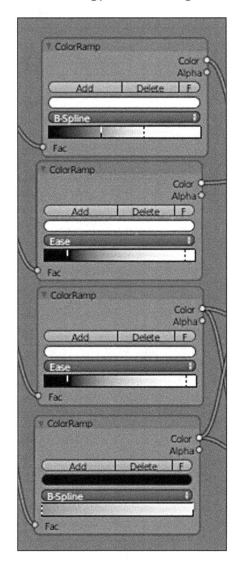

5. In the first **Noise Texture** node, set the **Scale** value to `500.000`. In the second, to `100.000`. In the first **Voronoi Texture** node, set the **Scale** value to `100.000` and in the second to `90.000`.

6. Add a **Texture Coordinate** node (press *Shift + A* and go to **Input | Texture Coordinate**) and a **Mapping** node (press *Shift + A* and go to **Vector | Mapping**). Connect the **UV** output of the **Texture Coordinate** node to the **Vector** input of the **Mapping** node and then its **Vector** output to the **Vector** input sockets of the four texture nodes.

7. Add a **Mix** node (press *Shift + A* and go to **Color | Mix**), set the **Blend Type** to **Subtract** and the **Fac** value to 1.000. Connect the **Color** outputs of the first two texture nodes to the **Color1** and **Color2** input sockets of the **Mix** node.

8. Select the **Mix** node, press *Shift + D* to duplicate it and set the **Blend Type** to **Multiply**. Connect the **Color** outputs of the third and fourth texture nodes to the **Color1** and **Color2** input sockets of this **Mix** node.

9. Again duplicate the **Mix** node, set the **Blend Type** to **Difference**, and again connect the **Color** outputs of the third and fourth texture nodes to the **Color1** and **Color2** input sockets of this third **Mix** node.

10. Duplicate the **Mix** node one more time, set the **Blend Type** to **Lighten**, and lower the **Fac** value to 0.500. Connect the **Color** output of the **Multiply** node to the **Color1** input of the **Lighten** node, and the **Color** output of the **Difference** node to the **Color2** input socket.

11. Add an **Invert** node (press *Shift + A* and go to **Color | Invert**) and move it to the link connecting the **Difference** and the **Lighten** nodes, to be automatically pasted in between.

12. Add a new **ColorRamp** node, connect the **Lighten** node output to its **Fac** input, and then move the white marker at the middle of the slider and the black one at a quarter to the right.

13. Add a new **Mix** node, set the **Blend Type** to **Subtract** and the **Fac** value to 1.00, and then connect the **ColorRamp** color output to the **Color1** input and the output of the first **Subtract** node to the **Color2** input socket.

14. Add an **RGB to BW** node (press *Shift + A* and go to **Convertor | RGB to BW**), a **Bump** node (press *Shift + A* and go to **Vector | Bump**) and a **Diffuse BSDF** shader (press *Shift + A* and go to **Shader | Diffuse BSDF**).

15. Connect the last **Subtract** node output to the **RGB to BW** node, the output of this one to the **Height** input of the **Bump** node and the **Normal** output to the **Normal** input of the **Diffuse** shader. Set the **Bump** node's **Strength** value to **0.010**, as shown in the following screenshot:

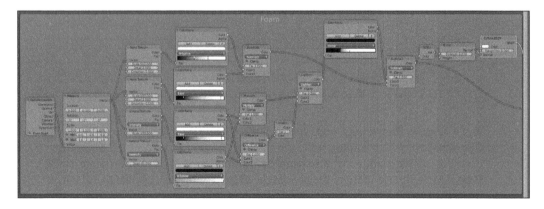

16. Select all these nodes and press *Crtl* + *G*, confirm on **New**, and rename the group as Foam.

17. Drag the **Color** output of the last **Subtract** node on the right-hand side of the group box to expose it. Do the same with the **BSDF** output of the **Diffuse** shader and press *Tab* to close the group.

Third - creating the stencil material for the foam location

What we now need is a way to limit the presence of the foam only to the upper parts of the waves:

1. Add a **Gradient** texture node (press *Shift* + *A* and go to **Texture | Gradient Texture**) and a **Voronoi** texture node (press *Shift* + *A* | **Texture | Voronoi Texture**), select them and press *Shift* + *D* to duplicate them.

2. Set both the **Gradient** node's types to **Easing**, the **Scale** value of the first **Voronoi** node to 250.000, and of the second to 50.000.

3. Add three **Mapping** nodes (press *Shift* + *A* and go to **Vector | Mapping**, then press *Shift* + *D*).

4. Add a **Texture Coordinate** node (press *Shift* + *A* and go to **Input | Texture Coordinate**) and a **Geometry** node (press *Shift* + *A* and go to **Input | Geometry**).

5. Connect the **Normal** output of the **Geometry** node to the **Vector** input of the first **Mapping** node. Connect the **Position** output of the **Geometry** node to the **Vector** input of the second **Mapping** node. Then connect the **UV** output of the **Texture Coordinate** node to the **Vector** input of the third **Mapping** node.

6. In the second **Mapping** node, change the **X** location's value to 0.500 and the **Y** rotation's value to 90°.

7. Connect the output of the first **Mapping** node to the input of the first **Gradient** texture, the output of the second **Mapping** to the input of the second **Gradient** texture, and the output of the third **Mapping** to both the **Vector** inputs of the last two **Voronoi** texture nodes.

8. Add a **ColorRamp** node (press *Shift* + *A* and go to **Convertor | ColorRamp**) and connect the **Color** output of the last **Voronoi** texture to the **Fac** input; set the interpolation to **B-Spline**. On the **ColorRamp** node, click on the little **Add** button. This adds a new medium gray marker in the middle of the slider. Change its color to total black and move it to the left, very close to the first black one.

9. Add a **Math** node (press *Shift* +*A* and go to **Convertor | Math**) and set the operation to **Multiply** and connect the **Color** output of the second **Gradient** texture node to the first **Value** input socket of the **Math** node.

10. Add a **Mix** node (press *Shift + A* and go to **Color | Mix**), set the **Blend Type** to **Difference** and the **Fac** value to 1.00. Connect the **Color** output of the first **Gradient** texture to the **Color1** and the **Value** output of the **Math** node to the **Color2** input socket.

11. Press *Shift + D* to duplicate the **Mix** node, set the **Blend Type** to **Subtract**, and connect the **ColorRamp** color output to both the **Color2** and to the **Fac** input sockets. Connect the **Color** output of the first **Voronoi** texture to the **Color1** input socket.

12. Add a new **ColorRamp** node, connect the output of the **Difference** node to the **Fac** input, and then move the white marker two-thirds to the left.

13. Duplicate the **Mix** node, set the **Blend Type** to **Burn**, and connect the color output of the last **ColorRamp** node to the **Color1** input. Connect the output of the **Subtract** node to the **Color2** input socket, as shown here:

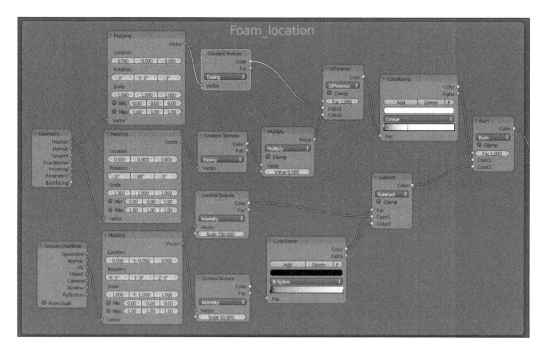

14. Now select all these nodes, press *Crtl + G*, confirm **New**, and rename the group as Foam_location. Drag the **Burn** node on the right to expose the color output and press *Tab* to close the group.

Fourth - putting everything together

What is left at this point is just to connect these three groups to build the final shader:

1. Add a **Mix Shader** node (press *Shift + A* and go to **Shader | Mix Shader**). Connect its output to the **Surface** input of the **Material Output** node.

2. Connect the **Shader** output of the **Ocean_water** group to the first **Shader** input of the **Mix Shader** node. Then connect the **BSDF** output of the **Foam** group to the second **Shader** input.

3. Add two **Mix** nodes and set the **Blend Type** of the first one to **Multiply** and the **Fac** value to 0.550. Set the second node **Blend Type** to **Burn** and the **Fac** value to 0.200.

4. Connect the **Color** output of the **Foam_location** group to the **Color1** input of the **Multiply** node and the **Color** output of the **Foam** group to the two **Color2** inputs of both the **Multiply** and **Burn** nodes.

5. Connect the **Multiply** node output to the **Color1** input of the **Burn** node. Connect the output of the **Burn** node to the **Fac** input of the **Mix Shader** node, as shown here:

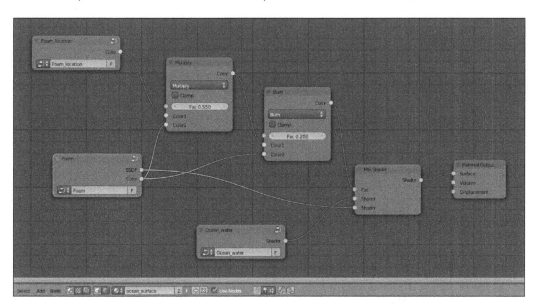

How it works...

This material, which looks quite complex, is actually easy to understand by splitting the entire process in three stages corresponding to the three group nodes:

> ▸ **The first stage**: Here, we created the basic ocean water shader by mixing a **Glass** shader with a **Transparent** shader on the ground of the **Facing** value of the **Layer Weight** node, and then with a **Glossy** shader driven by the water index of refraction (the **IOR** value of the **Fresnel** node, which for water at 20° C is of 1.333). In short, this means that the ocean surface is nicely reflecting the environment, but for the faces looking towards the camera (the **Facing** factor), it is transparent and lets the "underwater" show through. Very important is the bottom ocean plane, used to mimic the water volume, the underwater perspective, and also emitting light to enhance the effect of the sun bouncing from the ocean surface to any floating object:

> ▸ **The second stage**: This is where we worked on the material for the foam, a simple white **Diffuse** shader. In fact, the peculiarity of the foam shader is mostly in the frothy bumpiness and in the lacy-shaped outline cut out by the procedural textures:

▸ **The third stage**: This group of nodes establishes the location of the foam, which in the real world is mainly created in the higher parts of the waves, behaving as a gray-scale "stencil" map. This is a bit more complex, but basically a gradient texture is mapped on the (vertexes) **Position** and multiplied for the **Normal** coordinates of the ocean mesh that, being created by the **Ocean** modifier, is constantly changing. So, only as the waves rise up they show foam at the top. The effect has been lessened and made a bit random, to show some foam also scattered around the rest of the surface. This works not only for stills but also in animation. In the following image, you can see the resulting black and white "mask" used as stencil for the foam location:

See also

The Blender **Ocean** modifier is able to create its own foam effect, generated as vertex colors and baked to a series of images (frames) saved in a directory. These images are then automatically mapped on the surface and can be used also as stencil masks instead of the **Foam_location** group node. To know more about the **Ocean** modifier, you can have a look at the Wiki documentation at `http://wiki.blender.org/index.php/Doc:2.6/Manual/Modifiers/Simulate/Ocean`.

Creating underwater environment materials

In this recipe, we will create an underwater environment, looking especially at a fake caustic effect projected by the water's wavy surface and at the deep "atmospheric" perspective, obtained by a per material dedicated node group, as shown here:

Getting ready

Let's start by preparing the scene:

1. Start Blender and switch to the Cycles rendering engine. Select the cube and go in edit mode, scale it 21 times bigger (press *A* to select all the geometry and then press *S*, digit *21*, and hit *Enter*), then scale it on the Z axis to `0.300` (press *S*, followed by *Z*, digit *.3*, and hit *Enter*).

2. Go out of edit mode, switch to the **Objects Modifiers** window, and assign a **Subdivision Surface** modifier. Set the type of subdivision to **Simple** and the **Subdivision** value for both the **View** and the **Render** levels to 4.

3. Add a second **Subdivision Surface** modifier and set the type of subdivision to **Simple** and the **Subdivision** value for both the **View** and the **Render** levels to 2.

4. Now assign an **Ocean** modifier. Set **Geometry** to **Displace**, **Spatial Size** to 20, and **Resolution** to 12.

5. Go in the **Object Data** window and click on the **+** icon under **UV Maps** to add a set of **UV** coordinates. There is no need to unwrap the cube.

6. Press *N* and in the **Transform** panel set these values for the cube: **Location** to **X 3.22600**, **Y 2.79600**, **Z -0.20400**.

7. Be sure to be at frame **1** and place the mouse in the modifier's **Time** slot, press *I* to add a key for the animation. Go at frame **25**, change the **Time** value from 1.00 to 2.00 and press *I* again to set a second key.

8. In the **Screen lay-out** button at the top, switch from **Default** to **Animation**. In the **Graph Editor** window, press *T* and go to **Linear** and press *Shift + E* to go to **Linear Extrapolation** to make the ocean animation constant and continuous.

9. Rename the cube as Ocean_surface.

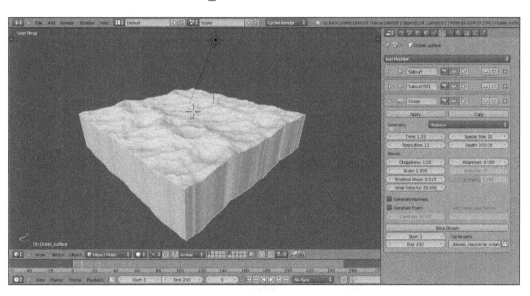

10. Move the camera below the ocean surface (**Location** set to **X 20.000**, **Y 0.15000**, **Z -2.50000**, and **Rotation** set to **X 92°**, **Y 0°**, and **Z 90°**) and then go in **Camera** view (press *0* from numpad).

11. Add a cube, a UV Sphere, and or whatever other object you want, floating under the ocean surface. Provide them very simple and colored **Diffuse** materials. Also add a big cylinder on the background, close to the end of the ocean's cube, half immersed in the water and half standing in the air and assign a simple **Diffuse** material to it too.

12. Go to the **World** window, click on **Use Nodes**, and then click on the little square with a dot on the right-hand side of the color slot. From the resulting menu, select **Sky Texture**.

13. Select the lamp, click on **Use Nodes**, and set a yellowish color for the light (**R 1.000, G 0.989, B 0.700**). Turn it to **Sun** and set the **Size** value to 0.010 and the **Strength** value to 2.500. Set **Rotation** values as: **X 22°, Y -7°**, and **Z 144°**; as you already know, the location doesn't matter for a **Sun** lamp.

14. Go to the **Render** window and under the **Sampling** tab set the **Clamp** value to 1.00 and the samples to 50 for **Preview** and 100 for **Render**. Under the **Light Paths** tab, check the **No Caustics** option.

15. Now add a plane, place it at **Z** location equal to -5.70000, and go in edit mode. Scale it 30 times bigger (press *A* to select all the geometry, followed by *S*, digit *30*, and hit *Enter*). Using the **Specials** menu (press *W*), subdivide the plane five or six times. Activate the **Proportional Editing** (PET) tool, randomly select vertexes, and move them up to model the dunes of the ocean bed. Next, come out of edit mode, smooth using the **Tools** panel, and assign a **Subdivision Surface** modifier at level 2. Rename it Ocean_bed.

16. Add a cube, in edit mode subdivide it a couple of times (press *W* and go to **Subdivide Smooth**). In the **Proportional Editing** mode and by selecting vertexes, quickly model a big round rock. Duplicate it three or four times, rotating and scaling the copies and place them scattered on the ocean bed.

 As alternative, just open the 1301OS_05_ underwater_start.blend file and use the already made scene (you, lazy ones!).

How to do it...

First, the easy steps, where we'll append already made materials to re-use them:

1. From the 1301OS_03_rock_procedural.blend file, append the Rock_ procedural_01 material. Select the rocks and assign the just appended material. Change the two **Diffuse** colors to **R 0.553, G 0.576, B 0.608** and **R 0.567, G 0.391, B 0.314** respectively.

2. From the 1301OS_03_ground.blend file, append the ground_01 material, select the ocean bed and assign this material.

Now, to the more complex steps:

1. From the `13010S_05_ocean.blend` file, append the `ocean_surface` material, select the ocean surface's cube and assign this material. Rename it as `ocean_surface_under`.

2. Go in edit mode, select only the upper faces of the ocean cube. Press *Crtl + I* to invert the selection. In the **Material** window under the **Properties** panel, click on the **+** icon on the right (**Add a new material slot**), rename the new material as `Null` (or whatever makes sense for you), and click on the **Assign** button. Now the ocean cube has two materials: the transparent water surface and the opaque sides/bottom (a simple white **Diffuse** material). After this, go out of edit mode.

3. In the **Material** window, click on the **ocean_surface_under** material to select it. In the **Node Editor** window, delete the **Foam** and the **Foam_location** node groups and also delete the two **Mix** nodes. Just to make things clearer, ungroup (press *ALT + G*) the remaining **Ocean_water** node group.

4. For the moment, place the **Ocean water** and the **Mix Shader** nodes ideally aside. Add a **Texture Coordinate** node (press *Shift + A* and go to **Input | Texture Coordinate**), a **Mapping** node (press *Shift + A* and go to **Vector | Mapping**), and an **Image Texture** node (press *Shift + A* and go to **Texture | Image Texture**). Connect the **UV** output of the **Texture Coordinate** node to the **Vector** input of the **Mapping** node and the **Vector** output of this one to the **Vector** input socket of the **Image Texture** node.

5. In the **Image Texture** node, load the `caustics_tileable_low.png` texture and set the color space to **Non-Color Data**.

6. Add a **Diffuse BSDF** shader and a **Transparent BSDF** shader. Add a new **Mix Shader** node. Connect the **Diffuse** output to the first **Shader** input of this **Mix Shader** node and the **Transparent** shader output to the second one. Connect the color output of the **Image Texture** node to the color input socket of the **Transparent BSDF** shader and the **Alpha** output to the **Fac** input of the same **Mix Shader** node.

7. Now connect the output of this second **Mix Shader** node to the first and still empty **Shader** input socket of the first **Mix Shader** node.

8. Add a **Light Path** node (press *Shift + A* and go to **Input | Light Path**) and connect the **Is Camera Ray** output to the **Fac** input of the first **Mix Shader** node, as shown here:

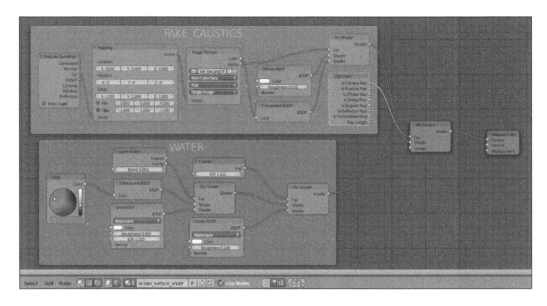

And here we are so far:

What is missing now is the underwater deep **atmospheric perspective** effect. There are several ways to obtain this, for example, by compositing a **Mist** pass rendered in Blender Internal, but we are going to do it with a node group assigned to each one of the different materials:

1. Add a **Camera Data** node (press *Shift + A* and go to **Input | Camera Data**), a **Math** node (press *Shift + A* and go to **Convertor | Math**), an **Emission** node (press *Shift + A* and **Shader | Emission**), and a **Mix Shader** node (press *Shift + A* and go to **Shader | Mix Shader**).

2. Connect the **View Z Depth** output of the **Camera Data** node to the first **Value** input of the **Math** node. Set the **Math** node operation to **Multiply** and the second **Value** to 0.030, check the **Clamp** option. Connect the **Multiply** node output to the **Fac** input socket of the **Mix Shader** node.

3. Connect the **Emission** output to the second **Shader** input of the **Mix Shader** node and set the color to **R 0.040, G 0.117, B 0.124**.

4. Select all these new nodes and press *Crtl + G* to make a group. Click and drag the first **Shader** input socket of the **Mix Shader** node to expose it on the left, do the same on the right for the **Shader** output socket. Rename the group as **Fog_underwater**, as shown here:

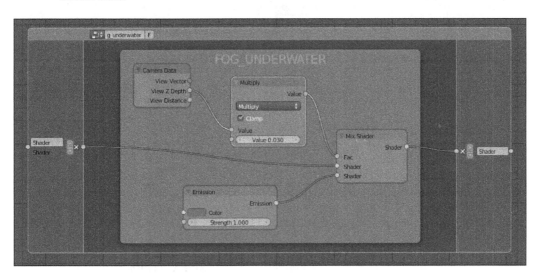

5. Close the group (press *Tab* to go out of edit mode) and paste it just before the **Material Output** node of every material (in our scene, it will show eight users if the **Fake User** option is also selected).

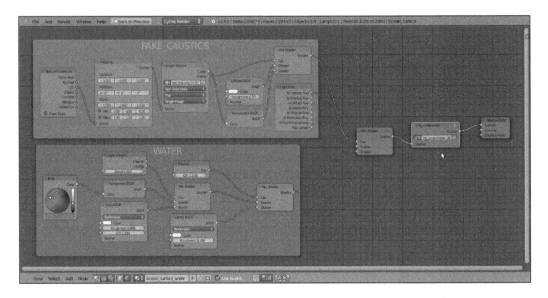

How it works...

First of all, why a cube for the ocean surface instead of the simpler plane?

The reason is very simple: in Cycles the **World** emits light and the only way to avoid this is to set its color to a pitch black (or by a combination of the **Light Path** node with the **World** materials, but this is another story). In our scene, the **World** is set to a bright blue sky color and, with a plane, the underwater objects and the ocean bed as well would have been lit too much from the sides and from the bottom, thereby giving an unnatural result. A cube, instead, envelops all the underwater elements, limiting the lighting to the **Sun** lamp passing through the surface and projecting the image textured caustics—which is a more natural behavior.

The image texture that we assigned to the water material is to obtain a textured transparency effect. The water surface now is actually opaque and transparent accordingly to the black and white values of the textures, so as to allow the **Sun** lamp's light to pass through and project the caustics.

Thanks to the **Is Camera Ray** output of the **Light Path** node, the caustics image texture is not directly renderable on the ocean surface but still has an effect on the other materials. Because **Is Camera Ray** is equal to **1**, the rays starting from the camera and directly hitting the ocean surface can render only the "clean" water material plugged in the second input socket of the **Mix Shader** node, while the transmitted caustics (plugged in the first socket equal to 0) get rendered.

Finally, the **Fog_underwater** node group is simply an emitter material colored as the background (in this case, a deep green) and mapped on every underwater material accordingly to the Z depth of the camera (but it works also out of camera view). The "density" of the fog is set by the **Multiply** node's second **Value**; for the ocean body, a value of 0.030 seems good enough. The camera's Z axis *must not be confused* with the global coordinate's Z axis, which in Blender is the vertical blue line visible in the 3D view. The camera's Z axis, instead, is the ideal line connecting the starting point of view to any visible element in the scene.

Note that we didn't expose the values of the nodes in the **Fog_underwater** group. This is so because we can tweak, in edit mode, the internal values of just one node to automatically update all the fog group instances assigned to the other materials, and we know that the values exposed on the group interface would overwrite the internal settings working only for that single node instance.

Creating a snowy mountain landscape with procedurals

In this recipe, we will make a snowy mountain landscape by re-using already made shaders, precisely the **Rock_procedural** and the **Snow** materials. We will improve these materials by grouping them and exposing the useful values; we will then create a new group node working as a stencil to arrange the snow in a more natural-looking manner on the rocks, as shown here:

Getting ready

As usual, let's start with the preparation of the scene, even if in this case we start with an almost readymade blend file:

1. Start Blender and open the 1301OS_05_rocksnow_start.blend file, where there is a scene with a placed camera, a simply modeled mountain, and a plane already set as emitter.

2. Select the **Mountain** object, go to the **Object Modifiers** window and assign a **Subdivision Surface** modifier. Set the levels for both for **View** and **Render** to 2.

3. Assign a second **Subdivision Surface** modifier with the same settings simply by clicking on the **Copy** button of the first one.

4. Assign a **Displace** modifier. Click on the **Show texture in texture tab** button on the extreme right of the **Texture** name slot to go to the **Textures** window and assign a **Voronoi** procedural texture. Set the **Size** value to 1.00. Go back to the **Displace** modifier and set the **Strength** value to -0.200.

5. Assign a second **Displace** modifier, in the **Texture** window assign a new **Voronoi** texture and set **Distance Metric** to **Manhattan** and the **Size** value to 050. In the **Displace** modifier, set the **Strength** value to -0.050.

6. Assign a third **Displace** modifier and select a **Clouds** texture. Set **Noise** to **Hard** and the **Displace** modifier's **Strength** value to 0.040.

7. Go to the **World** window and click on **Use Nodes**, and then click on the little square with a dot on the right side of the color slot. From the resulting menu, select **Sky Texture** and set the **Strength** value to 0.300.

8. Go to the **Render** window and under the **Sampling** tab set the **Clamp** value to 1.00 and the samples to 10 for **Preview** and 25 for **Render**. Under the **Light Paths** tab, check the **No Caustics** option.

How to do it...

Appending and grouping the rock and the snow shaders

First, let's append the already made materials to be improved from our library:

1. From the 1301OS_03_snow.blend file, append the Snow_01 material and, for the moment, assign it to the **Mountain** object.

2. In the **Node Editor** window, select all the nodes except for **Texture Coordinates** and **Material Output** and press *Crtl* + *G* to group them.

3. Move the **Snow_Diffuse** frame to the right of the **Snow_Bump** frame. Delete the **Value** output at the right of the group interface by clicking on the little **X** icon and also delete the last **Multiply** node inside the **Snow_Bump** frame.

4. Select the **Snow_Diffuse** frame and add a **Bump** node (press *Shift* + *A* and go to **Vector** | **Bump**). Connect the **Value** output of the **Add** node inside the **Snow_Bump** frame to the **Height** input of the **Bump** node, and connect the **Normal** output of the **Bump** node to the **Normal** input sockets of both the **Diffuse** and **Glossy** shaders inside the **Snow_Diffuse** frame.

5. Set the **Bump** node's **Strength** value to 0.010. Set the **Scale** value of the **Mapping** node to 1.000.

6. Close the group and rename it **Snow**. Just to be sure, check the **Fake User** option.

7. From the 1301OS_03_rock_procedural.blend file, append the Rock_procedural_01 material and assign it to the **Mountain** object.

8. In the **Node Editor** window, again select all the nodes except for **Texture Coordinates** and **Material Output** and press *Crtl* + *G* to group them. Rename the group as Rock_procedural.

9. First, we expose the colors: click on the **Color** input socket of the first **Diffuse** shader inside the **Color** frame and drag it to the extreme left to the border of the group interface. Rename the newly created input socket as `Diff_Color1`. Do the same with the second **Diffuse** shader and rename the new socket as `Diff_Color2`. Repeat this for the **Color** socket of the **Glossy** shader and rename the input as `Spec_Color`.

10. Now click on the **Fac** socket of the second **Mix Shader** node inside the **Color** frame and drag it to the left as well; rename it as `Spec_Amount`.

11. Expose, too, the **Roughness** socket of the **Glossy** shader.

Now we have to find a way to expose a single input value to drive the scale of all the texture nodes and also need one single input value to drive the three **Bump** nodes piped to the **Normal** sockets of the three shaders, keeping at the same time their individual starting values.

1. Add a **Math** node (press *Shift + A* and go to **Convertor | Math**) and move it closer to the first **Voronoi** texture inside the **2nd Bump** frame. Set the operation to **Multiply** and, in the first **Value** slot, copy the **Scale** value of the **Voronoi** texture. Connect the **Value** output to the texture's **Scale** input. Set the second **Value** to `1.000` and drag it to the left; rename the new interface input as `Scale`.

2. Press *Shift + D* to duplicate the **Math** node, move it close to the following **Musgrave** texture node, copy the **Scale** value, and drag the second **Value** input to connect it to the **Scale** new input on the interface. Connect the output of the duplicated **Math** node to the **Musgrave** scale input.

3. Repeat the same process for all the textures inside the **1st Bump** and **2nd Bump** frames, at the end you should have added and connected eight **Math** nodes.

4. By clicking on the little upper arrow on the side of the **Scale** interface input, move it before the **Spec_Amount** node.

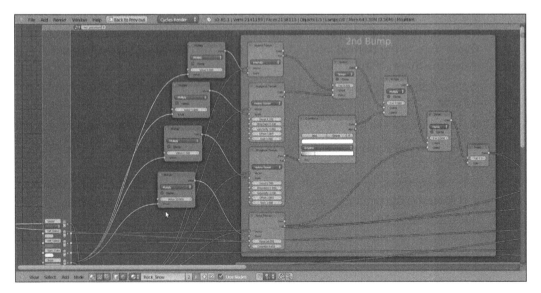

5. Repeat the same process for the other three **Bump** nodes connected to the shaders' **Normal** inputs by copying the **Strength** value. This time, drag the first **Multiply** socket to create a new interface input and connect the other two to it as well. Rename it as Bump and finally close the group.

Mixing the materials groups

Now we can start building the real shader, by mixing the **Rock_procedural** and the **Snow** materials:

1. Delete the Rock_procedural_01 material by clicking on the **X** icon on the **Node Editor** window's header.

2. Click on **New** in the **Material** window under the **Properties** panel or in the **Node Editor** header and rename this material as Rock_Snow.

3. In the **Material** window on the right, under the **Properties** panel, switch the **Diffuse BSDF** shader with a **Mix Shader** node. In the first **Shader** slot, load the **Rock_procedural** node group and in the second **Shader** slot load the **Snow** node group (they are available in a pop-up menu, under **Group**, by clicking on both the **Shader** buttons).

4. Add a **Texture Coordinate** node (press *Shift + A* and go to **Input | Texture Coordinate**) and connect the **Object** output to the **Vector** input of both the node groups, as shown here:

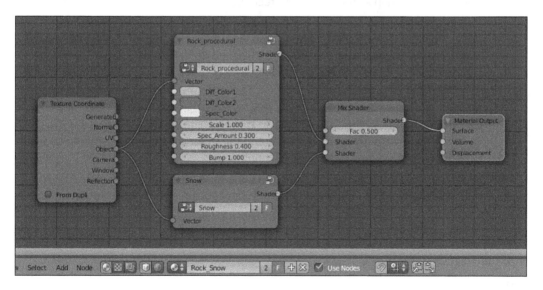

Creating the stencil material

At this point, both the materials are assigned to the **Mountain** object, but if you render the preview now, they will show everywhere on the mesh mixed at 50 percent. We must build a separator to decide where the surface must show only the rock and where only the snow:

1. Add a **Geometry** node (press *Shift + A* and go to **Input | Geometry**), a **Mapping** node (press *Shift + A* and go to **Vector | Mapping**), a **Gradient Texture** node (press *Shift + A* and go to **Texture | Gradient Texture**), a **Mix** node (press *Shift + A* and go to **Color | Mix**), and a **ColorRamp** node (press *Shift + A* and go to **Convertor | ColorRamp**).

2. Connect the **Normal** output of the **Geometry** node to the **Vector** input of the **Mapping** node, and then connect the **Mapping** node to the **Gradient** texture. Connect the **Color** output of the texture to the **Color1** input socket of the **Mix** node and the **Color** output of this latter to the **Fac** input of the **ColorRamp** node.

3. Set the **ColorRamp** interpolation to **B-Spline** and move the black color marker to the middle of the slider. Move the white color marker to the left two-third of the remaining half of the slider. Click on the **Add** button to create a new marker in between them and change its color to pure black.

4. Set the **Mix** node **Blend Type** to **Add**. Go to the **Mapping** node and set **Y Rotation** to **90°**.

5. Now select all these nodes except for **Geometry** and press *Shift + D* to duplicate them; move them in a row under the preceding nodes.

6. Connect the **Position** output of the **Geometry** node to the duplicated **Mapping** node and change node's **X Location** value to `-1.200`. Change the second **Gradient** texture's type to **Quadratic**, then go to the second **ColorRamp** node and click on the **Delete** button to erase the middle black marker; move the white color marker to the extreme right.

7. press *Shift + D* to duplicate one of the **Mix** nodes and move it to the right, after the **ColorRamp** nodes. Set the **Blend Type** to **Burn** and increase the **Fac** value to `1.000`. Connect the first **ColorRamp** color output to the **Color1** input socket and the second **ColorRamp** color output to the **Color2** input socket.

8. Press *Shift + D* to duplicate the **Burn** node one more time and connect the **Color** output of the first **Burn** node to the **Color1** input socket of the duplicated node.

9. Add a **Frame** (press *Shift + A* and go to **Layout | Frame**), select all the nodes and the frame and press *Crtl + P* to parent them; rename the frame as SLOPE.

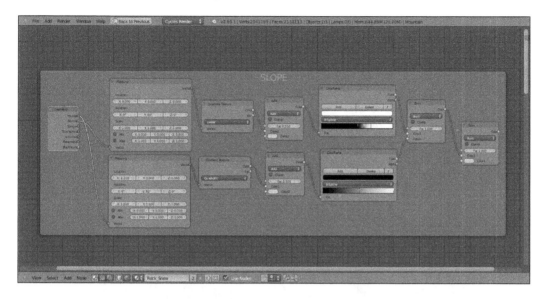

10. Now press *Shift + D* to duplicate one of the **Mapping** nodes (press *Alt + P* to unparent it from the frame) and move it under the **SLOPE** frame. Also, change its **X Location** value to -0.600.

11. Add a **Noise** node, a **Voronoi** node, and a **Musgrave** node (press *Shift + A* and go to **Texture**) and place them in a column aside of the **Mapping** node. Set the **Noise** texture's **Scale** value to 4.600. Set the **Voronoi** texture's **Coloring** value to **Cell** and the **Scale** value to 28.700. Set the **Musgrave** texture' type to **Ridget Multifractal**, the **Scale** value to 3.500, **Detail** to 16.000, **Dimension** to 0.900, **Lacunarity** to 0.600, **Offset** to 0.500, and **Gain** to 5.000.

12. Connect the **Vector** output of the **Mapping** node to the **Vector** inputs of the three textures, and then add a **Mix** node (press *Shift + A* and go to **Color | Mix**). Also, set the **Blend Type** to **Burn** and place it aside of the **Noise** and **Voronoi** texture nodes.

13. Connect the two texture's **Fac** outputs to the **Color1** and **Color2** input sockets of the **Burn** node. Press *Shift + D* to duplicate the latter and set its **Fac** value to 1.000; move it down and connect the color output of the first **Burn** node to the **Color1** input socket of the second **Burn** node, and then connect the **Fac** output of the **Musgrave** texture to its **Color2** input socket.

14. Add a **ColorRamp** node (press *Shift + A* and go to **Convertor | ColorRamp**) and paste it between the first and the second **Burn** nodes. Set the interpolation to **Ease** and move the white color marker to the middle of the slider.

15. Add a **Frame** (press *Shift + A* and go to **Layout | Frame**) and select all these nodes and the frame and press *Crtl + P* to parent them; rename the frame as DENSITY.

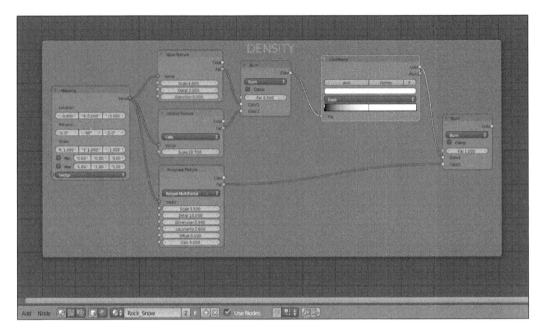

16. Select the two frames and all the nodes inside and press *Crtl + G* to make a group. Add a **Mix** node (press *Shift + A* and go to **Color | Mix**) and set the **Blend Type** to **Soft Light**, the **Fac** value to 1.000, and connect the **Color** output of the last **Burn** node inside the **SLOPE** frame to the **Color1** input socket. Then connect the **Color** output of the last **Burn** node inside the **DENSITY** frame to the **Color2** input socket.

17. Drag the **Color** output of the **Soft Light** node on the right border of the group envelope to create a new **Color** output on the interface.

18. Go to the **SLOPE** frame, click and drag to the left border of the envelope the **Fac** socket of the upper **Add** node. Rename the new input as Snow_amount and drag and connect to it also the **Fac** socket of the bottom **Add** node.

19. Go to the **DENSITY** frame and drag the **Vector** input of the **Mapping** node to the left border of the envelope. Move it up by clicking on the little arrow icon and press *Tab* to close the group; rename it as Separator.

20. Connect the **Object** output of the **Texture Coordinate** node to the **Vector** input socket of the **Separator** node group and its **Color** output to the **Fac** input socket of the **Mix Shader** node. On the group interface, set the **Snow_amount** value to 0.350.

Adding the atmospheric perspective

The very last thing we can do to improve our material is to append the **Fog_underwater** node group from the `1301OS_05_underwater_final.blend | Nodetree` file. Rename it as `Atmos_persp` and paste it just before the **Material Output** node. Then press *Tab* to open the group and by going in edit mode, set the **Multiply** node value to `0.010` and the color of the **Emission** shader to **R 0.078, G 0.133, B 0.250**.

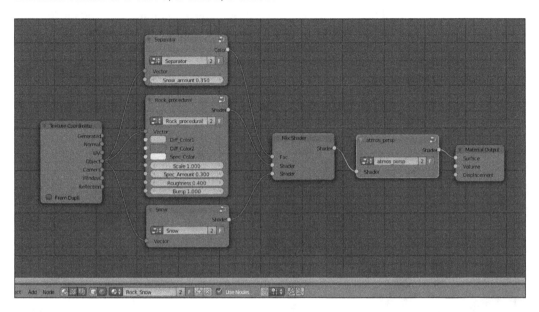

How it works...

Let's see now, by dividing the process in three parts, how this material actually works:

► First, we appended the **Snow** material and made a group, changing only the way the bump works, that is, deleting the output to the **Displacement** input of the **Material Output** node and implementing a "per shader" bump. This doesn't make a big difference, actually, in the final render. Just be aware that a bump piped in the **Displacement** socket can react to the **Ambient Occlusion** (which we didn't use in the scene, by the way), while this is not true with a "per shader" bump. We also appended the **Rock_procedural** material and made a group of it as well. All the necessary values have been exposed and, although in this scene we kept the material unaltered, the group can now be easily re-used for different kinds of rocks in other projects or on different objects. We added one **Math** nodes set to **Multiply** for every texture scale and bump strength value that needed to be driven by an exposed input. The first **Value**, set to the original scale or strength value, gets multiplied by the driven second **Value**, thereby increasing or decreasing (for values lower than 1) the effect.

▸ We then built the **Separator**, a node group outputting gray-scale values which, connected to the **Fac** input of the **Mix Shader** node, work as a "stencil map", separating the two different materials on the mesh surface accordingly to the black and white values. The two gradient textures in the **SLOPE** frame, mapped on the position and on the normals of the mesh and then blended together by the **Burn** nodes, make the snow material (the white color value of the "stencil map") appear more on the mesh's faces that have a more horizontal trend than a vertical one. Thanks to the **Add** nodes, driven by the exposed **Snow_amount** input and influencing the gradient of the **ColorRamp** nodes, it's possible to also set the quantity of snow (that is, of the white color in the stencil) on the whole object. The mixed textures in the **DENSITY** frame make the separation line between black and white more frayed and natural-looking.

In the preceding image, you can see the "mask" black and white values working as a separator between the rock and the snow materials.

Creating a realistic planet Earth as seen from space

In this recipe, we will create a realistic planet Earth using image textures available on the Web:

Getting ready

The image textures provided with this book have generally been heavily down-scaled and are good only for demonstration purposes (or, in this case, for a very distant Earth render). For better results with this recipe, just replace these low resolution images with hi-res versions that you can download, for example, from these addresses:

- http://www.shadedrelief.com/natural3/pages/textures.html
- http://www.shadedrelief.com/natural3/pages/clouds.html
- http://celestia.h-schmidt.net/earth-vt/
- http://www.celestiamotherlode.net/catalog/earth.php

Before you download anything, always have a look at the license of the images provided by any site you can find, to be sure they are released as freely usable, especially if you are going to use them for commercial works. The preceding links should be good enough, but on the Internet things can change quite quickly, so double-check!

The image maps you need are, at least, five:

- ▸ **Earth-color**: The color of the land/sea surfaces in daylight
- ▸ **Earth-night**: The color of the land/sea surfaces at night (usually provided with superimposed city lights)
- ▸ **Earth-bump**: A gray-scale high map of the continents
- ▸ **Earth-spec**: A black and white outline with the continents filled with black and the water masses perfectly white
- ▸ **Clouds**: A gray-scale map of the clouds

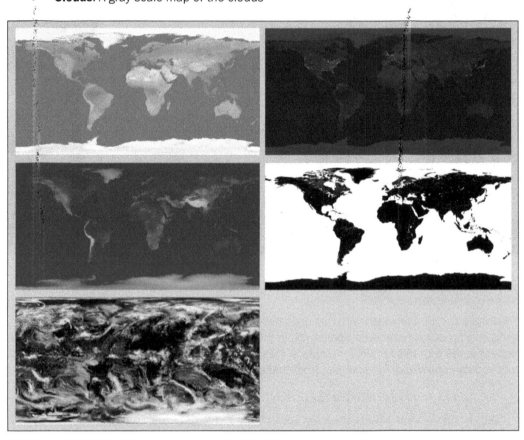

Note that, even if gray-scale, in Cycles all the image textures must be in RGB color space.

Actually, Cycles can also pretty well handle very big textures, reaching a size of 16 K (that is, 16.000 pixels for the longest side of the image), so you can use them at the best resolution you can find. In any case, be aware that the bigger the resolution of the textures, the longer the Cycles' rendering times.

However, besides the texture images, we also have to follow these steps:

1. Start Blender and switch to the **Cycles Render** engine.

2. Delete the default cube and add a UV Sphere (with the mouse cursor in the 3D view, press *Shift + A* and go to **Mesh | UV Sphere**). Rename it as `Earth_Surface`.

3. With the mouse cursor in the **Camera** view, press *1* from the numpad to go in orthogonal front view. Now, go in edit mode, select all the vertexes, and press *U*. In the **UV Mapping** pop-up menu, select **Sphere Projection**. Go out of edit mode and press *0* from the numpad to go back again to the **Camera** view.

4. Press *Shift + D* and hit *Enter* to duplicate the sphere. In the **Transform** panel to the right (press *N* if not already activated), set the **Scale** value for **X, Y,** and **Z** to `1.001`. Rename it as `Earth_Clouds`.

5. Duplicate it again, set the scale to `1.002`, and rename it as `Earth_Atmosphere`.

6. Add an **Empty** (press *Shift + A* and go to **Empty | Plain Axes**) and rename it as **Empty_Earth**. In the **Object Data** window, set its size to `2.00`. Select the three UV spheres and then the **Empty** and press *Crtl + P* to parent them to the **Empty**.

7. Select **Empty_Earth**, and in the **Transform** panel set the **Rotation** value to: **X= 18.387°, Y = 0.925°,** and **Z = -4.122°** (this is just to have a nice specular effect showing on the oceans at rendering time).

8. Select the camera and in the **Transform** panel set these values: **Location X = -0.64000, Y = - 4.70000,** and **Z = 0.12000; Rotation X = 89°, Y = 0°,** and **Z = -9°**. Go to the **Object Data** window and change the **Focal Length** value to `60.000` (Millimeters).

9. Go to the **World** window. Click on **New** and change the background color to pure black and set the **Strength** value to `0.000`.

10. Select the lamp and set it to **Sun**. Set the **Size** value to `0.100` and the **Strength** value to `8.000`. Set the color to **R 1.000, G 0.902, B 0.679**. In the **Transform** panel, set these values: **Location X = 145.00000, Y = -65.00000,** and **Z = 110.00000; Rotation X = 30.579°, Y = 48.615°,** and **Z = 14.078°**.

11. Go to the **Render** window, and under the **Sampling** sub-panel set the **Clamp** value to `1.00`, the **Preview** samples to `20`, and the **Render** samples to `50`.

How to do it...

In the **Outliner** hide, for the moment, the **Earth_Clouds** and **Earth_Atmosphere** spheres by clicking on the little eye icons to see only the **Earth_Surface** sphere in the viewport rendered and updated in real time as we work on the material.

1. Select the **Earth_Surface** sphere and click on **New** in the **Material** window under the **Properties** panel or in the **Node Editor** window's header. Rename the material as **Surface**.

2. In the **Material** window on the right, under the **Properties** panel, switch the **Diffuse BSDF** shader with an **Add Shader** node. In the first **Shader** slot, load a **Diffuse BSDF** shader. In the second **Shader** slot, load a **Glossy BSDF** node and set its **Roughness** value to 0.700.

3. Add an **Image Texture** node (press *Shift + A* and go to **Texture | Image Texture**) and connect its **Color** output to both the **Color** input sockets of the **Diffuse** and **Glossy** shaders. Click on the **Open** button on the **Image Texture** node and browse to your textures directory and load the Earth-col_low.png image (or a hi-res version if you have it).

4. Press *N* in the **Node Editor** window to bring up the **Active Node** panel. In the **Label** slot, rename the **Image Texture** node as **Color_Day**.

5. Add a new **Image Texture** node (press *Shift + A* and go to **Texture | Image Texture**) and a **Bump** node (press *Shift + A* and go to **Vector | Bump**). Connect the **color** output of this second **Image Texture** node to the **Height** input socket of the **Bump** node, and then connect the **Normal** output of the **Bump** node to the **Normal** input sockets of both the **Diffuse** and the **Glossy** shaders.

6. Rename the second **Image Texture** node as **Bump**, and then click on its **Open** button and load the **Earth-bump_low.png** image. Set **Color Space** to **Non-Color Data**. Select the **Bump** vector node, rename it as Bump_Lands, and set its **Strength** value to 0.002.

7. Add a **Frame** (press *Shift + A* and go to **Layout | Frame**), select the two image texture nodes, the **Bump_Lands** node, the **Diffuse** and **Glossy** shaders, and then the frame. Press *Crtl + P* to parent them and rename the frame as **LANDS**:

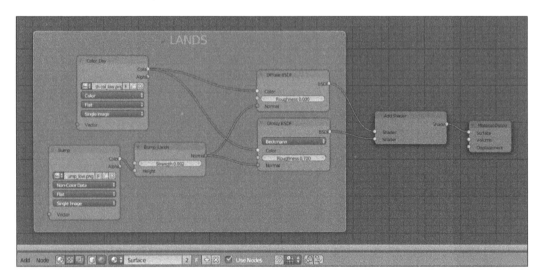

8. Now add a **Noise** texture (press *Shift + A* and go to **Texture | Noise Texture**), a **Bump** node (press *Shift + A* and go to **Vector | Bump**), a **Diffuse** shader (press *Shift + A* and go to **Shader | Diffuse BSDF**), and a **Glossy** shader (press *Shift + A* and go to **Shader | Glossy BSDF**).

9. Set the **Noise** texture's **Scale** value to `1000.000` and connect the **Color** output to the **Height** input socket of the **Bump** node. Rename the latter as `Bump_Oceans`, set the **Strength** value to `0.001`, and connect the **Normal** output to the **Normal** input sockets of the new **Diffuse** and **Glossy** shaders. Set the **Glossy** shader's **Roughness** value to `0.100`.

10. Add a Frame (press *Shift + A* and go to **Layout | Frame**), select the new nodes and the frame and press *Crtl + P* to parent them; rename the frame as `SEAS`.

11. Add a **Mix Shader** node (press *Shift + A* and go to **Shader | Mix Shader**) and place it just under the **Add Shader** node. Set the **Fac** value to `0.100` and connect the output of the **SEAS** frame's **Diffuse** to the first **Shader** input and the output of the **SEAS** frame's **Glossy** to the second **Shader** input socket.

12. Press *Shift + D* to duplicate the **Mix Shader** node and paste it between the **Add Shader** node and the **Material Output** node. Connect the output of the first **Mix Shader** node to the second **Shader** input.

13. Add a new **Image Texture** node (press *Shift + A* and go to **Texture | Image Texture**) and rename it as `Spec/Mask`. Connect the **Color** output to the **Fac** input socket of the last **Mix Shader** node. Click on the **Open** button to load the `Earth-spec_low.png` image and set **Color Space** to **Non-Color Data**.

14. Add a **Frame** (press *Shift + A* and go to **Layout | Frame**), select the **Spec/Mask** node and the frame, and press *Crtl + P* to parent them; rename the frame as `SEPARATOR LANDS/SEAS`.

15. Now click on the **Color** output of the **Color_Day** image texture inside the **LANDS** frame and connect it to the color input of the **Diffuse** shader inside the **SEAS** frame.

16. Add a **Mix** node (press *Shift + A* and go to **Color | Mix**) and paste it just before the **SEAS** frame's **Diffuse** shader. Switch the **Color1** connection to the **Color2** input socket and then set **Color1** to **R 0.0065, G 0.0065, B 0.024**.

17. Add a **ColorRamp** node (press *Shift+ A* and go to **Convertor | ColorRamp**) to the **SEAS** frame (just add it and parent it to the frame). Connect the **Color** output to the **Color** input of the **Glossy** shader. Set the interpolation to **B-Spline** and change the black color to pure white and the white color to **R 0.209, G 0.117, B 0.117**. Click on the **Add** button and change the new marker color to **R 0.965, G 0.462, B 0.223**.

18. Add a **Layer Weight** node (press *Shift + A* and go to **Input | Layer Weight**) to the **SEAS** frame, connect the **Facing** output to the **Fac** input socket of the **ColorRamp** node and to the **Fac** input socket of the **Mix** node.

19. Add an **Image Texture** node (press *Shift + A* and go to **Texture | Image Texture**), a **ColorRamp** node (press *Shift + A* and go to **Convertor | ColorRamp**), a **Mix** node (press *Shift + A* and go to **Color | Mix**), and an **Emission** shader (press *Shift + A* and go to **Shader | Emission**).

20. Rename the **Image Texture** node as `Color_Night` and connect its color output to the **Fac** input socket of the **ColorRamp** node and the color output of the latter to the **Color1** input socket of the **Mix** node. Connect the **Mix** node output to the color input of the **Emission** node.

21. In the **Color_Night** image texture node, load the `Earth-night_low.png` image. Set the **ColorRamp** node's interpolation to **B-Spline** and move the white color marker to the middle of the slider, then move the black color marker one-fourth to the right. Set the **Mix** node's **Blend Type** to **Multiply**, the **Fac** value to `1.000`, and change the **Color2** value to **R 1.000, G 0.257, B 0.090**. Set the **Emission** node's **Strength** value to `0.400`.

22. Add a **Frame** (press *Shift + A* and go to **Layout | Frame**), select the new nodes and the frame, and press *Crtl + P* to parent them; rename the frame as `NIGHT`.

23. Add a **Mix Shader** node (press *Shift + A* and go to **Shader | Mix Shader**) and paste it just before the **Material Output** node. Connect the **Emission** node output to the second **Shader** input socket of the last **Mix Shader** node.

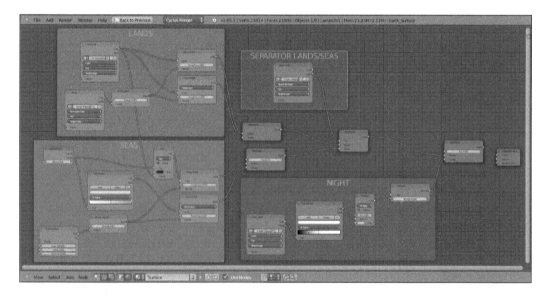

24. In the **Outliner**, unhide the **Earth_Clouds** sphere and select it. Click on **New** in the **Material** window under the **Properties** panel or in the **Node Editor** window's header. Rename the material as **Clouds**.

25. In the **Material** window on the right, under the **Properties** panel, switch the **Diffuse BSDF** shader with a **Mix Shader** node. In the first **Shader** slot, load a **Transparent BSDF** shader and in the second **Shader** slot load a new **Mix Shader** node. In its first **Shader** slot, load a **Diffuse BSDF** shader and in the second a **Glossy BSDF** shader. Set the Glossy shader's **Roughness** value to 0.800 and the colors of both the shader nodes to pure white.

26. Add an **Image Texture** node (press *Shift + A* and go to **Texture | Image Texture**), a ColorRamp node (press *Shift + A* and go to **Convertor | ColorRamp**) and a **Bump** node (press *Shift + A* and go to **Vector | Bump**).

27. Rename the **Image Texture** node as **Clouds** and connect its **Color** output to the **Fac** input of the **ColorRamp** and to the **Height** input socket of the **Bump** node.

28. Set the **ColorRamp** interpolation to **Ease** and connect its color output to the **Factor** input socket of the first **Mix Shader** node. Connect the **Bump** node output to the **Normal** inputs of both the **Diffuse** and **Glossy** shaders and set the **Strength** value to 0.002.

29. Click on the **Open** button of the **Clouds** image texture node and load the Clouds.png image. Set **Color Space** to **Non-Color Data**.

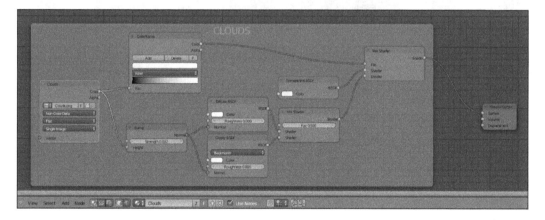

30. In the **Outliner**, unhide the **Earth_Atmosphere** sphere and select it. Click on **New** in the **Material** window under the **Properties** panel or in the **Node Editor** header. Rename the material as Atmosphere.

31. In the **Material** window on the right, under the **Properties** panel, switch the **Diffuse BSDF** shader with a **Mix Shader** node. In the first **Shader** slot, load a **Transparent BSDF** shader and in the second **Shader** slot load a new **Mix Shader** node. In its first **Shader** slot, load a **Diffuse BSDF** shader and in the second a **Glossy BSDF** shader. Set the **Glossy** shader's **Roughness** value to 0.800. Set the **Transparent** shader color to **R 0.640, G 0.692, B 0.753**.

32. Add a **Layer Weight** node (press *Shift + A* and go to **Input | Layer Weight**) and a **ColorRamp** node (press *Shift + A* and go to **Convertor | ColorRamp**) and connect the **Facing** output of the **Layer Weight** node to the **Fac** input of the **ColorRamp** node. Set the **ColorRamp** node's interpolation to **B-Spline** and move the black color marker one-fourth to the right of the slider.

33. Move them close to the first **Mix Shader** node and connect the **Color** output of the **ColorRamp** node to the **Fac** input of the first **Mix Shader** node. Set the **Layer Weight** node's blend factor to 0.200.

34. Select and press *Shift + D* to duplicate the **Layer Weight** and the **ColorRamp** nodes and move them close to the **Diffuse** and **Glossy** shaders. Connect the **ColorRamp** color output to the color inputs of the two shaders and set the blend factor of the **Layer Weight** node to 0.700.

35. Set the **ColorRamp** node's interpolation to **Ease** and move the white color marker to the middle of the slider. Set its color to **R 0.266, G 0.491, B 0.753**. Change the black color marker to **R 0.500, G 0.000, B 0.139**. Click on the **Add** button and change the new marker color to pure black.

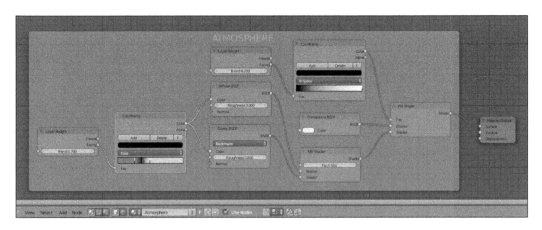

How it works...

The three overlapping spheres technique dates back almost to 2004 (at least for what relates to Blender), more precisely to the *How to make a realistic planet in Blender* tutorial that I wrote at that time for Blender Version 2.23/2.30. This tutorial is now outdated as far as materials are concerned, but the technique's basic concepts are still working even in Cycles, that is, the Earth surface on the smaller of the spheres, a clouds layer on a slightly bigger one, and the atmospheric Fresnel effect of the bigger one, thereby enclosing the other two.

At first, we built the more complex of all the three shaders—the **Surface** material— on the smallest of the three spheres:

- From step 1 to step 7, we built the shader for the continents, simply image textures connected as color factor to a **Diffuse** shader and a **Glossy** shader. And from step 8 to step 12, we built the basic shader for the oceans.

- At steps 13 and 14, we "split" the continent's component from the oceans by using the **Earth-spec** map, a black and white image working as a stencil for the factor input of the **Mix Shader** node. We also connected the **Earth-color** map to the **SEAS** frame's **Diffuse** shader, to bring back color to the oceans.

- From step 15 to step 18, we added to the **SEAS** frame, driven by a **Facing** Fresnel node, a **ColorRamp** node to enhance the coloration of the water's specularity (according to what often NASA satellite's photos show) and a deep blue color mixed to the color image map by a **Mix** node. Thanks to the **Facing** Fresnel, the blue color is mapped on the mesh faces perpendicular to the point of view, thereby resulting in darker water masses towards the center of the Earth sphere.

- From step 19 to step 23, we built the night shader. The **Earth-night** image has been clamped (contrasted) by the **ColorRamp** node and the resulting brighter values multiplied by a reddish color in the **Mix** node. All this is then assigned to an emission shader mixed at 50 percent with the rest of the components of the surface shader. Because the emission value is quite low, the "night surface" shows only in the shadow side of the Earth.

- Then, from step 24 to step 29, we built the **Clouds** layer on the second sphere.

- From step 30 to step 35, we built the atmosphere layer on the third sphere.

As you have probably noticed, we didn't use any **Texture Coordinate** or **Mapping** node to map the image maps. This is so because the spheres have been unwrapped and with **Image Textures** nodes the existing UV coordinate layer is taken automatically in account by Cycles for the mapping. For the ocean bump, instead, obtained by the **Noise** procedural, the **Generated** mapping option is automatically used (if you remember the section about the mapping of the textures in Cycles from *Chapter 1, Overview of Materials in Cycles*).

6
Creating More Complex Man-made Materials

In this chapter, we will cover:

- ▸ Creating cloth materials with procedurals
- ▸ Creating a leather material with procedurals
- ▸ Creating a synthetic sponge material with procedurals
- ▸ Creating a brick wall material with procedurals
- ▸ Creating a spaceship hull

Introduction

In this chapter we will see some more complex artificial material, starting from the simpler ones to the more complex. In any case, be aware that the procedure is basically always the same as for all the materials we have already seen: first the generic shader, then the color pattern, or the bump effect (one or more), depending on the preponderance of different components for the defining of the material itself.

The only difference is the level of complexity which they can reach (for example, just look at the spaceship hull shader or the brick wall).

Creating cloth materials with procedurals

In this recipe we will create a generic cloth material like the one shown in the following image:

Getting ready

1. Start Blender and load the file `13010S_cloth_start.blend`; in the scene there is an already set cloth simulation.

2. Press the play button on the timeline bar to see the simulation working and being cached in real-time: a plane (our tissue) draped on a sphere leaning on a bigger plane (the floor).

3. After the simulation has been totally cached (it's a total of 100 frames), in the **Physics** window on the right, under the **Cloth Cache** tab, click on the **Current Cache to Bake** button to save the simulation; the 100 frames simulation is now cached and saved inside a folder, named as the `blend file` and located in the same directory of the `blend file`.

From now on there is no need to calculate the simulation anymore, Blender will read the simulation data from that folder and so it will be possible to quickly scroll the timeline bar to immediately reach any frame inside the cached range.

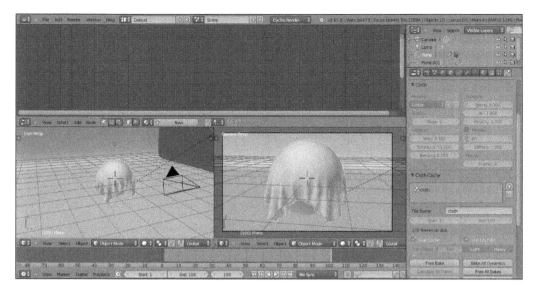

How to do it...

Now we are going to create the material:

1. Go to the frame 100.

2. Be sure to have the cloth plane selected and click on **New** in the **Material** window under the **Properties** panel or in the **Node Editor** header; rename the new material `cloth_generic`.

3. In the **Material** window switch the **Diffuse BSDF** node with a **Mix Shader** node; in the first **Shader** slot select a **Diffuse BSDF** node and in the second one a **Glossy BSDF** shader node.

4. Set the **Diffuse** roughness to **1.000**; set the **Glossy** roughness to **0.500**. Change the **Glossy** color to R 0.800, G 0.730, B 0.369 and the **Fac** value of the **Mix Shader** node to **0.160**.

5. Add a **Texture Coordinate** node (*Shift + A* | **Input** | **Texture Coordinate**) and two **Mapping** nodes (*Shift + A* | **Vector** | **Mapping**); connect the **UV** output of the **Texture Coordinate** node to the **Vector** input sockets of the two **Mapping** nodes.

6. Now add two **Wave Texture** nodes (*Shift + A* | **Texture** | **Wave Texture**) and a **Noise Texture** node (*Shift + A* | **Texture** | **Noise Texture**). Connect the output of the first **Mapping** node to the **Vector** input sockets of the first **Wave Texture** node and of the **Noise Texture** node; connect the output of the second **Mapping** node to the **Vector** input of the second **Wave Texture** node.

7. Add three **Math** nodes (*Shift + A* | **Convertor** | **Math**), each one for each texture node; set their operation mode to **Multiply** and connect the **Fac** output of each texture node to the first **Value** input socket of the respective **Math** node. Set the second **Value** of the first two **Math** nodes to **1.000**.

8. Go to the second **Mapping** node and set the **Rotation Y** to **90°**. Go to the **Wave Texture** nodes and for both of them set the **Scale** to **100.000**, **Distortion** to **2.000**, and **Detail Scale** to **2.000**. For the **Noise Texture** set the **Scale** to **80.000** and the **Distortion** to **5.000**.

9. Add a new **Math** node (*Shift + A* | **Convertor** | **Math**), set the operation to **Subtract**, and connect the outputs of the first two **Multiply** nodes to the first and to the second **Value** input sockets.

10. Press *Shift + D* to duplicate the last **Math** node, set the operation mode to **Add**, and connect the output of the **Subtract** node to its first **Value** socket, and the output of the third **Multiply** node, which is connected to the **Noise Texture** node, to the second **Value** input socket.

11. Press *Shift + D* to duplicate a **Multiply** node and connect the output of the **Add** node to the first **Value** input socket; set the second **Value** to **0.050**. Connect the last **Multiply** node output to the **Displacement** input socket of the **Material Output** node.

12. Add a frame (*Shift + A* | **Layout** | **Frame**), select the **Mapping** nodes, the **Textures**, and all the **Math** nodes, and then the frame and then press *Ctrl + P* to parent them. Rename the frame to **BUMP**.

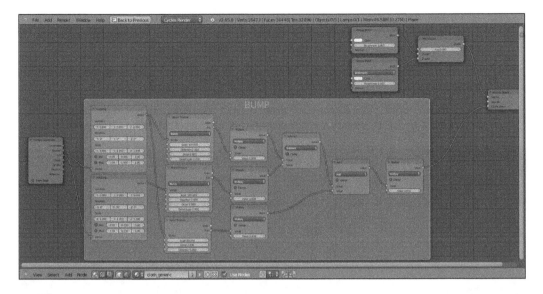

13. Add two new **Mapping** nodes (*Shift + A* | **Vector** | **Mapping**) and two **Wave Texture** nodes (*Shift + A* | **Texture** | **Wave Texture**). As before, connect the **UV** output of the **Texture Coordinate** node to the **Vector** inputs of each of the **Mapping** nodes, and these latter to the **Wave Texture** nodes.

14. Go to the first **Mapping** node and set the **Rotation Z** value to **-45°** and the **Scale Y** to **2.000**. Go to the respective **Wave Texture** and set the **Scale** to **10.900** and the **Detail** to **0.000**. Copy the same exact values in the second **Wave Texture** node and in the second **Mapping** node set the **Rotation Z** value to **45°**, and the **Scale X** to **2.000**.

15. Add two **ColorRamp** nodes (*Shift + A* | **Convertor** | **ColorRamp**) and connect the **Fac** output of the two **Wave Texture** nodes to the **Fac** input sockets of the two **ColorRamp** nodes.

16. Add a **Mix** node (*Shift + A* | **Color** | **Mix**) and connect the **Color** outputs of the two **ColorRamp** nodes to the **Color1** and **Color2** input sockets of the **Mix** node. Set its **Blend Type** to **Multiply** and the **Fac** value to **1.000**.

17. Connect the **Color** output of the Mix node to the **Color** input socket of the **Diffuse BSDF** node.

18. Add a frame (*Shift + A* | **Layout** | **Frame**), select the new nodes and then the frame, and press *Ctrl + P* to parent them; rename the frame to **COLOR**.

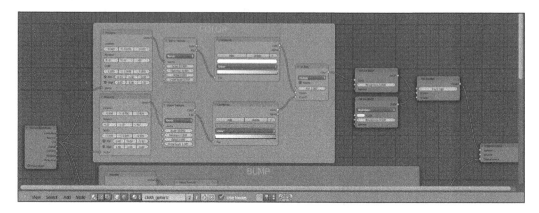

19. At this point we can change the colors inside the two **ColorRamp** gradients to obtain colored patterns; in my example, I set the first **ColorRamp** colors as a pure white going to a light blue, and to a violet for the second one.

How it works...

From step 1 to step 3 we just made the simple basic shader.

From step 4 to step 10 we built the bump texture of the tissue, by mixing with different orientations two wave textures, and by adding a little bit of noise.

From step 11 to step 18 we built a simple cross color pattern.

There's more...

A lot of variations can be obtained by setting different values for the bump but especially using different texture nodes and combinations for the color pattern:

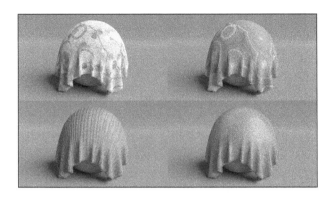

All these examples are included in the file `1301OS_06_cloth.blend`.

See also

To know more about Blender cloth simulation you can have a look at the following link:
`http://wiki.blender.org/index.php/Doc:2.6/Manual/Physics/Cloth`

Creating a leather material with procedurals

In this recipe we will create a leather-like material:

Getting ready

Start Blender and load the file `1301OS_06_start.blend`, where there is an already unwrapped Suzanne mesh.

How to do it...

Now we are going to create the material:

1. Click on **New** in the **Material** window under the **Properties** panel or in the **Node Editor** header; rename the new material `Leather_dark`.

2. In the **Material** window switch the **Diffuse BSDF** node with a **Mix Shader** node; in the first **Shader** slot select again a **Mix Shader** node and in the second one an **Anisotropic BSDF** shader node.

3. Add a **Fresnel** node (*Shift + A* | **Input** | **Fresnel**) and connect it to the **Fac** input sockets of both the **Mix Shader** nodes. Set the **IOR** value to **1.490**.

4. Set the **Anisotropic BSDF** node's **color** to a pure white and the **Roughness** value to **0.100**. Add a **Tangent** node (*Shift + A* | **Input** | **Tangent**), connect it to the **Tangent** input of the **Anisotropic** shader, and in its **Method to use for the tangent** slot select **UVMap**. Optionally, click on the blank slot at the right to select the name of the UV layer to be used (useful if the mesh has more than one UV layer).

5. Add a **Diffuse BSDF** shader (*Shift + A* | **Shader** | **Diffuse BSDF**) and a **Glossy BSDF** shader (*Shift + A* | **Shader** | **Glossy BSDF**); connect the **Diffuse** to the first **Shader** input socket of the second **Mix Shader** node and the **Glossy** to the second one. Set the **Diffuse Roughness** to **0.800**, the **Glossy** color to pure white, and its **Roughness** to **0.300**.

6. Add two **RGB** nodes (*Shift + A* | **Input** | **RGB**) and a **Mix** node (*Shift + A* | **Color** | **Mix**); connect the two **RGB** nodes to the **Color1** and **Color2** input sockets of the **Mix** node and then connect its **Color** output to the **Color** input socket of the **Diffuse** node.

7. Change the color of the first **RGB** node to **R 0.156, G 0.113, B 0.086** and the color of the second **RGB** node to **R 0.042, G 0.049, B 0.029**.

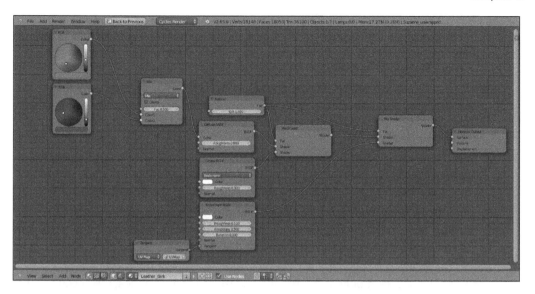

8. Add a **Texture Coordinate** node (*Shift + A* | **Input** | **Texture Coordinate**) and two **Mapping** nodes (*Shift + A* | **Vector** | **Mapping**). Connect the **Object** output of the **Texture Coordinate** node to the **Vector** input sockets of both the **Mapping** nodes, then in the second **Mapping** node change the **Rotation Y** value to **90°**.

9. Add two **Voronoi Texture** nodes (*Shift + A* | **Texture** | **Voronoi Texture**) and two **Wave Texture** nodes (*Shift + A* | **Texture** | **Wave Texture**); place them in a column to the side of the **Mapping** nodes like this: from the top, first the **Voronoi Texture**, below it the **Wave Texture**, below that again the second **Voronoi Texture**, and lastly the second **Wave Texture**.

10. Set the first **Voronoi Texture** node **Coloring** to **Cells** and the **Scale** to **60.000**; go to the first **Wave Texture** and set the **Scale** to **10.000**, **Distortion** to **10.000**, **Detail** to **16.000**, and **Detail Scale** to **0.300**. Set the **Scale** of the second **Voronoi Texture** node to **10.000** and copy the exact same values from the first **Wave Texture** to the second one.

11. Now connect the first **Mapping** node output to the **Vector** input sockets of the two **Voronoi Texture** nodes and of the first **Wave Texture** nodes; connect the output of the second **Mapping** node to the **Vector** input socket of the second **Wave Texture** node.

12. Add a **Mix** node (*Shift + A* | **Color** | **Mix**), set the **Blend Type** to **Difference** and the **Fac** value to **1.000**; connect the **Color** output of the first **Wave Texture** to the **Color2** input socket of the **Difference** node and the **Color** output of the second **Voronoi Texture** to its **Color1** input socket.

13. Press *Shift + D* to duplicate the **Difference** node and connect the **Color** output of the second **Voronoi Texture** node also to its **Color2** input socket; connect the **Color** output of the second **Wave Texture** to the **Color1** input socket of this second **Difference** node.

14. Press *Shift + D* to duplicate again a **Difference** node, change its **Blend Type** to **Multiply**, and connect the output of the first **Difference** node to the **Color1** input socket and the output of the second **Difference** node to the **Color2** input socket.

15. Add a **Math** node (*Shift + A* | **Convertor** | **Math**) and connect the output of the **Multiply** node to the second **Value** input socket; connect the **Color** output of the first **Voronoi Texture** node to the first **Value** input socket.

16. Add two **Bump** nodes (*Shift + A* | **Vector** | **Bump**); connect the first one to the **Normal** input socket of both the **Diffuse** and **Glossy** shader nodes, the second to the **Normal** input of the **Anisotropic** shader. Set the **Strength** of the first **Bump** node to **0.050** and the **Strength** of the second one to **0.025**. Connect the output of the **Add** node to the **Height** input sockets of both the **Bump** nodes.

17. Add a **ColorRamp** node (*Shift + A* | **Convertor** | **ColorRamp**) and paste it between the first **Difference** node and the **Multiply** node; set the **Interpolation** to **B-Spline** and move the white color marker 3/4 to the left. Press *Shift + D* to duplicate and paste it between the second **Difference** node and the **Multiply** node too.

18. Add a **Math** node (*Shift + A* | **Convertor** | **Math**) and paste it between the first **Voronoi Texture** node and the **Add** node; set the operation to **Multiply** and the second value to **-0.200**.

19. Press *Shift + D* to duplicate the **Multiply** math node and paste it between the multiply **Mix** node and the **Add** node; set its second value to **0.100**.

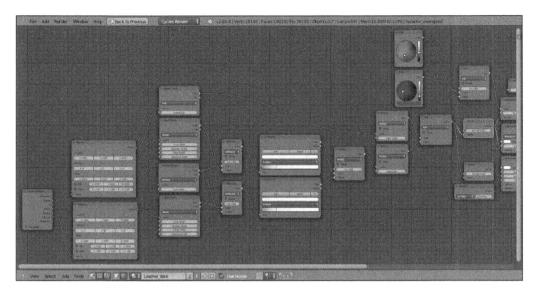

How it works...

From step 1 to step 7 we built the basic shader for the leather material; obviously there is not strictly the need to mix two different colors via **RGB** nodes inputs, one could be enough, but this way it can be easier to obtain certain hues.

From step 8 to step 19 we built the bump pattern for the leather. We used two different **Bump** nodes with different values for the **Diffuse** and **Glossy** and for the **Anisotropic** shader, to have slightly different light reflections on the surface.

Note that we used the **UVMap** layer information of the mesh for the **Tangent** node to be connected to the **Anisotropic** shader, and the **Object** mapping mode for the bump textures, instead; actually, because the mesh had been unwrapped already, we could have used the **UV** mapping output for the texture nodes too, but in that case the scale values for all the nodes would have been double and the flow of the textures on the polygons different (because forwarded by the flow of the unwrapped faces in the **UV** window).

Creating a synthetic sponge material with procedurals

In this recipe we will create a polyurethane sponge material, the type that you can usually find in any kitchen:

Getting ready

1. Start Blender and switch to the **Cycles Render** engine.

2. If not already selected, select the default cube and in the **Transform** panel to the right of the 3D view, under **Dimensions**, digit these values: **X 0.350, Y 0.235**, and **Z 0.116**. Press *Ctrl + A* to apply the scale.

3. Put the mouse in the 3D view and add a plane to the scene (*Shift + A* | **Mesh** | **Plane**). Go out of **Edit Mode** and in the **Transform** panel, **Dimensions** tab, write: **X 20.000** and **Y 20.000**. Again press *Ctrl + A* to apply the scale. Move the plane down (*G* | *Z* | *-0.05958* | *Enter*), to be the floor for the cube.

4. Select the Lamp, in the **Object Data** window click on the **Use Nodes** button and change the type to a Sun. Set the **Size** to **0.500**, the **Color** to pure white, and the **Strength** to **5.000**. In the **Transform** panel write these values: **Location X 3.44784, Y -1.15659, Z 14.12848; Rotation X 15°, Y 0°, Z 76°**.

5. Select the Camera and in the **Object Data** window, under the **Lens** tab, change the **Focal Length** to **60.000**. In the **Transform** panel write these values: **Location X 0.82385, Y -0.64613, Z 0.39382; Rotation X 68°, Y 0°, Z 51°**.

6. Go to the **World** window and click on the **Use Nodes** button under the **Surface** tab; click on the little square with a dot on the right side of the color slot: from the menu select **Sky Texture**. Set the **Strength** to **0.100**.

7. Go to the **Render** window and under the **Sampling** tab set the **Clamp** value to **1.00** and the **Samples** for **Render** and **Preview** to **50**.

8. Split the 3D view in two rows: change the upper one in a **Node Editor** window. Split the bottom view in two parts and change the left one into another 3D view. Put the mouse in the left 3D view and press *0* on the numpad to go in Camera view.

9. Select the cube and, with the mouse in the Camera view, press *Shift + S* | **Cursor to Selected** to place the cursor on the pivot of the cube (in case it's elsewhere): add a Lattice to the scene (*Shift + A* | **Lattice**), press *Tab* to go out of **Edit Mode** and in the **Transform** panel, under **Scale**, write **X 0.396**, **Y 0.264**, and **Z 0.129**. Go to the **Object Data** window and in the **Lattice** slot set the **U**, **V**, and **W** values to **3**.

10. Reselect the cube and go in the **Object Modifiers** window; assign a **Subdivision Surface** modifier, switch the type of subdivision algorithm from **Catmull-Clark** to **Simple**, and set the **Subdivisions** to **2** both for **View** and **Render**.

11. Assign a **Bevel** modifier and set the **Width** to **0.0010**. Assign a **Lattice** modifier and in the **Object** slot select the **Lattice** name. Reselect the **Lattice** and press *Tab* to go in **Edit Mode**; select the **Lattice** vertexes as indicated in the following image:

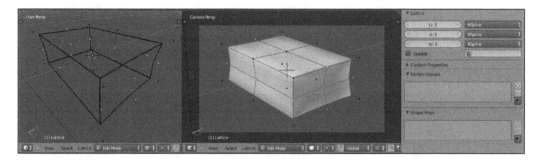

12. Scale a bit smaller the selected vertexes only on the **X** and **Y** axis (*S* | *Shift + Z* | *.9* | *Enter*), then scale a bit smaller only the upper vertexes, and so on, to obtain the result of a shape similar to a kitchen sponge. When done, go out of **Edit Mode** (*Tab*).

13. Reselect the cube and in the **Object Tools** panel, under **Shading**, select **Smooth**. With the mouse in the 3D view, press *N* and *T* to get rid of the **Transform** and **Object Tools** panels. Go to the **Material** window.

How to do it...

And now let's start with the creation of the material:

1. As first thing, select the plane and click on **New** in the **Material** window under the **Properties** panel or in the **Node Editor** header. In the **Material** window switch the **Diffuse BSDF** node with a **Mix Shader** node: in the first **Shader** slot select a **Diffuse BSDF** node and in the second **Shader** slot a **Glossy BSDF** shader node. Set the **Fac** value of the **Mix Shader** to **0.400** and the **Diffuse** color to a blue.

2. Now select the cube and click on **Use Nodes** in the **Material** window under the **Properties** panel or in the **Node Editor** header; rename the new material **sponge_ polyurethane**.

3. In the **Material** window switch the **Diffuse BSDF** node with a **Mix Shader** node: in the **Label** slot of the **Active Node** panel in the **Node Editor** window (if not present, press *N* to make it appear) rename it **Mix Shader1**. Go to the **Material** window on the right and in its first **Shader** slot select again a **Mix Shader** node and rename it **Mix Shader2**; in the second **Shader** slot select an **Add Shader** node.

4. In the first **Shader** slot of the **Mix Shader2** node select a **Diffuse BSDF** shader and in the second one a **Velvet BSDF**; set the **Diffuse** roughness to **1.000** and the **Velvet Sigma** value to **0.600**.

5. Connect the output of the **Velvet** shader also to the first **Shader** input of the **Add Shader** node; in its second **Shader** input load a **Glossy BSDF** shader and set the **Roughness** value to **0.350**.

6. Add a **Fresnel** node (*Shift + A* | **Input** | **Fresnel**) and connect it to the **Fac** input socket of the **Mix Shader1**. Set the **IOR** value to **1.496**. Add an **RGB** node (*Shift + A* | **Input** | **RGB**) and connect its output to the **Color** input sockets of the **Diffuse**, **Velvet**, and **Glossy** shaders. Set the **RGB** node **Color** to R 0.319, G 1.000, B 0.435 (but any other color can be fine).

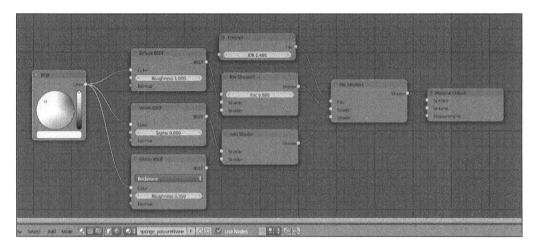

7. Add a **Texture Coordinate** node (*Shift + A* | **Input** | **Texture Coordinate**), a **Mapping** node (*Shift + A* | **Vector** | **Mapping**), two **Voronoi Texture** nodes (*Shift + A* | **Texture** | **Voronoi Texture**) and a **Noise Texture** node (*Shift + A* | **Texture** | **Noise Texture**).

8. Place the three textures horizontally in a row like this: **Voronoi**, **Voronoi**, and **Noise**. Rename the first texture **Voronoi Texture1** and the second one **Voronoi Texture2**.

9. Connect the **Object** output of the **Texture Coordinate** node to the **Vector** input socket of the **Mapping** node, and a the **Vector** output of this latter to the **Vector** input sockets of the three texture nodes.

10. Set the **Scale** of the **Voronoi Texture1** node to **38.000**, the **Scale** of the **Voronoi Texture2** node to **62.300**, and the **Scale** of the **Noise Texture** node to **300.000**.

11. Add three **ColorRamp** nodes (*Shift + A* | **Convertor** | **ColorRamp**) and connect the **Color** output of each texture to the **Fac** input socket of each **ColorRamp** node. Rename the first one **ColorRamp1**, the second one **ColorRamp2**, and the third **ColorRamp3**.

12. Add three **Math** nodes (*Shift + A* | **Convertor** | **Math**) and connect the color output of each **ColorRamp** node to the first **Value** input socket of each **Math** node. Set the operation for all the three math nodes to **Multiply** and rename the first one **Multiply1**, the second one **Multiply2**, and the third **Multiply3**. Set the second **Value** of the **Multiply1** and **Multiply2** nodes to **1.000** and the second **Value** of the **Multiply3** node to **0.100**.

13. Add a **Mix** node (*Shift + A* | **Color** | **Mix**) and connect the output of the **Multiply1** node to the **Color1** input socket and the output of the **Multiply2** node to the **Color2** input socket; change the **Blend Type** to **Add** and the **Fac** value to **1.000**. Rename the mix node **Add1**.

14. Press *Shift + D* to duplicate the **Add1** node and rename it **Add2**; connect the output of the **Add1** node to the **Color1** input socket and the output of the **Multiply3** node to the **Color2** input socket of the **Add2** node.

15. Add a Math node (*Shift + A* | **Convertor** | **Math**), set the operation to **Multiply**, and rename it **Multiply4**; connect the output of the **Add2** node to the first **Value** input socket and set the second **Value** to **1.000**.

16. Connect the output of the **Multiply4** node to the **Displacement** input socket of the **Material Output** node.

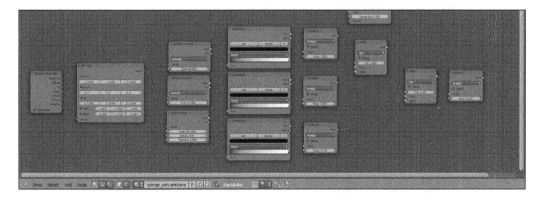

17. Now box select (press *B*, then click with the left mouse button to drag the selection on the objects) the **ColorRamp1** and **ColorRamp2** nodes, the **Multiply1** and **Multiply2** nodes, the two **Add** nodes, and the **Multiply4** node; press **G** and move them to the right, to make room for new nodes to the left side:

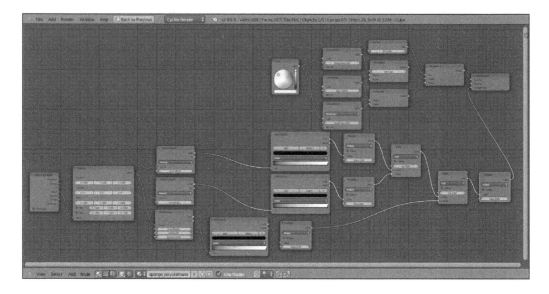

18. Add an **RGB Curves** node (*Shift + A | Color | RGB Curves*) and paste it between the **Voronoi Texture1** node and the **ColorRamp1** node. Rename it **RGB Curves1**. Click on the curve to add a control point and in the coordinates slots under the node main window set the **X = 0.26111** and the **Y = 0.50000**; click to add a second control point and write **X = 0.73889** and **Y = 0.51111**.

19. Press *Shift + D* to duplicate the **RGB Curves1** node, paste it between the **Voronoi Texture2**, and the **ColorRamp2** nodes and rename it **RGB Curves2**.

20. Go to the **ColorRamp1** node and move the white color marker 3/4 to the left; go to the **ColorRamp2** and do exactly the same. Go to the **ColorRamp3** node and move the white color marker to the middle of the slider.

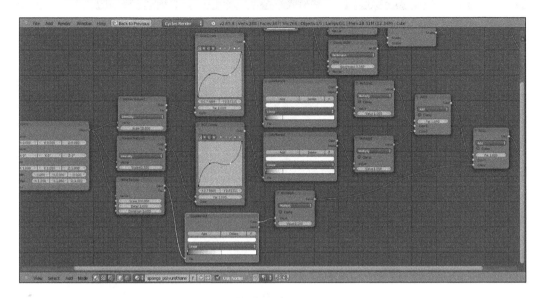

How it works...

From step 2 to step 6 we built the basic shader of the sponge material and the color. As you can see in the **Rendered** camera view, without the bump pattern, there is a visible artifact in the more distant side of the mesh; this is due to the **Smooth** shading we have set at step 13 of the *Getting ready* section of this recipe; setting the shading to **Flat** again will remove the artifact, but will show the blocky faces of the deformed sponge mesh. By the way, because of the bump pattern and of the fact that the mesh is subdivided, this is not trivial and anyone of the two solutions (smooth with artifact or flat but blocky) is fine.

From step 7 to step 20 we built the bump pattern.

Creating a brick wall material with procedurals

In this recipe we will create a wall made of bricks and concrete, like this one:

Getting ready

1. Start Blender and switch to the **Cycles Render** engine.

2. Select the default cube and, by typing the values in the **Dimensions** tab under the **Transform** panel located to the right of the 3D view (press *N* to make it appear if not visible), scale it like this: **X 10.000**, **Y 1.000**, and **Z 6.000**. Press *Ctrl + A* to apply the size.

3. Split the bottom row in two parts, change the left one to a **UV/Image Editor** window. Go in **Edit Mode** (*Tab*) and select the edges as indicated in the figure (the red edges in the image to the right):

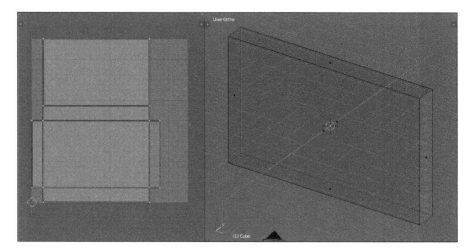

4. Press *Ctrl + E* | **Mark Seams** to seam the selected edges, then press *U*, and in the **UV Mapping** pop-up panel select **Unwrap**. Go out of **Edit Mode**.

5. Add a plane to the scene (mouse in the 3D view, *Shift + A* | **Mesh** | **Plane**) and still in **Edit Mode** scale it is 10 times bigger (press *A* to select all the vertexes, then *S* | *10* | *Enter*). Press *U* | **UV Mapping** | **Unwrap**. Go out of **Edit Mode** and move it three units down (*G* | *Z* | *-3* | *Enter*).

6. Join the bottom two windows in a single 3D view again to get rid of the **UV/Image Editor** window.

7. Select the Lamp and delete it. Add a new Plane to the scene (*Shift + A* | **Mesh** | **Plane**), go out of **Edit Mode** and scale it six times bigger (*S* | *6* | *Enter*). Rename it **Emitter**. In the **Transform** panel set these values: **Location X 87.00000, Y -39.70000, Z 58.00000** and **Rotation X 22°, Y 60°, Z 0°**.

8. Select the Camera and in the **Transform** panel set these values: **Location X 11.00000, Y -21.00000, Z 6.20000** and **Rotation X 74.7°, Y 0°, Z 26.5°**. Go to the **Object Data** window and set the **Focal Length** to **60.000**.

9. Go to the **World** window and click on the **Use Nodes** button under the **Surface** tab; click on the little square with a dot on the right side of the color slot: from the menu select **Sky Texture**. Set the **Strength** to **0.500**.

10. Go to the **Render** window and under the **Sampling** tab set the **Clamp** value to **1.00** and the **Samples** for **Render** and **Preview** to **25**. Under the **Performance** tab set the **Acceleration structure** to **Static BVH** and check both the **Use Spatial Splits** and **Cache BVH** options.

11. Press *N* to get rid of the **Transform** panel in the 3D view and split it in two rows: change the upper one to a **Node Editor** window.

How to do it...

Now we are going to create the material:

1. In the **Outliner** select the **Emitter** plane and click on **New** in the **Material** window under the **Properties** panel or in the **Node Editor** header; rename the new material **Emitter** and in the **Material window** switch the **Diffuse BSDF** node with an **Emission** node; set the **Strength** to **500.000**.

2. Select the floor plane and click on **New** in the **Material** window under the **Properties** panel or in the **Node Editor** header; rename the new material **Brickwall**. Select the cube and press *Shift* to select the floor plane, then press *Ctrl + L* | **Materials** to assign the same material to both the objects.

3. In the **Material** window switch the **Diffuse BSDF** node with a **Mix Shader** node; in the first **Shader** slot select a **Diffuse BSDF** node and in the second one a **Glossy BSDF** shader node.

4. Set the **Diffuse** roughness to **0.200** and the **Glossy** roughness to **0.800**. Add a **Layer Weight** node (*Shift + A* | **Input** | **Layer Weight**) and connect the **Fresnel** output to the **Fac** input socket of the **Mix Shader** node. Set the **Blend** to **0.200**.

5. Add two **Voronoi Texture** nodes (*Shift + A* | **Texture** | **Voronoi Texture**), a **Noise Texture** node (*Shift + A* | **Texture** | **Noise Texture**), and a **Musgrave Texture** (*Shift + A* | **Texture** | **Musgrave Texture**); place them vertically in a column in this order from the top: **Voronoi**, **Noise**, **Musgrave**, and **Voronoi**.

6. Add a **Texture Coordinate** node (*Shift + A* | **Input** | **Texture Coordinate**) and a **Mapping** node (*Shift + A* | **Vector** | **Mapping**); connect the **UV** output of the **Texture Coordinate** node to the **Vector** input of the **Mapping** node and the **Vector** output of this latter to the **Vector** input sockets of the four texture nodes.

7. Add four **ColorRamp** nodes (*Shift + A* | **Convertor** | **ColorRamp**) and place each one of them close to each one of the texture nodes; connect the **Color** output of each texture to the **Fac** input socket of the respective **ColorRamp**.

8. Go to the first **Voronoi Texture** node: set the **Coloring** to **Cells** and the **Scale** to **100.000**; set the **Interpolation** of its **ColorRamp** to **B-Spline** and move the black color marker to the middle of the slider, and the white color marker to the full left. Add a **Math** node (*Shift + A* | **Convertor** | **Math**) and connect the color **ColorRamp** output to the first **Value** input socket of the **Math** node; set the operation to **Multiply** and the second **Value** to **0.005**.

9. Go to the **Noise Texture** node and set the **Scale** to **80.000**. Set the respective **ColorRamp** interpolation to **Ease**, move the black color marker to the middle of the slider, and the white color marker 1/4 to the left. Add a **Math** node (*Shift + A* | **Convertor** | **Math**) and connect the color **ColorRamp** output to the first **Value** input socket of the **Math** node; set the operation to **Multiply** and the second **Value** to **0.050**.

10. Add a **Mix** node (*Shift + A* | **Color** | **Mix**), set the **Blend Type** to **Difference**, the **Fac** value to **1.000** and connect the outputs of the two **Multiply** math nodes to the **Color1** and **Color2** input sockets of the **Difference** node.

11. Go to the **Musgrave Texture** node and set the **Scale** to **96.900**, **Lacunarity** to **2.000**, and **Offset** to **1.000**. Set the respective **ColorRamp** interpolation to **B-Spline** and move the black color marker 1/4 to the right. Add a **Math** node (*Shift + A* | **Convertor** | **Math**) and connect the color **ColorRamp** output to the first **Value** input socket of the **Math** node; set the operation to **Multiply** and the second **Value** to **-3.000**.

12. Add a **Mix** node (*Shift + A* | **Color** | **Mix**), set the **Blend Type** to **Multiply**, the **Fac** value to **0.700**, and connect the output of the **Difference** node to the **Color1** and the output of the last **Multiply** math node to the **Color2** input socket.

13. Go to the second **Voronoi Texture** node and set the **Scale** to **600.000**. Set the respective **ColorRamp** interpolation to **Ease** and move the black color marker a little bit to the right (right under the E of the **Easy word**, to be clear) and the white color marker to the full left. Add a **Math** node (*Shift + A* | **Convertor** | **Math**) and connect the color **ColorRamp** output to the first **Value** input socket of the **Math** node; set the operation to **Multiply** and the second **Value** to **0.050**.

14. Add a **Mix** node (*Shift + A* | **Color** | **Mix**), set the **Blend Type** to **Divide**, the **Fac** value to **0.005**, and connect the output of the multiply **Mix** node to the **Color1** and the output of the last multiply **Math** node to the **Color2** input socket.

15. Add a **Bump** node (*Shift + A* | **Vector** | **Bump**) and connect the **Divide** node output to its **Height** input socket, then connect its **Normal** output to the **Normal** input sockets of the **Diffuse** and of the **Glossy** shaders. Set the **Strength** to **1.000**.

16. Add a **Brick Texture** node (*Shift + A* | **Texture** | **Brick Texture**) and connect the **Mapping** node output to the **Vector** input socket. Set these values: **Scale 5.500, Mortar Size 0.005, Row Height 0.150**; set the **Color1** as R 1.000, G 0.227, B 0.051, the **Color2** as R 0.462, G 0.051, B 0.012, and the **Mortar** color as RGB 0.555.

17. Add a Mix node (*Shift + A* | **Color** | **Mix**) and connect the color output of the **Brick Texture** to the **Color1** input socket; set the **Color2** to R 0.658, G 0.095, B 0.020, the **Blend Type** to **Color**, and the **Fac** value to **0.550**.

18. Add a new **Mix** node (*Shift + A* | **Color** | **Mix**) and connect the **Color** output of the color **Mix** node to the **Color1** input socket; set the **Color2** to R 0.597, G 0.056, B 0.012. Connect the color output of the **ColorRamp** of the last **Voronoi Texture** to the **Fac** input socket of the **Mix** node and the output of this latter to the **Color** input sockets of both the **Diffuse** and the **Glossy** shader nodes.

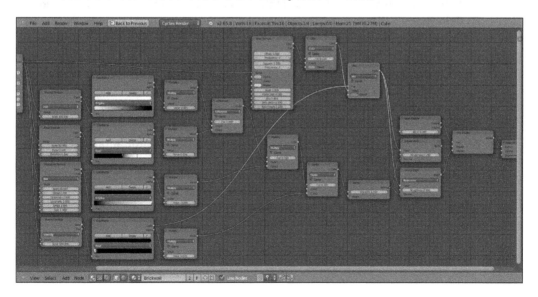

19. Add a Frame (*Shift + A* | **Layout** | **Frame**), select all the nodes except of the **Texture Coordinate**, the **Mapping**, and the **Material Output** nodes, then press *Shift* to select the Frame and *Ctrl + P* to parent them. Rename the frame **BRICKS**.

20. Now add a **Diffuse BSDF** shader, a **Glossy BSDF** shader, and a **Mix Shader** and connect them as usual; connect the **Mix Shader** output to the **Surface** input socket of the **Material Output** node (that is, to temporarily replace the connection of the brick material and see the result in the Rendered camera view).

21. Set the **Diffuse** roughness to **0.850**. Add a **Layer Weight** node (*Shift + A* | **Input** | **Layer Weight**) and connect the **Fresnel** output to the **Fac** input socket of the **Mix Shader** node; set the **Blend** factor to **0.150**.

22. Add a **Voronoi Texture** node (*Shift + A* | **Texture** | **Voronoi Texture**), a **Noise Texture** node (*Shift + A* | **Texture** | **Noise Texture**), and two **Musgrave Texture** (*Shift + A* | **Texture** | **Musgrave Texture**) nodes; place them vertically in a column in this order from the top: **Voronoi**, **Noise**, **Musgrave**, and **Musgrave**.

23. Add four **ColorRamp** nodes (*Shift + A* | **Convertor** | **ColorRamp**) and place each one of them close to each one of the texture nodes; connect the **Color** output of each texture to the **Fac** input socket of the respective **ColorRamp**.

24. Connect the **Vector** output of the **Mapping** node to the **Vector** input sockets of the four new texture nodes.

25. Go to the **Voronoi Texture** node and set the **Scale** to **200.000**. Set the **Interpolation** of its **ColorRamp** to **Ease**, move the black color marker a bit to the right (right under the middle of the **Ease** word, between the letters a and s, to be clear), and the white color marker to the full left.

26. Go to the **Noise Texture** node and set the **Scale** to **800.000**. Set the **Interpolation** of its **ColorRamp** to **Ease**, move the black color marker to the middle of the slider, and the white color marker 1/4 to the left.

27. Add a **Math** node (*Shift + A* | **Convertor** | **Math**) and connect the output of the first two **ColorRamp** nodes to the first and to the second **Value** input sockets. Press *Shift + D* to duplicate the **Math** node, change the operation to **Multiply**, and connect the output of the first math node to the first **Value** input socket; set the second **Value** to **0.100**; rename the node **Multiply1**.

28. Go to the first **Musgrave Texture** node and set the **Type** to **Multifractal**, the **Scale** to **800.000**, **Lacunarity** to **2.000**, and **Offset** to **1.000**. Set the **Interpolation** of its **ColorRamp** to **Ease**, move the black color marker to the middle of the slider and the white color marker 1/4 to the left. Add a **Math** node (*Shift + A* | **Convertor** | **Math**) and connect the **Color** output of **ColorRamp** to the first **Value** input socket of the **Math** node; set the operation to **Multiply** and the second **Value** to **1.000**; rename the node **Multiply2**.

29. Go to the second **Musgrave Texture** node and set the **Type** to **Multifractal**, the **Scale** to **193.800**, **Lacunarity** to **2.000**, and **Offset** to **1.000**. Set the **Interpolation** of its **ColorRamp** to **Ease**, move the black color marker 1/4 to the right and the white color marker to the middle of the slider; click on the **Add** button and move the new middle gray marker to the right for 3/4 of the total length of the slider. Add a **Math** node (*Shift + A* | **Convertor** | **Math**) and connect the color **ColorRamp** output to the first **Value** input socket of the **Math** node; set the operation to **Multiply** and the second **Value** to **-0.400**; rename the node **Multiply3**.

30. Add a **Mix** node (*Shift + A* | **Color** | **Mix**), set the **Blend Type** to **Divide** and the **Fac** value to **1.000**; connect the output of the **Multiply1** node to the **Color1** input socket and the output of the **Multiply2** math node to the **Color2** input socket; rename the node **Divide1**.

31. Press *Shift + D* to duplicate the **Divide1** node and rename it **Divide2**. Connect the output of the **Divide1** node to the **Color1** input socket of the **Divide2** node, and the output of the **Multiply3** node to the **Color2** input socket.

32. Add a **Bump** node (*Shift + A* | **Vector** | **Bump**), connect the output of the **Divide2** node to the **Height** input socket of the **Bump** node, and its **Normal** output to the **Normal** input sockets of both the **Diffuse** and the **Glossy** shaders.

33. Add a Mix node (*Shift + A* | **Color** | **Mix**) and connect the output to the **Color** input sockets of both the **Diffuse** and the **Glossy** shaders; set the **Blend Type** to **Add**.

34. Press *Shift + D* to duplicate the **Add** node, change the Blend Type to **Mix** and connect its output to the **Color1** input socket of the add **Mix** node; set the **Color1** to RGB 0.103 and the Color2 to R 0.546, G 0.571, B 0.565. Set the **Fac** value to **0.200**.

35. Connect the **Color** output of the **ColorRamp** of the **Voronoi Texture** node to the **Color2** input socket of the add **Mix** node.

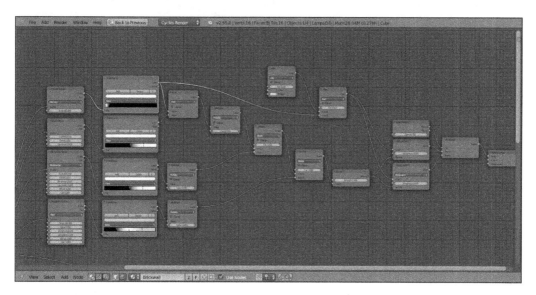

36. Add a Frame (*Shift + A* | **Layout** | **Frame**), select the nodes and then the frame, press *Ctrl + P* to parent them, and rename the frame **CONCRETE**.

37. Add a new **Brick Texture** node (*Shift + A* | **Texture** | **Brick Texture**) and connect the **Mapping** node output to its **Vector** input socket. Set these values: **Scale 5.500, Mortar Size 0.005, Row Height 0.150** (the same as in the first **Brick Texture** node we added). Set the **Color1** and **Color2** as pure white.

38. Add a **Voronoi Texture** node (*Shift + A* | **Texture** | **Voronoi Texture**), connect the **Mapping** node output to the **Vector** input socket, and set the **Scale** to **38.000**; add a **Mix** node (*Shift + A* | **Color** | **Mix**), set the **Blend Type** to **Multiply**, and the **Fac** value to **1.000**. Connect the **Voronoi Color** output to the **Color1** input socket and the **Brick Texture Color** output to the **Color2** input socket.

39. Now add a **Mix Shader** node (*Shift + A* | **Shader** | **Mix Shader**) and connect it to the **Surface** input socket of the **Material Output** node; connect the output of the **CONCRETE** frame to the first **Shader** input socket and the output of the **BRICKS** frame to the second one.

40. Connect the **Multiply** node output to the **Fac** input socket of the **Mix Shader** node.

41. Press *Shift + D* duplicate the **Brick Texture** node, connect the **Mapping** node output and change the **Mortar Size** value to **0.010**; add a **Mix** node (*Shift + A* |**Color** | **Mix**), paste it between the **Multiply** node and the **Material Output** node; set the **Blend Type** to **Screen**, the **Fac** value to **1.000**, click on the **Clamp** option, and connect the color output of the second **Brick Texture** node to the **Color2** input socket.

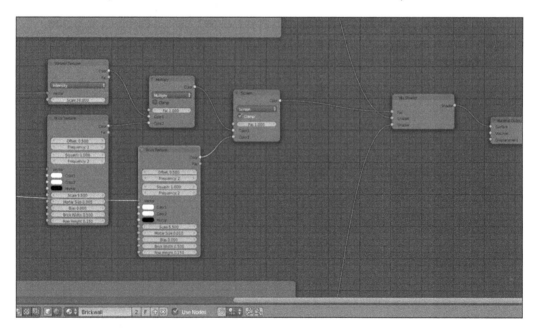

42. Add a **Frame** (*Shift + A* | **Layout** | **Frame**) and parent to it the last nodes; rename the frame **MASK_BRICKS**.

43. Go to the **BRICKS** frame and add a **Math** node (*Shift + A* | **Convertor** | **Math**); paste it between the **Bump** and the **Divide** nodes; add a new **Math** node (*Shift + A* | **Convertor** | **Math**) and connect its output to the first **Value** input socket of the former one (this way the connection of the **Divide** node is automatically moved to the second **Value** input socket). Set the operation to **Multiply** and connect the output of the **Screen** node inside the **MASK_BRICKS** frame to the first **Value** input socket. Set the second **Value** to **2.000**.

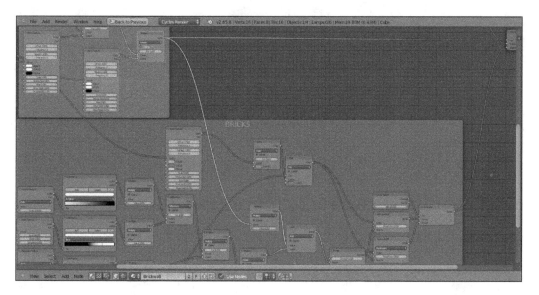

44. Add a **Voronoi Texture** (*Shift + A* | **Texture** | **Voronoi Texture**) and a **Musgrave Texture** (*Shift + A* | **Texture** | **Musgrave Texture**) and connect them as usual to the **Mapping** node output. Set the **Voronoi Scale** to **200.000** and the **Musgrave** scale to **154.200**.

45. Add a **Mix** node (*Shift + A* | **Color** | **Mix**), set the **Blend Type** to **Difference** and connect the **Voronoi** color output to the **Color1** input socket, and the **Musgrave** color output to the **Color2** input socket.

46. Go to the **BRICKS** frame and add a **Mix** node (*Shift + A* | **Color** | **Mix**); rename it **Mix1** and paste it between the **Diffuse** shader and the **Mix** node; move the connection of the **Mix** node from the **Color1** to the **Color2** input socket and set the **Color1 Color** to RGB 0.019.

47. Press *Shift + D* to duplicate the **Mix1** node, rename it **Mix2** and paste it between the **Mix1** node and the **Diffuse** shader. Move the connection of the **Mix1** node from the **Color1** to the **Color2** input socket and set the **Color1 Color** to pure white.

48. Connect the output of the **Difference** node to the **Fac** input sockets of the **Mix1** and **Mix2** nodes: add two **Bright/Contrast** nodes (*Shift + A | Color Bright/Contrast*) and paste them respectively between the **Difference** node and the **Mix1** and **Mix2** nodes.

49. For the **Bright/Contrast** node go to the **Mix1** node set the **Bright** to **1.300** and the **Contrast** to **1.550**; for the **Bright/Contrast** node go to the **Mix2** node set the **Bright** to **1.500** and the **Contrast** to **1.350**.

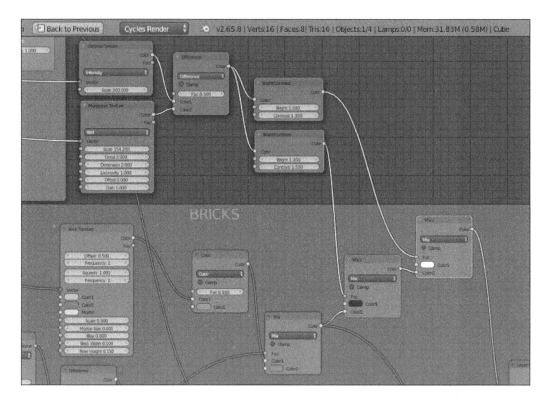

50. Add a Frame (*Shift + A | Layout | Frame*), select the **Voronoi**, the **Musgrave**, the **Difference**, and the two **Bright/Contrast** nodes and then the frame, and press *Ctrl + P* to parent them. Rename the frame **DIRT**.

How it works...

Even if this material can look quite complex, the concept behind is really simple: we built two separate materials, the brick and the concrete (mortar), and then we mixed them by a combination of **Brick Texture** nodes, arranged in such a way as to give a less regular and perfect result.

First, we started with the Brick material:

From step 1 to step 4 we built the basic shader, from step 5 to step 15 we built the bump component of the brick material, and from step 16 to step 18 we added the basic coloration of the bricks.

After this we built the Concrete material: from step 20 to step 21 again the basic shader combination, from step 22 to step 32 we built the bump for the concrete, and from step 33 to step 35 the color for the concrete.

Then it was the time of the brick masking, from step 37 to step 41; the second **Brick Texture** is combined with the first one so as to leave a distorted border only on the mortar space, to give an irregular shape to the bricks. At step 43 we added the black and white values of the brick masking to the overall bump effect.

As the last thing we added a slight dirty effect on the bricks, from step 44 to step 49.

Creating a spaceship hull

In this recipe we will create a spaceship hull material, adding also random light windows and the spaceship's name logo as if painted in red on the hull itself:

Getting ready

1. Start Blender and switch to the **Cycles Render** engine. Select the default cube and delete it.

2. With the mouse cursor in the 3D view press *Shift + A* on the keyboard and add a torus primitive (*Shift + A* | **Mesh** | **Torus**). Still in **Edit Mode** scale it at least two times bigger (press *A* to select all the vertexes, then digit *S* | *2* | *Enter*).

3. Go out of **Edit Mode** and in the **Outliner** select the lamp; in the **Object Data** panel to the right change it to a Sun, then set the **Size** to **0.100**. Click on the **Use Nodes** button and set the **Strength** to **10.000**. Change the color to RGB 0.800.

4. Go to the **World** window and click on the **Use Nodes** button under the **Surface** tab; click on the little square with a dot on the right side of the color slot: from the menu select **Sky Texture**. Set the **Strength** to **0.100**.

5. Select the Camera and in the **Transform** panel set these values: **Location X 6.10677, Y -0.91141, Z -2.16840; Rotation X 112.778°, Y -0.003°, Z 81.888°**.

6. Go to the **Render** window and, under the **Sampling** tab, set the **Samples** to **50** both for **Render** and **Preview**. Under the **Light Paths** tab check the **No Caustics** option and set the **Filter Glossy** to **1.000**. Under the **Performance** tab set the **Acceleration** structure to **Static BVH** and check the **Use Spatial Splits** and **Cache BVH** options.

7. Press *N* with the mouse cursor in the 3D view to get rid of the **Transform** panel and *T* to get rid of the **Object Tools** panel; split the 3D view in two rows and change the upper one in a **Node Editor** window.

8. Split the bottom window in two parts and change the left one in a **UV/Image Editor** window; select the torus, and press *Tab* to go in **Edit Mode**. In the window header change the selection mode to **Face** select and select only one face on the mesh (anyone); press *A* two times to select all the faces and keep the first selected face as the active one and then press *U*: in the **UV Mapping** pop-up menu select **Follow Active Quads**, then, in the following pop up, select **Even as Edge Length Mode** and click on the **OK** button.

9. Put the mouse cursor in the **UV/Image Editor** window and press *A* to select all the vertexes of the UV coordinates, then scale them 1/3 smaller (*S | .3 | Enter*). Press *Tab* to go out of **Edit Mode** and change the UV/Image Editor in a 3D view. Change the 3D view at the right in a Camera view by pressing *0* on the numpad (with the mouse cursor placed on the 3D view).

10. Go to the **Object Modifiers** window and assign to the torus a **Subdivision Surface** modifier: set the **Subdivisions** level to **4** both for **View** and **Render**; set the Camera view mode to **Rendered** and go to the **Material** window.

How to do it...

And now, to the material creation:

1. Click on **New** in the **Material** window under the **Properties** panel or in the **Node Editor** header; rename the new material **spacehull**.

2. In the **Material** window switch the **Diffuse BSDF** node with a **Mix Shader** node and rename it **Mix Shader1**; in the first **Shader** slot select a **Diffuse BSDF** node and in the second one a **Mix Shader** node, rename it **Mix Shader2**. In the first **Shader** slot of the **Mix Shader2** node select a **Glossy BSDF** and in the second one an **Add Shader** node. Connect the **Glossy** shader also to the first **Shader** slot of the **Add Shader** node and in the second one select an **Anisotropic BSDF**.

3. Add a **Tangent** node (*Shift + A* | **Input** | **Tangent**) and connect it to the **Tangent** input socket of the **Anisotropic** shader. In the **Method to use for the tangent** slot select **UV Map** and in the slot on the side select the name of the UV coordinates layer assigned to the torus.

4. In the **Anisotropic** shader node set the **Roughness** to **0.150**, the **Anisotropy** to **0.300**, and the **Rotation** to **0.250**.

5. Add a **Layer Weight** node (*Shift + A* | **Input** | **Layer Weight**), rename it **Layer Weight1**, and connect its **Fresnel** output to the **Fac** input sockets of both the **Mix Shader1** and **Mix Shader2** nodes. Set the **Blend** factor to **0.750**.

6. Add a **Mix** node (*Shift + A* | **Color** | **Mix**): set the **Color1** to R 0.400, G 0.458, B 0.500 and the **Color2** to **R 0.331, G 0.332, B 0.266**. Press *Shift + D* to duplicate it and change the **Blend Type** to **Color**: connect the output of the **Mix** node to the **Color1** input socket of the **Color** node and change the **Color2** to R 0.503, G 0.680, B 0.800.

7. Add a **Layer Weight** node (*Shift + A* | **Input** | **Layer Weight**), rename it **Layer Weight2** and connect the **Facing** output to the **Fac** input sockets of both the **Mix** and **Color** nodes. Set the **Blend** factor to **0.700**. Connect the output of the **Color** node to the **Color** input socket of the **Diffuse BSDF** shader.

8. Add a **Frame** (*Shift + A* | **Layout** | **Frame**), select all the nodes except for the **Material Output** one and then the frame and press *Ctrl + P* to parent them. Rename the frame **SHADER**.

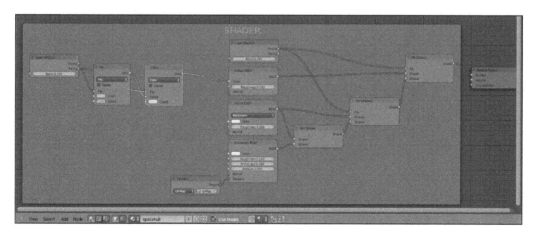

9. Add a **Texture Coordinate** node (*Shift + A* | **Input** | **Texture Coordinate**), a **Mapping** node (*Shift + A* | **Vector** | **Mapping**), an **Image Texture** node (*Shift + A* | **Texture** | **Image Texture**), and a **Musgrave Texture** node (*Shift + A* | **Texture** | **Musgrave Texture**).

10. Press *Shift + D* to duplicate the **Image Texture** node and place the textures vertically in a column like this from top: **Image**, **Image**, and **Musgrave**.

11. Press *Shift + D* to duplicate the **Mapping** node two times and place them in a column at the left side of the texture nodes. Connect the **UV** output of the **Texture Coordinate** node to the **Vector** input sockets of the three **Mapping** nodes. Connect the **Vector** output of each one of the **Mapping** nodes to the **Vector** input socket of each one of the textures.

12. Click on the **Open** button in the first **Image Texture** nodes to load the image `spacehull.png`; click on the little arrows on the left side of the button in the second **Image Texture** node to select the same image texture. Go to the **Musgrave Texture** and set the **Scale** to **115.500**, **Detail** to **4.500**, **Dimension** to **0.200**, and **Lacunarity** to **0.600**.

13. Go to the first **Mapping** node and set the **Scale X 2.000**, **Y 4.000**, and **Z 6.000**; go to the second **Mapping** node and set the **Scale Y 2.000** and **Z 3.000**; go to the third **Mapping** node and set the **Scale Z** to **0.100**.

14. Add a **Frame** (*Shift + A* | **Layout** | **Frame**), select the three **Mapping** nodes, the two **Image Texture** nodes, and the **Musgrave Texture** and then the frame, and press *Ctrl + P* to parent them. Rename the frame **HULL**.

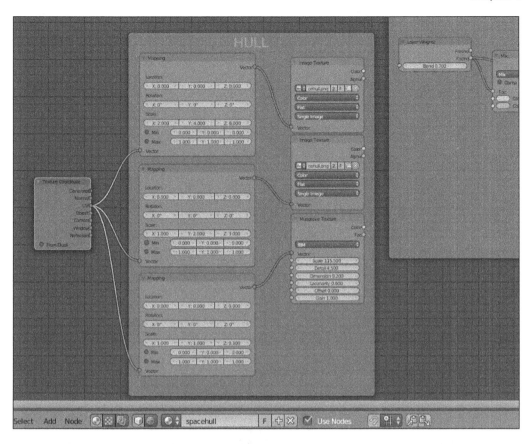

15. Add a **Mix** node (*Shift + A* | **Color** | **Mix**), a **Bump** node (*Shift + A* | **Vector** | **Bump**), and a **Frame** (*Shift + A* | **Layout** | **Frame**); select the **Mix** and the **Bump** nodes and then the frame and press *Ctrl + P* to parent them. Rename the frame **BUMP**. Set the **Mix** node **Blend Type** to **Multiply** and connect its output to the **Height** input socket of the **Bump** node. Set the **Strength** to **0.050** and connect the **Normal** output to the **Normal** input sockets of the **Diffuse**, **Glossy**, and **Anisotropic** shader nodes.

16. Connect the **Color** output of the first **Image Texture** node to the **Color2** input socket of the multiply **Mix** node; connect the **Color** output of the second **Image Texture** node to the **Color1** input socket.

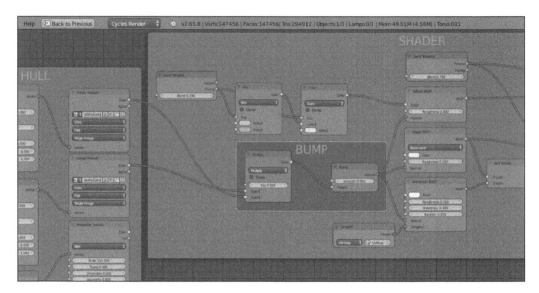

17. Now add a **Math** node (*Shift + A* | **Convertor** | **Math**) and set the operation to **Multiply**; connect the color output of the **Musgrave Texture** inside the **HULL** frame to the first **Value** input socket and set the second **Value** to **0.200**.

18. Add a **Bright/Contrast** node (*Shift + A* | **Color** | **Bright/Contrast**) and connect the **Color** output of the second **Image Texture** node to its color input socket; set the **Bright** to **-1.000** and the **Contrast** value to **1.500**. Add a **Mix** node (*Shift + A* | **Color** | **Mix**) and set the **Blend Type** to **Multiply**; connect the **Bright/Contrast** node output to the **Color1** input socket and the multiply **Math** node output to the **Color2** input socket. Connect also the **Bright/Contrast** node output to the **Fac** input socket of the multiply **Mix** node.

19. Connect the multiply **Mix** node output to the **Roughness** input socket of the **Glossy BSDF** shader.

20. Add a **Frame** (*Shift + A* | **Layout** | **Frame**), select the **Bright/Contrast** node, the multiply **Math** node, and the multiply **Mix** node and then the frame and, press *Ctrl + P* to parent them. Rename the frame **SPEC**.

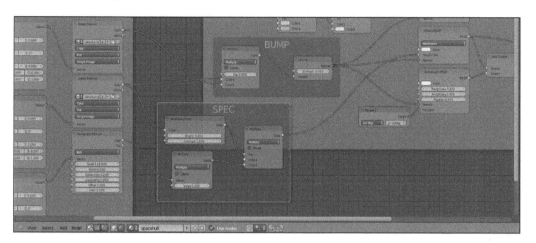

21. Add a new **Mapping** node (*Shift + A* | **Vector** | **Mapping**), an **Image Texture** node (*Shift + A* | **Texture** | **Image Texture**), a **Mix** node (*Shift + A* | **Color** | **Mix**), and an **Emission** shader node (*Shift + A* | **Shader** | **Emission**).

22. Add a **Frame** (*Shift + A* | **Layout** | **Frame**), select the former nodes and then the frame, and press *Ctrl + P* to parent them; rename the frame **WINDOWS**.

23. Connect the **UV** output of the **Texture Coordinate** node to the **Vector** input socket of the new **Mapping** node, then connect the **Mapping** node output to the **Image Texture Vector** input socket; rename the **Image Texture** node **WINDOWS**, and connect its **Color** output to the **Color1** input socket of the **Mix** node, then connect the output of this latter to the **Color** input socket of the **Emission** shader.

24. In the **Mapping** node set the **Scale** to **10.000** for all three axes; in the **WINDOWS Image Texture** node load the image `spacehull_windows.png` and set the **Color Space** to **Non Color Data**. Set the **Mix** node **Blend Type** to **Color**, the **Fac** value to **1.000**, and the **Color2** to **R 0.800**, **G 0.478**, **B 0.177**; finally set the **Emission** node **Strength** to **2.000**.

25. Now add a **Mix Shader** node (*Shift + A* | **Shader** | **Mix Shader**) and paste it just right before the **Material Output** node; rename it **ADD WINDOWS**. Connect the output of the **Emission** shader node to the second **Shader** input socket.

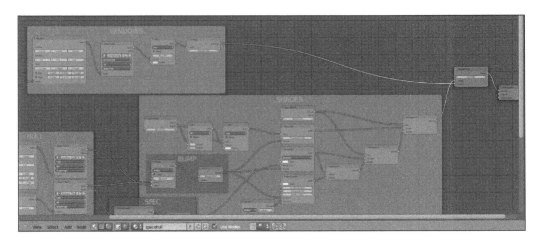

26. Add a new **Mapping** node (*Shift + A* | **Vector** | **Mapping**), a **Brick Texture** node (*Shift + A* | **Texture** | **Brick Texture**), a **Checker Texture** node (*Shift + A* | **Texture** | **Checker Texture**), and a **Mix** node (*Shift + A* | **Color** | **Mix**).

27. Add a **Frame** (*Shift + A* | **Layout** | **Frame**), select the former nodes and then the frame and press *Ctrl + P* to parent them; rename the frame **MASK WINDOWS**.

28. Connect the **UV** output of the **Texture Coordinate** node to the **Vector** input socket of this **Mapping** node, then connect the **Mapping** node output to the **Vector** input sockets of both the **Brick Texture** and **Checker Texture** nodes; connect the **Color** outputs of both the texture to the **Color1** and to the **Color2** input sockets of the **Mix** node.

29. Set the **Mapping** node **Scale** to **0.500** for all the three axes, then go to the **Brick Texture** node and set: the **Offset** and **Squash** frequency to **3**, the **Color1** to pure white, the **Color2** to RGB 0.500, and the **Scale** to **5.800**. Go to the **Checker Texture** node and set the **Color2** to total black and the **Scale** to **5.900**.

30. Set the **Mix** node **Blend Type** to **Burn** and the **Fac** value to **1.000**; connect its output to the **Fac** input socket of the **ADD WINDOWS** node. Press *Shift + D* to duplicate the **Burn** node and set the **Blend Type** to **Multiply**, then paste it right after the **Burn** node; connect the output of the **Bright/Contrast** node inside the **SPEC** frame to the **Color1** input socket of the just added **Multiply** node (this way the connection of the **Burn** node is automatically moved to the **Color2** input socket).

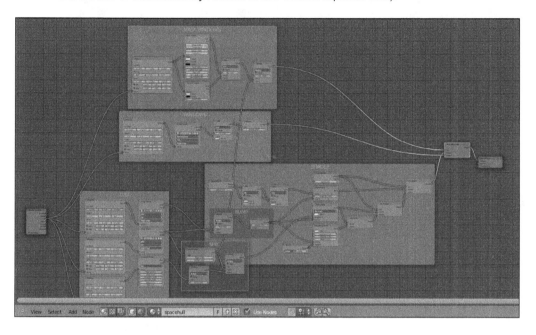

31. Add a **Mapping** node (*Shift + A* | **Vector** | **Mapping**) and an **Image Texture** node (*Shift + A* | **Texture** | **Image Texture**); rename this latter **NAME** and load the image `spacehull_name.png` (a simple logo made in Gimp with the alpha channel, that is a transparent background).

32. Connect the **UV** output of the **Texture Coordinate** node to the **Vector** input socket of this **Mapping** node, then connect the **Mapping** node output to the **Vector** input sockets of the **Image Texture** node.

33. Now go to the **SHADER** frame and add a **Mix** node (*Shift + A* | **Color** | **Mix**), paste it between the color **Mix** node and the **Diffuse** shader; connect the **Color** output of the **NAME Image Texture** node to the **Color2** input socket of the last added **Mix** node and the **Alpha** output to the **Fac** input socket.

34. In the **Mapping** node click to activate both the **Min** and **Max** clipping values, set the **Scale X 0.700** and **Y 1.600** and play with the **Location X** and **Y** values until you see the **ARGUS** logo appearing on the hull in the location you want (this is dependent on the location of the initial face you choose as the active one for the unwrapping, because every other face has been unwrapped following the location of that active face; in my example I had to set the **Location X** to **-1.900** and **Y** to **0.100**).

35. Add a **Frame** (*Shift + A* | **Layout** | **Frame**), select the **Mapping** and the **Image Texture** nodes and then the frame and press *Ctrl + P* to parent them; rename the frame **NAME**.

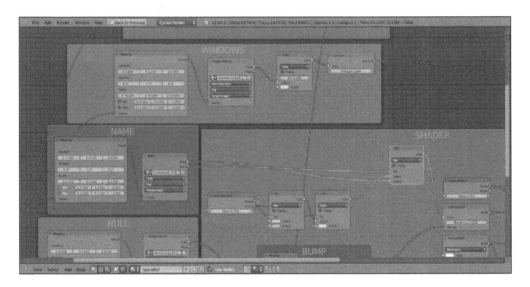

36. Go again to the **SHADER** frame and add a **Mix** node (*Shift + A* | **Color** | **Mix**), paste it between the **Color** node and the **Mix** node; set the **Blend Type** to **Multiply** and connect the **Bright/Contrast** node output to the **Color2** input socket, then connect the **Layer Weight2** facing output to its **Fac** input socket.

37. Go to the **SPEC** frame and add a **Mix** node (*Shift + A* | **Color** | **Mix**), set the **Blend Type** to **Subtract** and the **Fac** value to **0.800**, then paste it right after the **Multiply** node; connect the **Color** output of the **NAME Image Texture** to the **Color2** input socket.

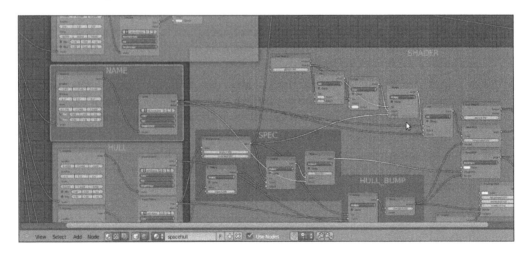

How it works...

From step 1 to step 8 we built the general shader for the metallic hull.

From step 9 to step 14 we built the **HULL** frame group, not immediately used by the shader but that will supply the basic pattern to be used for the bump and for the specular component (and for the color as well). At steps 15 and 16 we added the per-shader bump, by superimposing two differently scaled versions of the same hull panels image coming from the **HULL** frame group.

From step 17 to step 20 we built the **SPEC** frame group, by contrasting the **HULL** component then connected straight to the **Glossy** shader **Roughness**; the effect is added to the **Anisotropic** specularity by the **Add Shader** node, to give a metallic look. From step 21 to step 25 we built the frame group for the light windows to be added on the hull.

From step 26 to step 30 we made the masking for the windows, to give them a random and not uniform appearance. From step 31 to step 35 we added the name logo to the hull, by using the alpha channel of the image itself as mixing factor.

At step 36 we added a little improvement in the colors by multiplying the contrasted hull panels image and lastly at step 37 we subtracted the logo specularity from the hull, to make it less shiny.

There's more...

This is where we are so far:

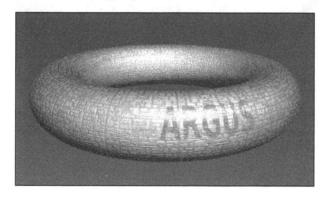

Actually, the appearance of the hull can be even more improved by using some displacement to add details to the spaceship shape, at the moment a little bit too smooth.

1. Go to the **Object Modifiers** window and assign to the **Torus** a second **Subdivision Surface** modifier; set the **Subdivisions** levels to **2** both for **View** and **Render**.

2. Assign a **Displace** modifier, then click on the **Show texture** in texture tab button on the right side of the **Texture** slot; in the **Textures** window click on the **New** button, then change the default **Clouds** texture with an **Image** or **Movie** texture.

3. Click on the **Open** button and load the texture spacehull_displ.exr. Go back to the **Object Modifiers** window and set the displacement **Strength** to **0.200**; in the **Texture Coordinates** slot select **UV**.

This way the displacement features get mixed with the hull panels of the shader, giving a nice result. The spacehull_displ.exr is a 32 bits float displacement map baked in the Blender Internal engine (at the moment Cycles doesn't have the possibility to bake textures or shaders). I modeled with planes and scaled cubes a simple greeble panel, then I baked the displacement on a different and unwrapped plane:

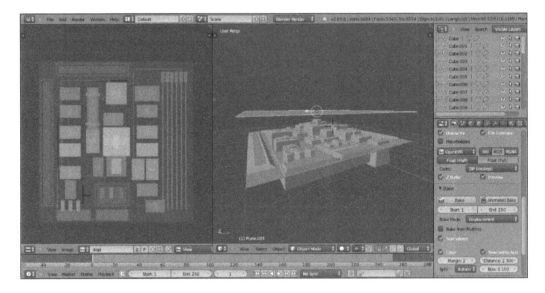

If you want to have a look at the scene, open the file 13010S_06_greeble.blend.

One last thing we can do to improve the model is to assign to the **Torus** mesh, after the **Displace** modifier, a **Decimate** modifier set to **Planar** with a ratio of **0.3000** or similar; you will inevitably lose some detail but will obtain a lot lighter mesh.

See also

There is an interesting and long thread about the displacement technique on the Blender Artist forum, at the following link: http://blenderartists.org/forum/showthread. php?273033-Sculpting-with-UVs-and-displacements

7
Creating Organic Materials

In this chapter, we will cover:

- ▶ Creating a snake-like scaly material with image maps and procedurals
- ▶ Creating a wasp-like chitin material with procedural textures
- ▶ Creating a beetle-like chitin material with procedural textures
- ▶ Creating a grass shader
- ▶ Creating tree shaders – the bark
- ▶ Creating tree shaders – the leaves
- ▶ Creating a Gray Alien skin material with procedurals

Introduction

Following the natural materials we have seen in *Chapter 3, Creating Natural Materials in Cycles*, and *Chapter 5, Creating Complex Natural Materials*, it's now time to have a look at organic shaders.

Again, we tried to use only the Cycles procedurals textures for building the materials but this hasn't been the case in several cases: on one side, because it hasn't been possible, such as in the snake-like shader where it seemed that at least at the moment there were no proper ways to make believable scales only with procedurals; on the other side, because some material image maps would have always worked better, such as in the leaf shader.

Anyways, procedurals have often been added to the material networks to refine the details or add "disorder" to a too much repeating pattern.

Creating a snake-like scaly material with image maps and procedurals

In this recipe we will create a snake-like scaly skin material, as shown here:

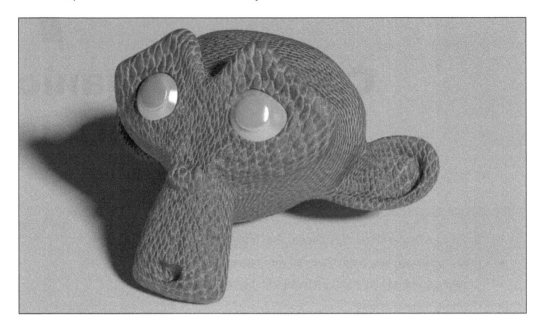

Getting ready

Start Blender and open the `1301OS_07_start.blend` file, where there is an already set scene with an unwrapped **Suzanne** primitive object.

How to do it...

Let's go straight to the material creation:

1. Click on **New** in the **Node Editor** window's header or in the **Material** window on the right and rename the new material as `scales`.

2. Press *Tab* to go in the edit mode and select the eyes' vertexes (put the mouse pointer on the part and press the *L* key to select all the connected vertexes). Click on the **+** icon in the top-left corner of the **Material** window to add a new material. Click on **New**, rename the material as `eyes`, and click on the **Assign** button. Press *Tab* to come out of the edit mode.

3. In the **Material** window, switch the **Diffuse** shader with a **Mix Shader** node. In the first **Shader** slot, select a **Diffuse BSDF** node and in the second one, a **Glossy BSDF** shader node.

4. Set the **Diffuse** shader's **Color** value to a yellowish hue (**R 0.800, G 0.655, B 0.105**) and the **Glossy** shader's **Color** value to pure white. Set the **Glossy** shader's **Roughness** value to 0.200.

5. Now, in the **Material** window, select the **scales** material. Switch the **Diffuse** shader with a **Mix Shader** node. In the first **Shader** slot, select a **Diffuse BSDF** shader node and in the second one, a **Glossy BSDF** shader node. Set the **Glossy** shader's **Roughness** value to 0.350 and its **Color** value to **R 0.529, G 0.709, B 0.800**.

6. Add a **Layer Weight** node (press *Shift + A* and go to **Input | Layer Weight**) and connect its **Fresnel** output to the **Fac** input socket of the **Mix Shader** node. Set the **Blend** value to 0.500.

7. Add a **Texture Coordinate** node (press *Shift + A* and go to **Input | Texture Coordinate**), a **Mapping** node (press *Shift + A* and go to **Vector | Mapping**), and an **Image Texture** node (press *Shift + A* and go to **Texture | Image Texture**). Connect the **UV** output of the **Texture Coordinate** node to the **Vector** input of the **Mapping** node and the **Vector** output of the latter to the **Vector** input of the **Image Texture** node.

8. Add a **Bump** node (press *Shift + A* and go to **Vector | Bump**) and connect the **Color** output of the **Image Texture** node to the **Height** input socket of the **Bump** node. Connect the **Normal** output of the **Bump** node to the **Normal** input sockets of both the **Diffuse** and the **Glossy** shader nodes. Set the **Bump** node's **Strength** value to 0.100.

9. Click on the **Open** button of the **Image Texture** node, browse to the `textures` folder, and load the `scales_tile.png` image map. Set **Color Space** to **Non-Color Data**.

10. Add an **Invert** node (press *Shift + A* and go to **Color | Invert**) and paste it between the **Image Texture** node and the **Bump** node. Go to the **Mapping** node and set **Scale** for all three axes to 2.000.

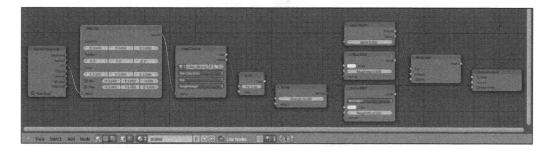

11. Now, box-select the **Texture Coordinate, Mapping, Image Texture,** and **Invert** nodes and move them to the left to make room for new nodes.

12. Add a **Noise Texture** node (press *Shift + A* and go to **Texture | Noise Texture**) and a **Voronoi Texture** node (press *Shift + A* and go to **Texture | Voronoi Texture**). To their **Vector** input sockets, connect the **Vector** output of the **Mapping** node. Set the **Noise** texture's **Scale** value to 30.000 and the **Voronoi** texture's **Scale** value to 400.000.

13. Add a **Math** node (press *Shift + A* and go to **Convertor | Math**) and paste it between the **Invert** node and the **Bump** node. Rename it as Add1 and connect the **Noise** texture's **Color** output to the second **Value** input socket.

14. Add a second **Math** node (press *Shift + A* and go to **Convertor | Math**), rename it as Add2, and paste it to the right of the Add1 math node. Connect the **Voronoi** texture's **Color** output to the second **Value** input socket of the **Add2** node.

15. Now, add a **Math** node again (press *Shift + A* and go to **Convertor | Math**), set the operation to **Multiply**, and paste it to the right of the **Noise Texture** node. Rename it as Multiply1 and set the second **Value** to 1.200.

16. Press *Shift + D* to duplicate the **Multiply1** node, rename it as Multiply2, and paste it to the right of the **Voronoi** texture. Set the second **Value** to 0.500.

17. Add a **ColorRamp** node (press *Shift + A* and go to **Convertor | ColorRamp**) and paste it between the **Voronoi** texture node and the **Multiply2** node. Set the interpolation to **Ease** and move the white colored marker to the left (right under the letter **a** of the word **Easy**).

18. Add a **Bright/Contrast** node (press *Shift + A* and go to **Color | Bright/Contrast**) and paste it between the **Invert** node and the **Multiply1** node. Set the **Bright** value to 0.100 and the **Contrast** value to -0.100.

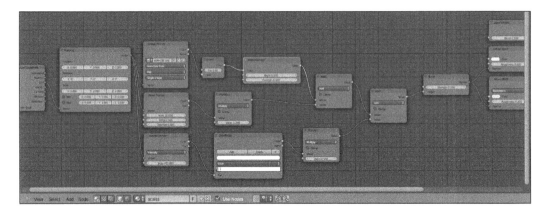

19. Add a new **Noise** texture node (press *Shift + A* and go to **Texture | Noise Texture**), connect it as usual to the **Mapping** node's output, and set the **Scale** to 10.600.

20. Add a **ColorRamp** node (press *Shift + A* and go to **Convertor | ColorRamp**) and connect the **Color** output of the last **Noise** texture node to its **Fac** input socket. Connect the output of the **ColorRamp** to the **Color** input socket of the **Diffuse BSDF** shader. Rename the node as ColorRamp_pattern.

21. Set the interpolation to **Constant** and change the second **Color** to pure black (that is, both the colored markers are now black). Click on the **Add** button to add a new colored marker in the middle of the slider and let it be black as well. Then, click again on the **Add** button but change the color to pure white this time. Click, one last time, on the **Add** button, move the new marker to the right, three-fourths of the total length of the slider, and change its color to pure white as well.

22. Add a **Mix** node (press *Shift + A* and go to **Color | Mix**) and paste it between the **ColorRamp_pattern** node and the **Diffuse** node. Rename it as `connective_color` and change the **Color2** value to **R 0.500, G 0.361, B 0.295**.

23. Add a new **ColorRamp** (press *Shift + A* and go to **Convertor | ColorRamp**) and rename it as `ColorRamp_scales`. Connect the **Color** output of the **Image Texture** node to the **Fac** input socket of the **ColorRamp_scales** node and the **Color** output of the latter to the **Fac** input socket of the **connective_color** mix node.

24. Set the interpolation of the **ColorRamp_scales** node to **Ease**. Move the white colored marker to the middle of the slider and the black colored marker one-fourth of the slider length to the right.

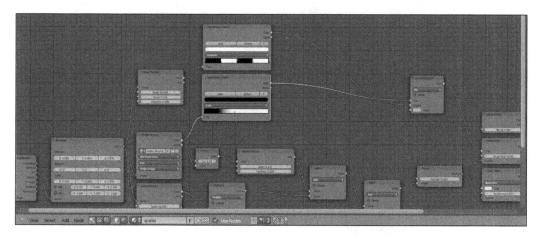

25. Press *Shift + D* to duplicate the **Mix** node and paste it to the immediate right of the **ColorRamp_pattern** node. Move the connection from the **Color1** socket to the **Fac** input socket and rename the node as `scales_pattern`. Change the **Color1** to **R 0.500, G 0.350, B 0.00** and the **Color2** value to **R 0.431, G 0.500, B 0.341**.

26. Add a new **Mix** node (press *Shift + A* and go to **Color | Mix**), set its blend type to **Darken**, and rename it as `scales_dark`. Connect the **Color** output of the **scales_pattern** node to the **Color2** input socket and set **Color1** to **R 0.132, G 0.051, B 0.032**. Connect the **Color** output of the **scales_dark** node to the **Color1** input socket of the **connective_color** node.

27. Add a **ColorRamp** node (press *Shift + A* and go to **Convertor | ColorRamp**) and rename it as `ColorRamp_darken`. Connect the **Color** output of the **Image Texture** node to the **Fac** input socket of the **ColorRamp_darken** node and the **Color** output of the latter to the **Fac** input socket of the **scales_dark** mix node. Move both the black and white colored markers to one-fourth of the slider length from the left (very close together).

28. Add a **Mix** node (press *Shift + A* and go to **Color | Mix**), rename it as `scales_dark_amount` and paste it to the right of the **scales_dark** mix node. Set the **Fac** value to `0.150` and connect the **Color** output of the **scales_pattern** mix node to the **Color2** input socket.

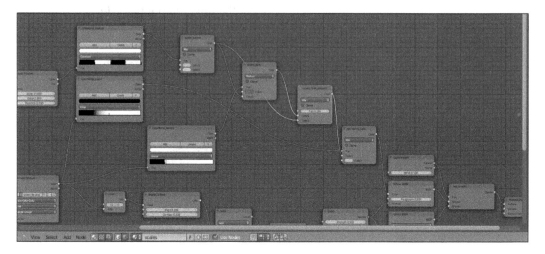

How it works...

This is how the preceding steps work to create a snake-like scaly material:

▶ From step 3 to step 6, we built the ground for the shader by mixing, as usual, a diffuse and a glossy node, factored by the output of a **Fresnel** node.

▶ From step 7 onwards, we started building the scales bump pattern by using a tile-able image map. And from step 11 onwards, we refined the details in the scales pattern by adding the outputs of some procedural textures. With step 18, the bump pattern is complete.

▶ From step 19 to step 28, we build the color pattern by mixing the values of the image texture in a noise procedural to add uneven dark coloration to the scales and by using the scales' image edges as a stencil for the **connective_color** node.

Creating a wasp-like chitin material with procedural textures

In this recipe, we will create a material similar to an insect chitin, colored with a wasp-like yellow and black pattern, as shown here:

Getting ready

Start Blender and open the `13010S_07_start.blend` file, where there is an already set scene with an unwrapped **Suzanne** primitive object.

How to do it...

Let's immediately start with the material creation:

1. Click on **New** in the **Node Editor** window's header or in the **Material** window on the right and rename the new material as `chitin_wasp`.

2. Press *Tab* to go in the edit mode and select the eyes' vertexes (put the mouse pointer on the part and press the *L* key to select all the connected vertexes). Click on the **+** icon in the top-left corner of the **Material** window to add a new material. Click on **New**, rename the material as `eyes`, and click on the **Assign** button. Press *Tab* to come out of the edit mode.

3. Now, in the **Material** window, select the **chitin_wasp** material. Switch the **Diffuse** shader with a **Mix Shader** node. In the first **Shader** slot, select a new **Mix Shader** node and in the second one, a **Glossy BSDF** shader node. Set the **Glossy** shader's **Roughness** to 0.040 and its **Color** to **R 0.500, G 0.440, B 0.086**. Set the **Fac** value of the **Mix Shader** node to 0.025.

4. Go to the second **Mix Shader** node and in the first **Shader** slot, select a **Diffuse BSDF** shader and in the second one, a new **Glossy BSDF** shader node. Set the **Glossy** shader's **Roughness** to 0.100 and its **Color** to **R 0.039, G 0.138, B 0.046**.

5. Add a **Layer Weight** node (press *Shift + A* and go to **Input | Layer Weight**) and connect its **Facing** output to the **Fac** input socket of the second **Mix Shader** node. Set the **Blend** value to 0.500.

6. Add a **Texture Coordinate** node (press *Shift + A* and go to **Input | Texture Coordinate**) and a **Mapping** node (press *Shift + A* and go to **Vector | Mapping**). Connect the **UV** output of the **Texture Coordinate** node to the **Vector** input of the **Mapping** node.

7. Add a **Voronoi Texture** node (press *Shift + A* and go to **Texture | Voronoi Texture**) and a **Noise Texture** node (press *Shift + A* and go to **Texture | Noise Texture**). Connect the **Mapping** output to their **Vector** input sockets. Set the **Voronoi** texture's **Scale** value to 300.000 and the **Noise** texture's **Scale** value to 300.000 as well.

8. Add a **Bump** node (press *Shift + A* and go to **Vector | Bump**) and connect the **Color** output of the **Voronoi Texture** node to the the **Height** input socket of the **Bump** node. Connect the **Normal** output of the latter to the **Normal** input sockets of the **Diffuse** and both the two **Glossy** shader nodes. Set the **Bump** node's **Strength** value to 0.500.

9. Add a **ColorRamp** node (press *Shift + A* and go to **Convertor | ColorRamp**) and paste it between the **Voronoi Texture** node and the **Bump** node. Set the interpolation to **Ease** and move the white colored marker to the left (right under the **E** letter of the word **Ease**).

10. Add a **Math** node (press *Shift + A* and go to **Convertor | Math**), set the operation to **Multiply** and connect the **Fac** output of the **Noise Texture** node to the first **Value** input socket of the **Math** node. Set the second **Value** to 0.100 and connect the **Value** output to the **Displacement** input socket of the **Material Output** node.

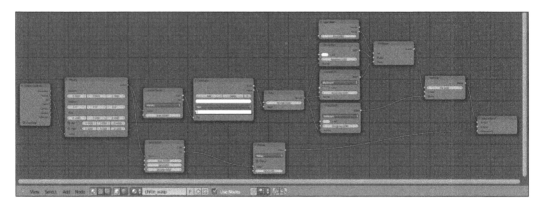

11. Add a new **Mapping** node (press *Shift + A* and go to **Vector | Mapping**) and connect the **UV** output of the **Texture Coordinate** node to the **Vector** input socket of the **Mapping** node. Set the **Rotation Y** value to **90°** and the **Rotation Z** to **45°**. Set the **Scale** value for all the three axes to 5.000.

12. Add a **Noise Texture** node (press *Shift + A* and go to **Texture | Noise Texture**) and a **ColorRamp** node (press *Shift + A* and go to **Convertor | ColorRamp**). Connect the output of the second **Mapping** node to the **Vector** input socket of the last **Noise** texture and the **Fac** output of the latter to the **Fac** input socket of the new **ColorRamp**. Connect the output of the last **Noise** texture to the **Color** input socket of the **Diffuse** shader node.

13. Go to the **Noise Texture** node and set both the **Scale** and **Distortion** values to 2.000. Go to the **ColorRamp** node and set the interpolation to **Constant**. Then, select the white colored marker and change the color to **R 1.000, G 0.429, B 0.000**.

14. Click on the **Add** button to add a new marker in the middle of the slider. Then, click again on the **Add** button. Click, one more time, on the **Add** button but this time move the new marker three-fourth of the slider length to the right. At this point, you have a **ColorRamp** node with four black markers and a yellow one at the end.

15. Add three more markers, change their color to the same yellow as that of the last one and move them in between the already present black markers, so as to have the slider subdivided in eight parts, four black and four yellow.

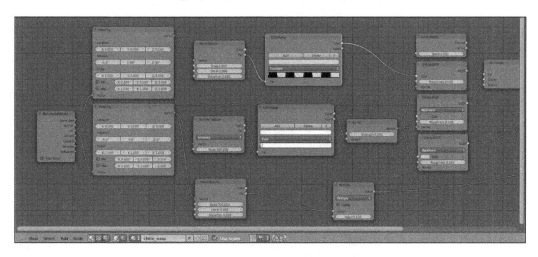

How it works...

This is how the preceding steps work to create a wasp-like chitin material:

- From step 3 to step 5, we built the basic shader using two **Glossy** shaders with different colors to mimic a color shifting in the "specularity" areas.

- From step 6 to step 10, we built the chitin bump, assigning the pores to the *pre-shader* bump and a general noise pattern to the displacement output (which still works as a simple bump in this case).

- From step 11 to step 15, we built a simple and random wasp colored pattern. Obviously, this can be changed and modified as you prefer. Actually, to use it on a more appropriate model, it would be better to make use of a painted color texture map to build a more appropriate and less random color pattern.

Creating a beetle-like chitin material with procedural textures

In this recipe we will create a material similar to a beetle's iridescent chitin, as shown here:

Getting ready

Start Blender and open the 1301OS_07_start.blend file, where there is an already set scene with an unwrapped **Suzanne** primitive object.

How to do it...

Let's start with the creation of the chitin material by assigning a second default material to the eyes of the **Suzanne** mesh (which, although not connected to the face vertexes, are part of the same object):

1. Click on **New** in the **Node Editor** window's header or in the **Material** window on the right and rename the new material as `chitin_beetle`.

2. Press *Tab* to go in the edit mode and select the eyes' vertexes (put the mouse pointer on the part and press the *L* key to select all the connected vertexes). Click on the **+** icon in the top-left corner of the **Material** window to add a new material. Click on **New**, rename the material as `eyes`, and click on the **Assign** button. Press *Tab* to come out of the edit mode.

3. Now, in the **Material** window, select the **chitin_beetle** material. Switch the **Diffuse** shader with a **Mix Shader** node. In the first **Shader** slot select a new **Mix Shader** node and in the second one, a **Glossy BSDF** shader node. Set the **Glossy** shader's **Roughness** value to `0.100` and its **Color** value to **R 0.800, G 0.574, B 0.233**.

4. Go to the second **Mix Shader** node and in the first **Shader** slot, select a **Diffuse BSDF** shader and in the second one, a new **Glossy BSDF** shader node. Set the **Glossy** shader's **Color** value to **R 1.000, G 0.000, B 0.562**.

5. Add a **Layer Weight** node (press *Shift + A* and go to **Input | Layer Weight**) and connect its **Facing** output to the **Fac** input socket of the first **Mix Shader** node. Set the **Blend** value to `0.500`.

6. Add a new **Layer Weight** node (press *Shift + A* and go to **Input | Layer Weight**) and connect its **Facing** output to the **Fac** input socket of the second **Mix Shader** node. Set the **Blend** value to `0.800`.

7. Add a **Texture Coordinate** node (press *Shift + A* and go to **Input | Texture Coordinate**) and a **Mapping** node (press *Shift + A* and go to **Vector | Mapping**). Connect the **UV** output of the **Texture Coordinate** node to the **Vector** input of the **Mapping** node.

8. Add a **Voronoi Texture** node (press *Shift + A* and go to **Texture | Voronoi Texture**) and a **Noise Texture** node (press *Shift + A* and go to **Texture | Noise Texture**). To their **Vector** input sockets, connect the **Mapping** output. Set the **Voronoi** texture's **Scale** value to `300.000` and the **Noise** texture's **Scale** to `300.000` as well.

9. Add a **Bump** node (press *Shift + A* and go to **Vector | Bump**) and connect the **Color** output of the **Voronoi Texture** node to the the **Height** input socket of the **Bump** node. Connect the **Normal** output of the **Bump** node to the **Normal** input sockets of the **Diffuse** and both the two **Glossy** shader nodes. Set the **Bump** node's **Strength** value to `0.025`.

10. Add a **ColorRamp** (press *Shift + A* and go to **Convertor | ColorRamp**) and paste it between the **Voronoi Texture** node and the **Bump** node. Set the interpolation to **Ease** and move the white colored marker to the left (right under the **E** letter of the word **Ease**).

11. Add a **Math** node (press *Shift + A* and go to **Convertor | Math**), set the operation to **Multiply**, and connect the **Fac** output of the **Noise Texture** node to the first **Value** input socket of the **Math** node. Set the second **Value** to 0.050 and connect the **Value** output to the **Displacement** input socket of the **Material Output** node.

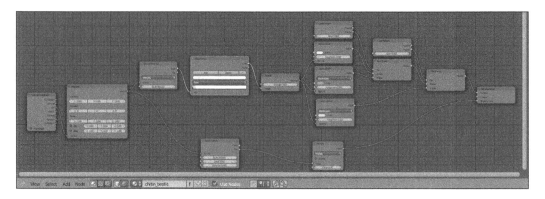

12. Add a **Layer Weight** node (press *Shift + A* and go to **Input | Layer Weight**), two **Math** nodes (press *Shift + A* and go to **Convertor | Math**) and a **Hue Saturation Value** node (press *Shift + A* and go to **Color | Hue Saturation Value**).

13. Connect the **Facing** output of the **Layer Weight** node to the first **Value** input socket of the first **Math** node. Set the operation to **Multiply** and the second **Value** to 0.700.

14. Connect the **Multiply** node's output to the first **Value** input socket of the second **Math** node and the output of the latter to the **Hue** input socket of the **Hue Saturation Value** node. Connect the output of the **Hue Saturation Value** node to the **Color** input socket of the **Diffuse** shader node.

15. Change the **Hue Saturation Value** node's **Color** value to **R 0.103**, **G 0.500**, **B 0.229** and, just for this example, let the other values be as they are.

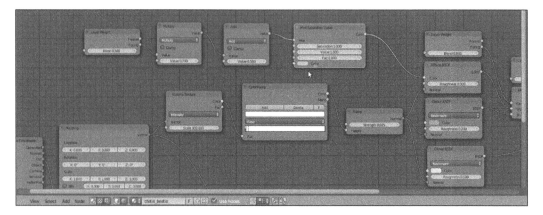

How it works...

This is how the preceding steps work to create a beetle-like chitin material:

▶ The first parts of this shader work almost the same as that of the **chitin_wasp** material, that is the basic shader from step 3 to step 6 and the chitin bump from step 7 to step 11.

▶ From step 12 to step 15, we built the color component coming from the **Hue Saturation Value** node and that, thanks to the combination of the **Layer Weight** and of the **Math** nodes, shows mainly in the mesh faces perpendicular to the point of view, and is moreover sliding in the other spectrum colors on the facing-away mesh sides. The adding of the **Hue Saturation Value** node is also for further color tweaking. Especially, the **Fac** value is useful to set the intensity of the mixture of the iridescent colors with the green base color.

Creating a grass shader

In this recipe, we will create a generic grass shader using grass leaves meshes instanced on a particle system, as shown here:

Getting ready

Start Blender and open the `1301OS_07_grass_start.blend` file, where there is an already set scene with an emitter plane working as light source, an uneven plane to perform the ground, and several grass leaves objects grouped and instanced on the ground plane by a particle system.

How to do it...

Let's start by assigning a ground material to the ground plane and with the creation of the grass shader working on the grass blades meshes to be instanced:

1. Select the ground plane and click on the **New** button in the **Node Editor** window's header or in the **Material** window to the right. Rename the material as `ground` and set the **Color** value of the **Diffuse** shader to **R 0.141, G 0.082, B 0.031**.

2. Select one of the grass leaves objects and again click on the **New** button in the **Node Editor** window's header or in the **Material** window to the right. Rename the material as `grass`.

3. Box-select (press *B* and drag with the left mouse button pressed) the other grass leaves object and then press *Ctrl + L*. In the **Make Links** pop-up menu select **Material** to assign the **grass** shader to all the selected objects.

4. In the **Material** window, switch the **Diffuse** shader with a **Mix Shader** node. In the first **Shader** slot, select a new **Mix Shader** node and in the second one, a **Glossy BSDF** shader node.

5. Go to the second **Mix Shader** node and in the first **Shader** slot, select a **Translucent BSDF** node and in the second one, a **Diffuse BSDF** shader node.

6. Add a **Texture Coordinate** node (press *Shift + A* and go to **Input | Texture Coordinate**), a **Mapping** node (press *Shift + A* and go to **Vector | Mapping**) and an **Image Texture** node (press *Shift + A* and go to **Texture | Image Texture**). Connect the **UV** output of the **Texture Coordinate** node to the **Vector** input of the **Mapping** node and the output of the latter to the **Vector** input socket of the **Image Texture** node.

7. Connect the **Color** output of the **Image Texture** node to the **Color** input sockets of the **Translucent**, **Diffuse**, and **Glossy** shader nodes. Click on the **Open** button on the **Image Texture** node, browse to the `textures` folder, and load the image `grass.png`.

8. Add a new **Image Texture** node (press *Shift + A* and go to **Texture | Image Texture**). Connect the output of the **Mapping** node to the **Vector** input socket of the second **Image Texture** node and its **Color** output to both the **Roughness** input socket of the **Glossy** shader node and the **Fac** input socket of the second **Mix Shader** node.

9. Click on the **Open** button on the second **Image Texture** node, browse to the `textures` folder, and load the `grass_spec.png` image. Set the **Color Space** to **Non-Color Data**.

10. Add a **Bump** node (press *Shift + A* and go to **Vector | Bump**), connect the **Color** output of the second **Image Texture** node to the **Height** input socket and the **Normal** output of the **Bump** node to the **Normal** input sockets of the **Translucent**, **Diffuse**, and **Glossy** shader nodes. Set the **Strength** value to 0.010.

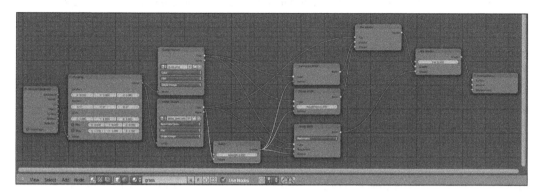

How it works...

This is a very simple material. The translucent component is mixed with the diffuse component by the grass_spec.png texture, a gray-scale image acting as a stencil for the mixing factor and also as a very slight per-shader bump map. Then, the glossy component is mixed as well and the grass_spec.png image is used as its roughness factor.

Note that the color image map is connected to the **Color** input sockets of all the three shader nodes: **Translucent**, **Diffuse**, and **Glossy**. This is necessary to avoid white transparencies and specularity, and to obtain a more natural look.

Creating tree shaders – the bark

There are several different ways to build trees in a 3D package: starting from the simpler low poly objects such as the billboards used in video games (simple planes mapped with tree images on a transparent background) to slightly complex objects where a trunk mesh is attached to a foliage mass made of little alpha textured planes, each one representing a leaf or even a twig, to more complex and heavy meshes where every little branch and leaf is actually modeled.

For this two-parts tree shader recipe, we will use a model coming from the many environment assets of the CG short film *Big Buck Bunny*, the second Open Movie produced by the Blender Foundation. All the movie assets are free to be downloaded, distributed, and reused, even for commercial projects, because they are licensed under the Creative Commons Attribution 3.0 (`http://creativecommons.org/licenses/by/3.0/`).

The general shape of the tree and of the leaves as well is pretty "toyish". This is because they are the elements that have been drawn to match the toon style of the furry characters, but actually, it's perfectly suited for our demonstration purposes.

The tree model is made up of several parts: on the first layer there are the **tree_trunk**, **tree_branch**, and **tree_branches** meshes and on the second layer the leaves, made up of a single leaf object dupliverted on the tiny faces of the **leaves_dupli** object (that is the **leaf_tobeswitched** object is parented to the **leaves_dupli** object and then, in the **Object** window, under the **Duplication** tab, the **Faces** duplication method has been selected, the **Scale** option checked and the **Inherit Scale** value set to 1110.000. This way the **leaf_tobeswitched** object is instanced on the many **leaves_dupli** faces according to their location, rotation, and scale).

On the eleventh layer, there are three leaf objects with three different levels of detail: a simple flat plane, a subdivided and curved plane, and a modeled leaf. Their presence is only to supply the low, middle, and high resolution mesh data—by selecting the **leaf_tobeswitched** object and going to the **Object Data** window, it is possible to switch between the **leaf_generic_low**, **leaf_generic_mid**, and **leaf_generic_hi** foliage level of resolution.

In the first part of this two-parts recipe, we will create the material for the bark:

Getting ready

Start Blender and open the `1301OS_07_tree_start.blend` file. For this recipe, deactivate the second layer and select the **tree_trunk** object.

How to do it...

Let's start by creating the bark material:

1. Click on the **New** button in the **Node Editor** window's header or in the **Material** window and rename the material as `bark`.

2. In the **Material** window switch the **Diffuse BSDF** shader with a **Mix Shader** node. In the first **Shader** slot, select a **Diffuse BSDF** shader node and in the second one, a **Glossy BSDF** shader node. Set the **Glossy** shader's **Roughness** value to `0.800` and the **Mix Shader** factor value to `0.200`.

3. Add a **Texture Coordinate** node (press *Shift + A* and go to **Input | Texture Coordinate**), a **Mapping** node (press *Shift + A* and go to **Vector | Mapping**), and an **Image Texture** node (press *Shift + A* and go to **Texture | Image Texture**).

4. Connect the **UV** output of the **Texture Coordinate** node to the **Vector** input socket of the **Mapping** node and the output of the latter to the **Vector** input socket of the **Image Texture** node. Connect the **Color** output of the **Image Texture** node to the **Color** input sockets of both the **Diffuse** and **Glossy** shader nodes.

5. Click on the **Open** button of the **Image Texture** node, browse to the `textures` folder and load the `bark_color_tile.png` image.

6. Press *Shift + D* to duplicate the **Image Texture** node and connect the **Mapping** node's output to its **Vector** input socket as well. Click on the **2** little icon to the right of the texture image name to make the node single user. Click on the **Open Image** button (the one with the folder icon), browse again to the `textures` folder, and load the `bark_norm_tile.png` image. Set the **Color Space** to **Non-Color Data**.

7. Add a **Normal Map** node (press *Shift + A* and go to **Vector | Normal Map**), connect the **Color** output of the second **Image Texture** node to the **Color** input socket of the **Normal Map** node, and set the **Strength** value to `2.000`. Click on the **UV Map for tangent space maps** button above the **Strength** one and select **UVMap** (the trunk mesh has two different sets of UV coordinates, as we'll see this later).

8. Connect the **Normal** output of the **Normal Map** node to the **Normal** input sockets of both the **Diffuse** and the **Glossy** shader nodes.

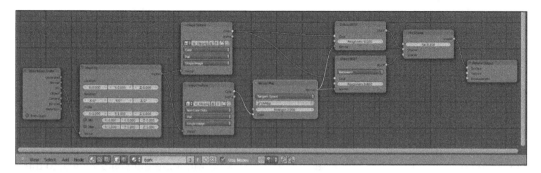

9. Now, box-select all the nodes except the **Texture Coordinate** and the **Material Output** ones and press *Shift + D* to duplicate them. Move them down. Connect the **UV** output of the **Texture Coordinate** node to the **Vector** input socket of the duplicated **Mapping** node and set the **Scale** value of the latter to 0.350 for all the three axes.

10. Add a **Mix Shader** node (press *Shift + A* and go to **Shader | Mix Shader**) and paste it to the immediate left of the **Material Output** node. Connect the output of the duplicated **Mix Shader** node to the second **Shader** input socket of the last added **Mix Shader** node.

11. Add a **Noise Texture** node (press *Shift + A* and go to **Texture | Noise Texture**), connect the **UV** output of the **Texture Coordinate** node to the **Vector** input socket of the **Noise** texture, and connect the **Fac** output of the latter to the **Fac** input socket of the last added **Mix Shader** node.

12. Set the **Noise** texture's **Scale** value to 15.000.

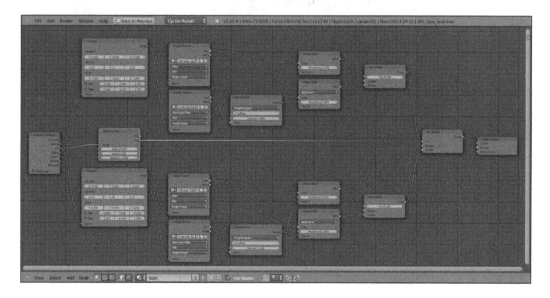

13. Now, press *Shift* and select the **tree_branch** and **tree_branches** meshes and, as last one, reselect the **tree_trunk** mesh to make it the active object. Then, press *Ctrl + L*. In the **Make Links** pop up, select **Materials** to assign the bark material to the other two meshes.

How it works...

For this material, we built a simple shader using two tile-able image maps—a colored one for the diffuse and glossy components and a normal map for the bump component. Then, we duplicated everything and mixed the second material copy, with different scale values, to the first one by the factor of a **Noise** procedural texture, to add variety to the bark pattern and to avoid the unpleasant repeating effect that often shows up with tile-able image textures.

There's more...

At this point, if you look carefully at the **Rendered** view of the tree trunk, you'll see that, sadly, there are ugly seams where the trunk's main body joins with the big low branches:

Obviously, this is due to the fact that the unwrap of the mesh has separated the branches' UV isles from the main trunk ones, although the effect is barely visible. Let's say that you absolutely want to avoid this. That's why, we are now going to see a solution for the problem by using a second set of UV coordinates and a **Vertex Color** layer:

1. Select the trunk mesh and go in the vertex paint mode. The mesh turns totally white because that is the color assigned to the vertexes by default. Start painting with a pure black color the vertexes located at the joinings of the low branches with the trunk, achieving this result:

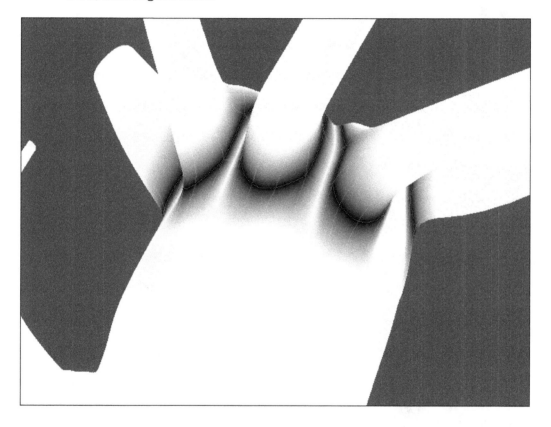

2. As you can see, the "joining vertexes" edge-loops are black but smoothly blending into the white of the default mesh vertex color. This will be used as a stencil map to blend two different instances of the same bark material. Go to the **Object Data** window and rename the **Vertex Color** layer as Join_branches.

3. Go in the edit mode and select all the faces enveloping the vertexes at the joinings of the branches with the trunk. In the **Object Data** window, under the **UV Maps** tab, click on the **+** icon (**Add UV Map**). Rename the new UV coordinates layer as UVMap2, put the mouse pointer on the 3D view-port, press *U*, and select **Unwrap** in the **UV Mapping** pop-up menu.

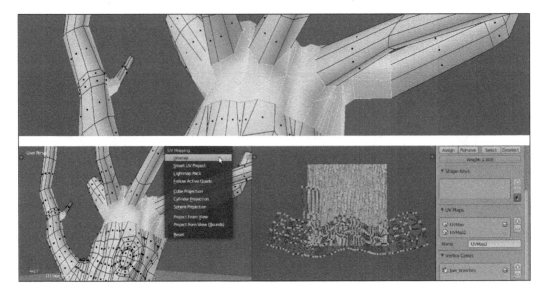

4. Come out of the edit mode. Click on the user number to the right of the material name in the **Node Editor** window's header and rename the new material as bark_ seamless. Now, by looking at the following image, it will be clear what you have to do:

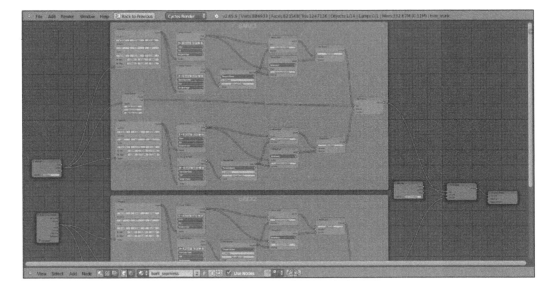

5. Make a duplicate of the bark material and blend the two shaders with a **Mix Shader** node, factored by the **Join_branches** vertex color stencil. Use an **Attribute** node for both the **Vertex Color** layer output and to set the **UVMap2** coordinates layer for the second copy of the bark material.

As you can see in the previous image, there are no more visible seams. The two differently UV mapped materials smoothly blend together.

Creating tree shaders – the leaves

In this second tree recipe we will create the leaves shaders, as shown here:

Getting ready

Carrying on with the blend of the previous recipe, now press *Shift* and activate the second and the eleventh layers also and select the **leaf_generic_mid** object.

How to do it...

Let's go straight to creating the leaves shader:

1. Click on the **New** button in the **Node Editor** window's header or in the **Material** window and rename the material as `leaf_alpha`.

2. In the **Material** window switch, the **Diffuse BSDF** shader with a **Mix Shader** node and rename it as `Mix Shader Cutout`. In the first **Shader** slot, select a **Transparent BSDF** shader node and in the second one, a new **Mix Shader** node that will be renamed as `Mix Shader Add Translucency`.

3. Add an **Image Texture** node (press *Shift + A* and go to **Texture | Image Texture**), rename it as MASK, and connect its **Alpha** output to the **Fac** input socket of the **Mix Shader Cutout** node.

4. Click on the **Open** button of the **Image Texture** node, browse to the textures folder, and load the leaf_generic_mask.png image (which actually is a simple black silhouette of a leaf, with a transparent alpha channel). Set the **Color Space** to **Non-Color Data**.

5. Add a **Diffuse BSDF** node (press *Shift + A* and go to **Shader | Diffuse BSDF**), a **Glossy BSDF** node (press *Shift + A* and go to **Shader | Glossy BSDF**), and a **Translucent BSDF** node (press *Shift + A* and go to **Shader | Translucent BSDF**).

6. Add two new **Mix Shader** nodes (press *Shift + A* and go to **Shader | Mix Shader**) and rename them as Mix Shader1 and Mix Shader2.

7. Connect the output of the **Diffuse** shader to the first **Shader** input socket of the **Mix Shader1** node and the output of the **Glossy** shader to the second one. Set the **Glossy** shader's **Color** value to **R 0.794, G 0.800, B 0.413** and the **Roughness** value to 0.500.

8. Connect the output of the **Mix Shader1** node to the first **Shader** input socket of the **Mix Shader2** node and the output of the **Translucent** node to the second one. Connect the output of the **Mix Shader2** node to the second **Shader** input socket of the **Mix Shader Add Translucency** node.

9. Connect the output of the **Diffuse** shader node to the first **Shader** input socket of the **Mix Shader Add Translucency** node. Set its **Fac** value to 0.300 (this value establishes the amount of translucency in the shader).

10. Add an **Image Texture** node (press *Shift + A* and go to **Texture | Image Texture**), rename it as TRANSLUCENCY, and connect its **Color** output to the **Fac** input socket of the **Mix Shader2** node. Click on the **Open** button, browse to the textures folder, and load the leaf_generic_trans.png image. Set the **Color Space** to **Non-Color Data**.

11. Add a **Fresnel** node (press *Shift + A* and go to **Input | Fresnel**), connect it to the **Fac** input socket of the **Mix Shader1** node and set the **IOR** value to 1.500.

12. Add an **Image Texture** node (press *Shift + A* and go to **Texture | Image Texture**), rename it as COLOR, and connect its **Color** output to the **Color** input socket of the **Diffuse** shader node and to the **Color** input socket of the **Translucent** node. Click on the **Open** button, browse to the textures folder, and load the leaf_generic_col.png image.

13. Add a **Hue Saturation Value** node (press *Shift + A* and go to **Color | Hue Saturation Value**) and paste it between the **COLOR** node and the **Translucent** shader node. Set the **Hue** value to 0.350 and the **Value** to 2.000.

14. Add a last **Image Texture** node (press *Shift + A* and go to **Texture | Image Texture**) and rename it as BUMP. Add a **Bump** node (press *Shift + A* and go to **Vector | Bump**) and connect the **Image Texture** node's **Color** output to the **Height** input socket of the **Bump** node and the **Normal** output socket of the latter to the **Normal** input sockets of the **Diffuse**, **Glossy**, and **Translucent** nodes.

15. Click on the **Open** button, browse to the textures folder, and load the leaf_generic_bump.png image. Set the **Color Space** to **Non-Color Data** and the **Bump** node's **Strength** value to 0.002.

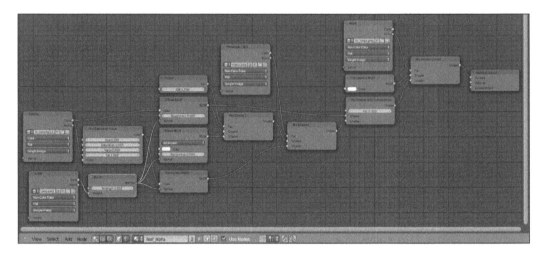

How it works...

▶ From step 1 to step 11, we built the basic shader of the leaf, using an alpha channeled image to "cut-out" the leaf shape on the plane and a gray-scale image to drive the translucency effect.

▶ From step 12 to step 15, we added the color of the leaf, using it also with a hue and intensity variation for the translucency effect. Then, we added the bump, keeping the amount very low.

There's more...

Now, assign the same material to both the **leaf_generic_low** and **leaf_generic_hi** meshes on the eleventh layer.

The modeled leaf mesh doesn't need the alpha channel. So, select the **leaf_generic_hi** object and in the header of the **Node Editor** window, click on the user data number to make it single user. Rename the new material as simply `leaf` and delete the **MASK** and **Transparent BSDF** nodes. Press *Alt + D* to remove the **Mix Shader Cutout** node from the link and delete it as well.

Remember that the examples in the preceding and following images are made with very stylish models coming from the *Big Buck Bunny* short movie. Real objects have more subtle details and more randomly repeating patterns, but in this case this just depends on the image textures you are going to use for your material.

Such a shader is of good use not only for leaves but also for other kinds of plants. In many cases, it's enough to give variations to the color.

Creating a Gray Alien skin material with procedurals

In this recipe, we will create a Gray Alien-like skin shader using Cycles procedural textures, as shown here:

Getting ready

Start Blender and open the `1301OS_07_alienskin_start.blend` file, where there is an already set scene with an unwrapped **Suzanne** primitive object. The **Suzanne** mesh has been "alienized" by a shape key to morph its monkey-like features into the head of a Gray Alien-like creature (in the **Object Data** window, under the **Shape Keys** tab, the **alien** shape keys with a **Value** of `1.000`, and sliding the slider towards `0.000` gradually restore the original **Suzanne** shape).

On the second layer, there is a plane tracked (by a **Damped Track** constraint, in the **Object Constraints** window) to the **Camera** to stay perpendicular to the point of view, which we'll use to create a simple star backdrop for our alien **Suzanne**.

How to do it...

Let's start by setting the background image material first:

1. Select the background plane and click on the **New** button in the **Node Editor** window's header or in the **Material** window. Rename the material as `star_backdrop` and in the **Material** window switch the **Diffuse BSDF** shader with an **Emission** shader. Set the **Strength** value to `0.500`.

2. Add an **Image Texture** node (press *Shift + A* and go to **Texture | Image Texture**) and connect the **Color** output to the **Color** input socket of the **Emission** node. Click on the **Open** button and browse to the `textures` folder. Load the `galaxy-constellation-star-background.png` image (courtesy of `nasaimages.org`).

3. Add a **RGB Curves** node (press *Shift + A* and go to **Color | RGB Curves**) and paste it between the **Image Texture** node and the **Emission** node. Click on the curve window to add a control point and set these coordinates—**X** = `0.36667` and **Y** = `0.12778`. Click again on the curve window to add a second control point and set these coordinates—**X** = `0.65556` and **Y** = `0.81111`.

Now, let's go ahead with the creation of the alien skin shader (with a different material for the eyes):

1. Select the alien **Suzanne** object. Click on the **New** button in the **Node Editor** window's header or in the **Material** window and rename the material as `alienskin`.

2. Go in the edit mode (press *Tab*), select the eyes' vertexes, and click on the **+** icon to the right of the **Material** window to add a second material. Click on the **New** button and rename the material as `alieneyes`. Then, click on **Assign** to assign it to the selected vertexes. Come out of the edit mode.

3. Switch the **Diffuse** shader with a **Mix Shader** node. In the first **Shader** slot, select a **Diffuse** shader and in the second one, a **Glossy Shader**. Set the **Mix Shader** node's **Factor** value to `0.600`, the **Diffuse** shader's **Color** value to **R 0.010, G 0.006, B 0.010**, the **Glossy** shader's **Color** value to **R 0.345, G 0.731, B 0.800** and the **Roughness** value to `0.100`.

4. Select the **alienskin** material and in the **Material** window switch the **Diffuse BSDF** shader with a **Mix Shader** node. In the first **Shader** slot, select a **Diffuse BSDF** node and in the second one, an **Add Shader** node. Set the **Diffuse** shader's **Roughness** value to `0.800`.

5. Add a **Layer Weight** node (press *Shift + A* and go to **Input | Layer Weight**) and connect its **Facing** output to the **Fac** input socket of the **Mix Shader** node. Set the **Blend** node's **Factor** value to `0.400`.

6. In both the **Shader** slots of the **Add Shader** node, select a **Glossy BSDF** shader node. Rename the first one as `Glossy BSDF 1` and the second one as `Glossy BSDF 2`. Set the **Roughness** value of the first one to `0.450` and the **Roughness** value of the second one to `0.225`.

Now that we have set the basic shader for the alien skin, let's go ahead with the main component of the material, that is the bump:

1. Add a **Texture Coordinate** node (press *Shift + A* and go to **Input | Texture Coordinate**) and two **Mapping** nodes (press *Shift + A* and go to **Vector | Mapping**). Connect the **UV** output of the **Texture Coordinate** node to the **Vector** input sockets of both the **Mapping** nodes.

2.   Add two **Voronoi Texture** nodes (press *Shift + A* and go to **Texture | Voronoi Texture,**) rename them as `Voronoi Texture1` and `Voronoi Texture2`, and connect the first **Mapping** node's output to their **Vector** input sockets. Set the **Scale** value of the **Voronoi Texture1** to `100.000` and the **Scale** value of the **Voronoi Texture2** to `20.000`.

3.   Set the **Rotation Y** value of the first **Mapping** node to **60°**.

4.   Add two **Wave Texture** nodes (press *Shift + A* and go to **Texture | Wave Texture**) and rename them as `Wave Texture1` and `Wave Texture2`. Connect the first **Mapping** node's output to the **Vector** input socket of the **Wave Texture1** node, set the **Scale** value of the texture to `20.000`, **Distortion** value to `10.000`, **Detail** to `16.000`, and **Detail Scale** to `0.300`.

5.   Connect the second **Mapping** node output to the **Wave Texture2** node's **Vector** input socket and set the values of the texture exactly as the former one. Set the **Rotation Y** value of the second **Mapping** node to **20°**.

6.   Add a **Noise Texture** node (press *Shift + A* and go to **Texture | Noise Texture**), rename it as `Noise Texture1`, and connect the second **Mapping** node's output to its **Vector** input socket and set the texture's **Scale** value to `120.000` and the **Detail** value to `7.000`.

7.   Add a **ColorRamp** node (press *Shift + A* and go to **Convertor | ColorRamp**), rename it as `ColorRamp1`, and connect the **Voronoi Texture1** node's **Color** output to its **Fac** input socket. Set the interpolation to **Ease** and move the white colored marker to the left, very close to the black colored one (to be more exact, under the end of the last **e** of the word **Ease**).

8.   Add a **Math** node (press *Shift + A* and go to **Convertor | Math**), change the operation to **Multiply**, and rename it as `Multiply1`. Connect the **Color** output of the **ColorRamp1** node to the first **Value** input socket of the **Multiply1** node and set the second **Value** to `0.050`.

9.   Add a **Mix** node (press *Shift + A* and go to **Color | Mix**) and connect the **Color** output of the **Voronoi Texture2** to the **Color1** input socket and the **Color** output of the **Wave Texture1** node to the **Color2** input socket. Set the **Blend Type** to **Difference** and the **Fac** value to `1.000`. Rename it as `Difference1`.

10. Add a second **Mix** node (press *Shift + A* and go to **Color | Mix**) and connect the **Color** output of the **Voronoi Texture2** to the **Color1** input socket and the **Color** output of the **Wave Texture2** node to the **Color2** input socket. Set the **Blend Type** to **Difference** and the **Fac** value to `1.000`. Rename it as `Difference2`.

11. Add two **ColorRamp** nodes (press *Shift + A* and go to **Convertor | ColorRamp**), rename them as `ColorRamp2` and `ColorRamp3`. Connect the **Difference1** node's **Color** output to the **Fac** input socket of the **ColorRamp2** node and the output of the **Difference2** node to the **Fac** input socket of the **ColorRamp3** node.

12. Set the interpolation to **B-Spline** for both of them. And, move the white colored marker three-fourths of the slider length to the left for both of them.

13. Add a **Mix** node (press *Shift + A* and go to **Color | Mix**) and connect the **Color** output of the **ColorRamp2** node to the **Color1** input socket and the **Color** output of the **ColorRamp3** node to the **Color2** input socket. Set the **Blend Type** to **Multiply** and the **Fac** value to `1.000`. Rename it as `Multiply2`.

14. Add a **Math** node (press *Shift + A* and go to **Convertor | Math**), change the operation to **Multiply**, and rename it as `Multiply3`. Connect the output of the **Multiply2** node to the first **Value** input socket of the **Multiply3** node and set the second **Value** to `0.050`.

15. Add a **Bump** node (press *Shift + A* and go to **Vector | Bump**) and connect the output of the **Multiply3** node to the **Height** input socket. Set the **Strength** value to `0.400` and connect the **Bump** node's **Normal** output to the **Normal** input sockets of the **Diffuse BSDF** node. Rename the node as `Bump_diff`.

16. Press *Shift + D* to duplicate the **Bump** node, rename it as `Bump_spec`, and connect its output to the **Normal** input sockets of the **Glossy BSDF 1** and **Glossy BSDF 2** nodes. Connect the **Fac** output of the **Voronoi Texture1** node to the **Height** input socket. Set the **Strength** to `-0.015`.

17. Press *Shift + D* to duplicate the **Add2** node, rename it as `Add5`, and paste it in between the **Voronoi Texture1** node and the **Bump_spec** node.

18. Add a **Math** node (press *Shift + A* and go to **Convertor | Math**) and paste it to the immediate left of the **Bump** node. Rename it as `Add1` and connect the output of the **Multiply1** node to the first **Value** input socket, so as to automatically switch the former connection to the second **Value** input socket.

19. Add a new **Math** node (press *Shift + A* and go to **Convertor | Math**) and paste it in between the **Add1** node and the **Bump** node. Rename it as `Add2`. Connect the **Noise Texture1** node's **Color** output to the second **Value** input socket.

20. Add a **Math** node again (press *Shift + A* and go to **Convertor | Math**) and paste it between the **Noise Texture1** node and the **Add2** node. Set the operation to **Multiply** and the second **Value** to `0.175`. Rename it as `Multiply4`.

21. Connect the output of the **Add2** node to the second **Value** input socket of the **Add5** node.

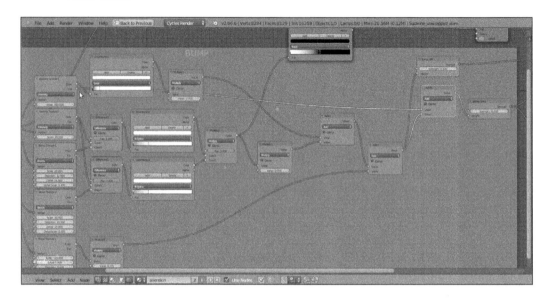

We are done with the bump part, so now let's go with the color pattern:

22. Add a **ColorRamp** node (press *Shift + A* and go to **Convertor | ColorRamp**), rename it as ColorRamp4, and connect the **Color** output of the **Multiply2** node to its **Fac** input socket. Set the interpolation to **Ease**, move the black colored marker to the middle of the slider, and the white colored marker to the extreme left.

23. Add a **Mix** node (press *Shift + A* and go to **Color | Mix**), set the **Blend Type** to **Add**, and rename it as Add3. Connect the **Color** output of the **ColorRamp4** node to the **Fac** input socket and set the **Color2** value to **R 0.553, G 0.599, B 0.473**. Connect its output to the **Color** input socket of the **Diffuse** shader node.

24. Add a **Noise Texture** node (press *Shift + A* and go to **Texture | Noise Texture**) and rename it as Noise Texture2. Connect the first **Mapping** node's output to its **Vector** input socket and set the texture's **Scale** value to 60.000 and the **Detail** value to 7.000.

25. Add a **ColorRamp** node (press *Shift + A* and go to **Convertor | ColorRamp**), rename it as ColorRamp5, and connect the **Noise Texture2** node's **Color** output to its **Fac** input socket. Set the interpolation to **B-Spline**, move the black colored marker to the middle of the slider, and the white colored marker one-fourth the slider length to the left.

26. Add a **Mix** node (press *Shift + A* and go to **Color | Mix**), set the **Blend Type** to **Add**, and rename it as Add4. Paste it between the **Add3** node and the **Diffuse** shader. Set the **Color2** value to **R 0.235**, **G 0.198**, **B 0.132**. Connect the **Color** output of the **ColorRamp5** node to the **Fac** input socket of the **Add4** node.

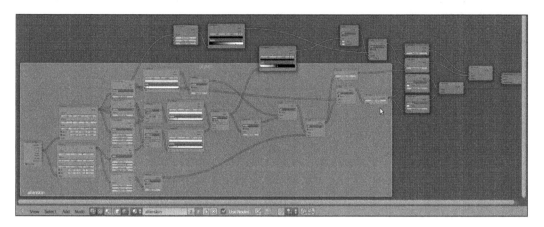

How it works...

This is how the preceding steps work to create a Gray Alien skin material:

▸ From step 1 to step 3, we built a simple and quick shader for the starry background. Note that the background is actually emitting light (off course, according to the black and white values of the image mapped on the plane), so affecting the **Suzanne** alien mesh. But in this case, this doesn't matter because it's not visible from the **Camera** point of view. To see how to set a bright, but not a light-emitting background, that is a shader behaving as a shadeless material you have in the Blender Internal engine, go to *Chapter 9, Special Materials*, of this cookbook.

▸ From step 6 to step 9, we built the basic shader for the alien **Suzanne** skin. The diffuse component is mixed, on the ground of the **Facing** output of a **Layer Weight** node, with a specular component made up of two summed **Glossy** nodes with different **Roughness** values, so as to have a crisper specular effect on a more diffuse one.

▸ From step 10 to step 30, we built the quite complex bump pattern for the skin. Note that there are two separate bump effects, one for the diffuse component and the same one, summed with the bare **Voronoi** texture, connected to the specular component nodes.

▸ Finally, from step 31 to step 35, we built a very simple color pattern.

There's more...

The reality of this material would benefit a lot from at least a little Sub Surface Scattering effect. In the 2.66a official Blender version, there is no **SSS** shader in Cycles yet (even if not totally developed, it will be present in the official 2.67 release coming out soon), but we'll see different ways to "fake" it in *Chapter 8, Human Skin Materials and Faking Sub Surface Scattering in Cycles*, of this cookbook.

Index

Thank you for buying
Blender 2.6 Cycles: Materials and Textures Cookbook

About Packt Publishing

Packt, pronounced 'packed', published its first book "*Mastering phpMyAdmin for Effective MySQL Management*" in April 2004 and subsequently continued to specialize in publishing highly focused books on specific technologies and solutions.

Our books and publications share the experiences of your fellow IT professionals in adapting and customizing today's systems, applications, and frameworks. Our solution based books give you the knowledge and power to customize the software and technologies you're using to get the job done. Packt books are more specific and less general than the IT books you have seen in the past. Our unique business model allows us to bring you more focused information, giving you more of what you need to know, and less of what you don't.

Packt is a modern, yet unique publishing company, which focuses on producing quality, cutting-edge books for communities of developers, administrators, and newbies alike. For more information, please visit our website: www.packtpub.com.

About Packt Open Source

In 2010, Packt launched two new brands, Packt Open Source and Packt Enterprise, in order to continue its focus on specialization. This book is part of the Packt Open Source brand, home to books published on software built around Open Source licences, and offering information to anybody from advanced developers to budding web designers. The Open Source brand also runs Packt's Open Source Royalty Scheme, by which Packt gives a royalty to each Open Source project about whose software a book is sold.

Writing for Packt

We welcome all inquiries from people who are interested in authoring. Book proposals should be sent to author@packtpub.com. If your book idea is still at an early stage and you would like to discuss it first before writing a formal book proposal, contact us; one of our commissioning editors will get in touch with you.

We're not just looking for published authors; if you have strong technical skills but no writing experience, our experienced editors can help you develop a writing career, or simply get some additional reward for your expertise.

Blender 3D Basics
Beginner's Guide

ISBN: 978-1-84951-690-7   Paperback: 468 pages

The complete novice's guide to 3D modeling
and animation

1. The best starter guide for complete newcomers to 3D modeling and animation

2. Easier learning curve than any other book on Blender

3. You will learn all the important foundation skills ready to apply to any 3D software

WebGL Beginner's Guide

ISBN: 978-1-84969-172-7   Paperback: 376 pages

Become a master of 3D web programming in WebGL and JavaScript

1. Dive headfirst into 3D web application development using WebGL and JavaScript.

2. Each chapter is loaded with code examples and exercises that allow the reader to quickly learn the various concepts associated with 3D web development

3. The only software that the reader needs to run the examples is an HTML5 enabled modern web browser. No additional tools needed.

Please check **www.PacktPub.com** for information on our titles

Blender Game Engine: Beginner's Guide

ISBN: 978-1-84951-702-7   Paperback: 206 pages

The non programmer's guide to creating 3D video games

1. Use Blender to create a complete 3D video game

2. Ideal entry level to game development without the need for coding

3. No programming or scripting required

Unity 3D Game Development by Example Beginner's Guide

ISBN: 978-1-84969-054-6   Paperback: 384 pages

A seat-of-your-pants manual for building fun, groovy little games quickly

1. Build fun games using the free Unity 3D game engine even if you've never coded before

2. Learn how to "skin" projects to make totally different games from the same file – more games, less effort!

3. Deploy your games to the Internet so that your friends and family can play them

4. Packed with ideas, inspiration, and advice for your own game design and development

Please check **www.PacktPub.com** for information on our titles

www.ingramcontent.com/pod-product-compliance
Lightning Source LLC
Chambersburg PA
CBHW060527060326
40690CB00017B/3405